GOD SAID YES

GOD SAID YES

HEATHER HORNBACK-BLAND

and Ninie Hammon

BERKLEY PRAISE, NEW YORK

THE BERKLEY PUBLISHING GROUP
Published by the Penguin Group
Penguin Group (USA) Inc.
375 Hudson Street, New York, New York 10014, USA
Penguin Group (Canada), 90 Eglinton Avenue East, Suite 700, Toronto, Ontario M4P 2Y3, Canada
(a division of Pearson Penguin Canada Inc.)
Penguin Books Ltd., 80 Strand, London WC2R 0RL, England
Penguin Group Ireland, 25 St. Stephen's Green, Dublin 2, Ireland (a division of Penguin Books Ltd.)
Penguin Group (Australia), 250 Camberwell Road, Camberwell, Victoria 3124, Australia
(a division of Pearson Australia Group Pty. Ltd.)
Penguin Books India Pvt. Ltd., 11 Community Centre, Panchsheel Park, New Delhi—110 017, India
Penguin Group (NZ), 67 Apollo Drive, Rosedale, North Shore 0632, New Zealand
(a division of Pearson New Zealand Ltd.)
Penguin Books (South Africa) (Pty.) Ltd., 24 Sturdee Avenue, Rosebank, Johannesburg 2196, South Africa

Penguin Books Ltd., Registered Offices: 80 Strand, London WC2R 0RL, England

This book is an original publication of The Berkley Publishing Group.

Interior text design by Tiffany Estreicher.

FIRST EDITION: October 2007

Library of Congress Cataloging-in-Publication Data

Hornback-Bland, Heather.
God said yes / Heather Hornback-Bland and Ninie Hammon. — 1st ed.
p. cm.
ISBN 978-0-425-21723-8
1. Hornback-Bland, Heather—Health. 2. Traffic accident victims—United States—Biography. 3. Wounds and injuries—Religious aspects—Christianity. I. Hammon, Ninie. II. Title.

RD93.8.H67 2007
617.10092—dc22
[B]

2007022848

PRINTED IN THE UNITED STATES OF AMERICA

10 9 8 7 6 5 4 3 2 1

Most Berkley Books are available at special quantity discounts for bulk purchases for sales promotions, premiums, fund-raising, or educational use. Special books, or book excerpts, can also be created to fit specific needs.

For details, write: Special Markets, The Berkley Publishing Group, 375 Hudson Street, New York, New York 10014.

I would like to dedicate my life story to a few people. First and foremost, thank you to my Savior Jesus Christ for loving me unconditionally and for showing me in my best and worst days he is with *me. His grace is my shining light every day. Second, to my husband, DeWayne (BUDA), you are my very best friend and you truly have shown me I am lovable and given me the courage not only to do this book but to know that it will be a story of hope to those who hurt. I look forward to the rest of my life with you and thanks for loving my heart, my soul, my scarred body, and my mind. You are worth everything I have been through. Also, to my* precious *daughter, Mackenzie, you are the brightest point of my every day and I am so proud of you. You are beautiful inside and out and one of the most compassionate people I have ever known. Being your mom is the greatest gift Jesus has ever given me. I love you forever and a day, Baby Girl. Last but not least, Mom and Dad. You both have been my example of a Christ-centered love and you knew that DeWayne was my forever love—like Dad is yours, Mom. You have given when it was too hard for anyone else and shown me how to depend on my Savior like you always have. I pray every day to be a spouse, a parent, and a friend like I have watched both of you be. Mom, my accident may have started out a tragedy, but our walk is a true testament to trusting that joy in pain is a real blessing.*

—Heather

HEATHER'S ACKNOWLEDGMENTS

This book has been a long walk with many people and this is where I want to share my heart with several that have been on this journey with me. Some of them have always been by my side and some are in and out of my life—but they have each been a piece of this book whether their names are in it or not.

To Ninie, thanks for the time, love, and support you and Tom have given me. Ninie, thanks for the hours of writing and praying, the laughter and tears to make this the best book. I believe God knew you would tell it as honest and straightforward as I always hoped it could be. THANKS.

I want to thank Southeast Christian Church for thirty years of growth in my faith and I want to thank a few specific people. Bob, wow, what a true teacher and faithful friend you have been to me. Mike, you are one of my best friends and you have been such an inspiration in my life. You are a true example of having grace through life's storms. Greg, you crazy guy, thanks for sticking by me—from high school through today—and showing me to trust that God has always had a plan for my life. Dave, God bless this new road you're on and keep your heart on Christ—thanks for always caring about and supporting me. To Debra and Debbie, thanks so much for your behind-the-scenes support and for showing me faith in prayer all this time. Also, to the VINE, you rock my heart; and, Rachel, thanks for sharing this with me—trust in God's plan for you. Dare to DREAM! Also, to the high school kids at Christian Academy, thanks for showing me my true speaking voice.

To all of my doctors, nurses, lab and x-ray staff, the friends I have made in all the different hospitals is a gift. It was a miracle how God placed so many people in my life that not only cared but also never let me quit. I also want to say to those who bailed when insurance failed or they saw no hope: God showed me the way to get to the next day and placed new people to pick me up. To those few that have gone above and beyond, THANKS will never be enough.

To some friends that keep me sane, like Laura, Rachel, Vicki, Sheri, Susan, Linda S., Linda P., ReRe, Tammy, Kelli, Kim, Bill, and Kelly, it has been a rough road but a blessed one because of you. You have seen me at my worst and loved me through it, and I am a better person for the things each of you has brought to my life. I have had so many people come in and out of my life, and as much as that hurt, I am now stronger and better for it. Mom has always told me two things: (1) If you can count your true friends on one hand, you are truly blessed, and (2) people always disappoint. For anyone I have disappointed or for those that walked away, I wish you all the happiness life has to offer.

Malcolm, Jimbo, Ann, and Carolyn are new to my crew, but I look forward to all the memories to come. Kenny W., I am so thankful that you are such a special part of my life. Thanks for giving me courage and friendship all these years. You have helped me keep it real. To Melanie, Whitney, and Savannah, you girls stay true to your hearts and I'll always be here for you. Matthew, you stay true to yourself and stay strong with your walk. You are a little hottie! Go #11! Phil C., thanks for loving us. We miss you. Shawn, thanks for all your help and for being a friend. I believe giving people like you will be blessed greatly one day. To the M word and V., love like you have never been loved, dream like never before, and trust one another and cherish a real soul mate!

To my father, Will, I am glad you are in my life now and I am praying for you and my family out west. I can never thank my siblings and family—step, half, and whole, Mamaw and Poppy, Jimmy, Sissy, aunts, uncles, and cousins—enough for keeping me real. For loving me and for supporting me. To my cousin Suzie, never forget *Coal Miner's Daughter.* I love you all for the things each of you has brought to my life. Also, to my grandmother, grandpa, my son, Christopher, and Aunt Nina, I miss you everyday, but I have a peace knowing I will see each of you again.

To Jamey, I want to thank you for the greatest joy and gift in my life: Mackenzie. I hope you and Terri are happy; and, Terri, thanks for being such a good stepmom and friend to Kenzie. I am glad she has all of us.

To Rebel, thanks for always loving me and for believing in me. God made us so different but he has brought us full circle. I love you and will always be one of your biggest fans. Tim, thanks for loving her so well and for loving Christ so much. And to Jack and Sam, your aunt Heather loves you heart and soul.

To DeWayne's parents, Joe and Virginia, thanks for raising such a wonderful, loving son and for instilling such a strong faith in his heart. He is my best friend. Thanks to all who have taken Mackenzie and me in as part of your family. I hope that we all get closer as the years go by.

I know that my book is dedicated to them but, DeWayne (Buda), Mackenzie, Mom, and Dad, "thanks" will never be enough and, wow, isn't our Savior amazing! Buda, I can't wait to love you the rest of our lives here on Earth and in heaven.

Thanks to everyone who has been a part of my life and touched me in some way. Each of you has given me the courage to share, and my prayer every day is that this book can give hope to someone who hurts, and that they can see how my joy has always outweighed my pain.

—Heather

NINIE'S ACKNOWLEDGMENTS

I would like to thank my husband, Tom, for being my biggest fan, my rock of support, and my best friend through the process of writing this book (and all the rest of the time, too). Thanks for putting up with my insane, middle-of-the-night writing schedule, and for picking me up, dusting me off, and pushing me back into the ring when I was convinced I didn't have another word left in me.

I would like to thank my children and grandchildren for breathing in and out on a regular basis. You guys give me joy just by existing. To Shane, the filmmaker: You are the oldest son every mother prays for. To Jeremy, the police officer: I am so very, very proud of you. To Joshua, the computer geek: Your sunny disposition has brightened my world since the day you were born. To Jana and Karen: Thanks for putting up with my boys. To Anjel, Dakota, Caleb, Logan, Megan, Jacob, and the bun in the oven: You make me glad I didn't eat my young. To my new children, Luke, Jamie, and Brett: Thank you for sharing your father with me, and for the richness and joy each of you has brought into my life. To my sister-in-law Sharon: I'm sorry Tom put gum in your hair.

And a very special thanks to Heather for granting me the privilege of telling her incredible story.

—Ninie

AUTHORS' NOTES

When I became a mom, I learned what it meant to love someone enough to die for them. When I look at Mackenzie, I get a tiny glimpse of how much God loves me. I am profoundly grateful that the experiences of my life have allowed me to see in extraordinary ways that I am precious beyond measure to my Heavenly Father, that he tiptoes into my room at night, looks down on me, and is filled with unconditional love.

The path God picked out for my life isn't what I would have chosen if he had consulted me. He didn't. I would never have picked suffering. I would have selected an innocent childhood, a carefree adolescence, a houseful of children, a healthy body—a basic, garden-variety, normal life. Over the years, I have learned that this is my normal. For me, normal was growing up in a hospital, greeting pain every morning with the sunrise, struggling with fear, anger, and despair. That's all I've ever known.

But because my life has been hard, it has also been normal for me to see God do astonishing things, to watch him lovingly care for my needs in remarkable ways. No matter how bad my day has been, God always shows me my blessings.

The process of telling my story has been an incredible gift because it gave me a chance to step back and look at my life from a different perspective. What I saw was not just how awful it had been, but how all that I went through has shaped who I am today. God will meet you wherever circumstances have taken you, and if you'll let him, he will walk beside you—sometimes pick you up and carry you—every step along your life's journey. I wouldn't trade what my experiences have taught me about God's grace, care, comfort, healing, and faithfulness for all the health and happy memories in the world.

If no one ever reads a word Ninie has written about me, unpacking my life has still been worth every bit of effort we put into telling this story.

And there was effort. We sat together in my living room every day for months. When Ninie turned on her tape recorder and picked up her notepad, that was my cue to relive my life. Not just remember it, *relive* it. Ninie asked hard questions; she wanted details. So I climbed back into the ten-year-old Heather and relived the nightmare of abuse. I became nineteen again, riding a stallion free across a golden meadow. I stepped into the heart of a young mother, cradling her dead baby in her arms.

I shed buckets of tears during those months of interviews. We both did. And we laughed, too. The joy, the humor, the laughter, the private jokes that only my mom and I knew—those were God's grace shining down on me.

I also discovered just how many of my memories were "borrowed" memories. "How do you know what your mother and your grandmother did that afternoon?" Ninie—forever the journalist—would ask. "You were in the operating room hanging upside down being cut open." Of course, I knew because my mother told me about it later. Over the years, I've heard the fill-in-the-gap stories so often, they feel like my own memories.

Ninie spent hours interviewing my mother, who could fill in the gaps better than anyone else. And Ninie talked to other significant people in my life to get their firsthand memories, too.

May I ask you to do something for me? When you read my memories—both borrowed and my own—in this book, will you look beyond a little girl/teenager/young woman's pain and suffering? Allow yourself to be touched, not by the sadness, but by God's gifts of joy that turned my tragedy into victory!

—Heather Hornback-Bland

I met Heather in 1996 when I wrote a story about her for the newspaper where I served as executive editor. We became friends. I had written several other stories about her through the years before the day in 2005 when I commented in casual conversation: "Heather, I've always wanted to write a book about your life." That's where it started.

After that came months of interviews, of asking her painful questions and watching her crumble under the weight of some of the memories, of crying with her as she spilled her guts, of writing, writing, and writing—speaking in Heather's voice, sharing her heart. Though I spent a quarter of a century as a journalist, Heather's is the most challenging story I have ever told. How do you tack words onto the kind of suffering she has endured; how do you describe the way God has held her so tenderly in the palm of his hand?

Before I wrote this book, I thought I knew how difficult Heather's daily life was. I didn't have a clue. Few who know her do because she always looks perfectly normal, her hair fixed, her makeup on, wearing a cheerful smile. No one who sees her at lunchtime would ever guess she spent the morning throwing up pints of blood, had doctors stabbing injections directly into her lungs, and had nurses sticking IV needles over and over again into her neck and between her toes.

God's grace has been sufficient for Heather in a more profound way than the rest of us will ever be able to fathom. It is an honor and a privilege for me to take readers by the hand and lead them into a world they never imagined existed, where an incredibly courageous woman depends for every breath on a God who is always faithful.

—Ninie Hammon

My mother's memories of the sunny spring day thirty-two years ago when she ran over me are seared into her brain like mental snapshots, freeze-frames with the detailed clarity of digital photographs.

Click, click.

The open car door, the empty seat where I had been perched on my knees, babbling little-girl speak to my six-year-old sister in the backseat.

Click, click.

My four-year-old body lying faceup on the asphalt, blood spreading out in a crimson pool beneath me, the wide, racing-slick tire on the front of the Dodge Charger resting squarely on my tiny belly.

Click, click.

The doctor's face when he told her that I could not possibly survive, that my internal organs had been reduced to "ground meat," that Mom could see me briefly before they wheeled me into the operating room—so she could kiss her baby daughter good-bye.

Between the frozen images in my mother's mind are streams of moving scenes, some of them played out in an elongated slow motion, others in a kind of frenetic fast forward where events and people and life are moving way too fast.

Mom wanted so many times to scream, "Stop!" She wanted to grab hold of the out-of-control events and rein them in, to prove that this was all a huge mistake, that this raging nightmare wasn't really happening. She wanted to halt the freight-train rush of unthinkable horror long enough to convince somebody, somewhere, to grant her a do-over, a replay that would begin with the ritual car-door check she performed every time she put my sister and me into the car—every time except that time.

By all rights, my mother should have been overwhelmed by guilt and despair—hysterical, maybe, or in the uncomprehending haze of denial and shock. But she wasn't. In the middle of the chaos, she felt a strange peace. She was calm, not dazed, but serene. Mom got down on her knees beside me as I lay bleeding on the pavement, so close her face filled all of my view, and told me firmly that everything would be okay. She told me the same thing over and over again until the ambulance arrived, during the siren-shrieking ride to the hospital, and in the emergency room. And she whispered the words urgently into my ear as nurses in white, starched uniforms wheeled me toward the double doors of the operating room—everything will be okay! And strange as it seemed, my mother actually believed it would be.

ONE

When the Louisville Metro Police patrolman flipped on his blue lights and whipped his cruiser in a U-turn from the west- to the eastbound lane of Interstate 64 in the predawn darkness of a crisp Sunday morning in September 2005, he was certain he had a live one. He wouldn't have cut twin tire tracks across the wet grass in the median for just anything—but he had just watched the driver of a silver Jeep pull to a stop in the emergency lane on the other side of the road, stagger out of the vehicle, and begin violently throwing up. The officer called it in.

"Suspected DUI, eastbound I-64 one mile west of the Cannon's Lane exit," he told the dispatcher as his patrol car bounced up out of the median onto the pavement. Pulling up behind the Jeep, which wasn't even completely off the road out of the lane of traffic, he flicked his headlights on high beam to better illuminate the license plate, and read off the numbers into his hand-held mike. Then he waited, watching the tall, dark-haired woman heave uncontrollably, holding onto the driver's side door for support.

The response came back in less than a minute.

The 1998 Jeep Cherokee Jefferson County, Kentucky, license plate number 871-Adam-Charlie-Baker was registered to a thirty-six-year-old white female, the dispatcher told him. No priors, no warrants, no outstanding tickets. The owner's name was Heather Bland.

. . .

I had seen him coming. When I spotted the cruiser on the other side of the interstate, I knew he'd be all over me. They always were—particularly on Sunday mornings.

Please, God, let this one be a nice guy, I pleaded silently.

I gathered as much strength as I could muster and stood up straight as he walked up to me. I think I even managed a smile. It was a shaky smile, but it was the best I could do.

"Closed down the bar at Coyote's, did ya," the officer said. It was a statement not a question.

"No, sir," I replied courteously. "I didn't go to a bar last night. I don't drink. I went . . ."

He didn't let me finish.

"I need to see your driver's license, registration, and proof of insurance, please," he said.

I tried to comply. I was able to get the registration and insurance card out of the glove box, but I was still fumbling in my purse for my wallet when another round of nausea seized me. I had just enough time to sweep my hair back out of my face before the noxious, foul-smelling stream of stomach bile and old blood spewed out of my mouth onto the pavement, setting the ulcers in my throat and on my gums aflame in a dozen points of searing pain—and splattering on the policeman's shoes.

"I am sooo sorry . . . !" I began breathlessly when the reflexive gagging finally let up. "I didn't mean to . . ."

"Ma'am, I need you to step away from the vehicle, please," he said tightly, all business. "And I want you to hold your arms straight out to the sides, shoulder high . . ."

Oh, no, not a sobriety test. Not now!

". . . tilt your head back, close your eyes, and touch your right index finger to the tip of your nose . . . Can you do that for me, please?"

I gathered all the strength I could manage and looked the officer dead in the eye.

"No, I can't do that," I said firmly. "I can't lean my head back and close my eyes. It will just make me more nauseous. I'm not drunk; I'm sick."

I could tell the officer wasn't buying.

"What's wrong with you?" he asked, and the hint of sarcasm in his words hit my spirit like a drop of water in hot grease.

For one brief, wild moment, I ached to tell him *exactly* what was wrong with me, all of it, to spew the whole story out at him like I'd spewed vomit all over his shoes.

"You want to know what's wrong with me?" I shrieked at him in my head. "Okay, I'll tell you! I fell out of a car and my mother ran over me when I was four years old and I've been operated on 187 times in the past thirty-two years. Sixty-three of those surgeries lasted more than twelve hours, two of them took more than twenty, and during one of them I woke up while they were cutting me open. I've died on the operating table . . . what? half a dozen times, maybe—I've long since lost count of exactly how many. And of how many documented medical miracles I've racked up—twelve or thirteen at least. I owe more than $1.5 million in medical debt. And right now I'm being eaten alive!"

But I grabbed hold of the angry words before they lunged out of my mouth, and let the rage blow through me like a squall across a lake. Then the phrase showed up, as it always did eventually, on the projector screen of my mind. The old phrase, as worn as a tattered house shoe, was comforting somehow just because it was familiar, because it had defined my response to reality every day that I could remember: *Just suck it up and go on*. I half-smiled at the phrase. My mother must have said those words to me a thousand times. Self-pity simply was not an option. Mom never once allowed me to throw a poor-Heather party.

"I haven't been to a bar," I said politely, trying to sound calm, reasonable, and rational as I struggled fiercely to keep the nausea at bay. "I've been at the hospital all night."

I considered pulling up my sleeve to show him the recent IV punctures, but thought better of it. One look at the needle tracks on my arms and I'd never be able to convince him I wasn't a junkie. Instead, I felt around in the pocket of my sweatpants.

"Here's the stub from the parking garage," I said, handing it to him. "I take treatments that make me very, very sick. You can call the garage. The parking attendant will tell you I just left there. You have to talk kind of loud. He's an old guy and he's a little hard of hearing. He'll remember me, though. I'm there every night. Just tell him you want to know about the sassy lady who always teases him about his Yankee accent."

The policeman looked at the ticket for a moment, then turned and strode back to his cruiser. As soon as he was out of splatter range, I let fly again, retching until tears from the violent heaving spilled down my cheeks. I was no longer just throwing up old blood. Most of what came streaming out of my mouth was light, not dark, red. When I finished gagging, I leaned back against the Jeep, weak and breathless.

The officer would check out my story and find out it was true. Maybe he'd offer to escort me home. Twice, other policemen had done that when they found me sick on the side of the road. In fact, a team of officers had once found me on the other side of the I-64 tunnel, and one of them had actually gotten in my Jeep and driven me home while his partner followed. Nice guys. Those cops were really nice guys.

I got sick once more—vomiting nothing but fresh, bright red blood. At that rate, I knew I'd soon need another transfusion, and I'd already gone through twelve pints of blood and two of platelets—just in the past two weeks. Then I raised my head to find the policeman standing beside me. He held out something to me and I took it, thinking it was the parking stub. It wasn't. It was a traffic ticket.

"Your vehicle isn't pulled properly off the road into the emergency lane," the officer said. "Your court date is October 9th, in traffic court. That's in the courthouse downtown. Or you can mail in the ticket with a check to the Jefferson County Circuit Clerk's office. Just make sure they get your payment before your court date. The fine's on the citation."

I looked down at the ticket, dumbfounded. It took me a moment to locate the amount. Two hundred and fifty dollars!

"You need to move your car, ma'am," the officer told me, and before I could say a word, he turned on his heel and marched back to his patrol car. He called out something to me as he got into the cruiser, but the whooshing roar of a passing truck blew his words away. All I caught was ". . . and turn on your flashers."

I stumbled into the driver's seat, turned the key, and pulled the Jeep forward about ten feet—all the way into the emergency lane. I flicked the switch that set the twin red lights on the back blinking furiously. The officer turned off his blue lights, pulled around me, and drove away, leaving me there alone in the darkness on the side of the road.

I opened the Jeep door and dry-heaved, then pulled the door closed and put my head down on the steering wheel in utter exhaustion. Two hundred fifty dollars! Where on earth could I come up with that kind of money? And for what? Because my back tire was six inches over the white line? What kind of heartless robot gives out tickets to sick people? I guess if I'd been dead, he'd have arrested me. I was furious! And tired, so very, very tired. Suddenly, I felt myself teetering on the edge of collapsing in a sobbing heap.

But I refused to give in to the wave of emotion. I sat there for a time—five minutes? half an hour?—nausea making my head swim. Then slowly, deliberately, I shook off the trembling and steadied myself, summoning strength from some deep reservoir of faith—as I had done so often over the years.

"My life should come with a warning label," I whispered grimly. "Don't try this at home!"

Hey, that was pretty good, I thought, and in spite of myself a tiny bud of a smile popped into bloom on my face.

Joy. That's right, find the joy! Focus on the joy.

The words worked their magic and I began to relax, settling back into the worn leather seat. Every day of my life, God had given me a treasure beyond price—a joy so sweet and tender that it soothed my soul like warm breath on cold fingers.

I thought of DeWayne. With the image of his face, I let out a slow sigh and a genuine, though trembling, smile blossomed beneath the streaks of tears. DeWayne, my rock of support. The man who loved me unconditionally, not in spite of the scars and bags but because "they give you your heart, baby." If I concentrated, I could almost feel the warmth of his long arms, cuddling me close. He always slept better if he was touching me. I'd had to ease myself carefully out of his grasp that morning, sliding a pillow into his arms in my place to keep from waking him.

My routine was the same every morning, had been the same for almost six months.

. . .

The insistent *beep-beep-beep* of the alarm clock jarred me from a shallow, uneasy sleep at 2:30 A.M. My first waking thought was always the same, a simple prayer: *Please, let them get the needle in today—first try! Please, no digging . . . no digging!*

In the semidarkness of our bedroom, I turned the oscillating fan full force on my sleeping husband and staggered bleary-eyed to the bathroom. Though the pain was there almost every day of my life, it was still jarring to wake up to it. It seemed worse, somehow, in the vulnerability of sleepiness, before I could summon the will to relegate it to the special place in my mind I had created for it years before, where its presence simply was not acknowledged.

But in the early morning, I experienced my pain. I hurt. The usual suspects always showed up the moment I opened my eyes. Abdominal pain in the mother of all incisions—an eighteen-inch zipper of rubberized scar tissue from the back of my pelvis to my sternum. Aching in the tangled labyrinth of old adhesions and in the half-dozen hernias in the wire mesh that served as my abdominal wall and muscles.

Oh, I could do something about the pain if I wanted to. There were drugs that would make it all go away. But I refused to take daily doses of heavy-duty pain meds! Period. No discussion. For one thing, it would require a dosage big enough to fell an elephant to put a dent in my discomfort. My body's resistance to pain medication—and to anesthesia—was legendary among the army of medical professionals who had cared for me in the three decades since an accident in 1973 "exploded" most of my internal organs. Percocet. Dilaudid. Morphine. Darvocet. Vicodin. Two milligrams of any of them would launch the average person into la-la land. I required 15 to 18 milligrams just to take the edge off, more than that for any real relief. What I needed would kill most people.

And it wasn't just that they'd have to funnel pain meds into me through a fire hose. There was a more important reason why

I refused drugs, a reality I held to with ferocious determination. I had a life! I had a daughter to raise, a husband to care for, meals to cook, a house to clean. I went to church, coached cheerleading, and tutored special students. I couldn't do any of those things as a drugged-out zombie. I'd rather hurt.

But this new pain . . .

A cold fear snaked into my belly, curled up, and began to gnaw at my insides like a lazy rat. I was not yet awake enough to banish it, and my fever must have risen during the night—probably to 103, maybe higher—leaving me weak and vulnerable.

I've always been healthy! I cried out in silent defiance. *Injured, but healthy. I was hurt, not sick.*

And God brought me through it, beat the odds, proved them wrong—every time! If I had a nickel for every time a doctor has told me I wouldn't make it, I'd have enough money to— I stopped short in mid-rant, then completed the thought, sans defiance. *Enough money to pay for medicine to keep me alive.*

Standing on the cold tile of the bathroom floor, I unwillingly catalogued the new pain. My lungs hurt. My stomach hurt. My head hurt—from lack of sleep and fever. My kidneys hurt. My bowels hurt.

And the sores . . .

I slipped the oversized T-shirt I slept in over my head and turned on the tap to run a bath. As warm water filled the tub, I faced the full-length mirror on the back of the bathroom door and surveyed the open ulcers on my body.

My buttocks were covered with oozing lesions—from infection expelled during violent bouts of diarrhea. New sores had formed under my arms during the night—from infection in my perspiration. There were ulcers in every orifice of my body—my mouth, nose, ears, rectum, and vagina, and all around the port for the urostomy bag that collected my urine.

I stepped into the tub and sat down gingerly, the warm water stinging like wasp bites in dozens of places. And in the stillness, a single word began to ring in my head like some idiotic Chinese gong, keeping rhythm with the thudding pain of my headache, louder and louder until I wondered why the sound didn't awaken my husband.

Finally, I expelled the word from my mind into the room, speaking it in a hushed, almost quizzical whisper.

"Staph," I said softly, with a degree of incredulity still, even after all these months. "I have a staph infection that's eating me alive."

I picked up a big sponge, squirted sweet-smelling liquid soap onto it from a bottle on the edge of the tub, and began to lather my arms and chest, determined not to allow my mind to download images of the other people with staph who had begun taking the experimental German drug the same time I did that spring. People who had learned each other's life stories during the hours we spent together as the drug dripped slowly through IV tubes into our arms. There had been eight of us . . . but that was seven funerals ago.

And I struggled not to hear the doctors' voices. But I was just too tired. The tapes of their dire predictions turned on in my head and began to play whether I liked it or not.

Heather, you and DeWayne need to liquidate everything you have, travel around the country with Mackenzie, and enjoy yourselves this summer. You won't be here in September.

Heather, we're denying your request to become a part of our drug study because it is the belief of the doctors here at Johns Hopkins that we wouldn't have a good result with you. You're just too far gone.

Heather, I don't have any idea what it will do to you to double the dose of this medication. It's an experimental drug, all bets are off. Nobody else in the world has ever taken doses this high. But then nobody else on Earth is up walking around with staph in every major organ of their body, either. I'll sign off on the medicine because I don't see what we have to lose. The drug may kill you. But if you stop taking it, the staph most certainly will.

Double the dosage. The words sent a chill down my spine. Oh, not because I feared the physical consequences. That I could handle. I could take it. Bring it on. I'd seen worse. I was not afraid of the toll the strange concoction would take on my body. On the contrary, I welcomed the additional medication—because I believed it would work. I believed I was about to log yet another medical miracle, to add to the list of more than a dozen I had racked up over the years.

The trouble was that double the dosage meant double the expense. A month's supply of medicine, mailed to me from Germany, cost $4,200. Where were DeWayne and I going to get the money to pay for twice as much every month? And that was in addition to my normal monthly medical expenses—$2,200 for medication and $250 for urostomy supplies. The grand total was so staggering I couldn't fit it into my head without pieces of it hanging out my ears. So I stopped trying.

Instead, I softly recited the words that had become a mantra in the past six months, words that calmed me and granted me peace, words I believed as confidently as I believed in sunrise on Easter Sunday morning: *God didn't get me this far to let me die from a staph infection!*

I stood up, stepped out of the tub, and dried off carefully, gently patting my skin dry around the oozing sores. Then I took stock of my urostomy. Doctors had built a stoma in my side when I was twenty-six, surgically implanting a permanent tube that drained urine into a bag taped to my stomach.

What a battle that had been!

I had fought so hard against it. More than anything else in the world, I had wanted to be normal, "regular." As a kid, I underwent one surgical procedure after another—not just to repair the damage done to my body when my mother ran over me, but to rebuild my internal organs. Surgeon after surgeon tried to reconstruct the bladder and ureters that had exploded when the tire of the Dodge Charger crushed my belly. The surgeons honestly believed they could fix me; I had to give them that. And I had egged them on. More than half of the 187 surgeries I had undergone were attempts to rebuild organs that no longer existed. Failed attempts.

I remember the disappointment and the outrage I felt when I was finally forced to face the undeniable truth. There was no way to re-create the organs that had been destroyed. It just wasn't possible. I'd have to have a permanent urostomy and wear a bag for the rest of my life. It was perhaps the hardest adjustment I ever had to make—in a lifetime full of extraordinary adjustments.

It took time, lots of tears, lots of anger, lots of prayer, before I came to accept the bag as a simple fact of life, not the end-all evil of existence I thought it was when I was young.

But that morning I had other issues with the urostomy, issues plainly visible in the mirror on the back of the bathroom door. The urostomy had collapsed into my abdomen. I wasn't surprised. I'd seen it coming. For months, I had been postponing surgery to repair the stomas—holes—in the wire mesh surgeons used to replace the abdominal wall and muscle structure of my belly. Without a solid base to hold to, the urostomy was bound to cave in eventually. Bad as the collapse was, I couldn't have surgery to fix it. I couldn't have surgery period, for any reason. If doctors cut into my abdomen, the staph infection would get into my bloodstream and I'd be dead in minutes. And this time when I died on the table, they wouldn't be able to shock me back.

I would just have to live with the stomas, the doctors had said. But I couldn't live with the collapsed urostomy. When it caved into my belly, the opening squeezed partially shut, and it was crimping the tubing that drained urine out of my kidneys—like standing on a garden hose. That would have to be fixed . . . somehow.

Meanwhile, I had a compound dilemma. Not only did I have a collapsed urostomy, I was out of urostomy supplies. I had none of the special tape that held the cohesive ring around the opening in place and kept it from leaking. I'd used the last I had the day before—but I hadn't told DeWayne about it. We needed groceries. And the cost of urostomy supplies, which used to run $250 a month, had almost doubled because the staph kept my urostomy site constantly infected.

No tape. I sighed. There was nothing to do but use duct tape again. It wouldn't be the first time. I couldn't help smiling at the thought of adding mine to the ever-growing list of duct tape uses. Every good ole boy in Kentucky knew you could fix just about anything with duct tape—from patching a flat tire to mending a broken putter. One of my nurses at Boston Children's Hospital when I was sixteen told me her fiancé's friends duct-taped him naked to a freeway exit sign the night of his bachelor party.

I wondered if anybody ever thought of using duct tape on a urostomy. Maybe somebody would see humor in that, but I didn't. And I certainly wouldn't think it was funny when I had to peel the tape off to change the bag. Its super-stickiness would most likely take a layer of my skin with it, leaving behind a raw spot—a perfect human petri dish in which to grow staph.

But there was nothing else to do, so I wrapped a bath towel around me and went downstairs to retrieve the roll of tape from the toolbox in the storage closet under the stairs. Back in the bathroom, I taped my bag securely in place and then reached for my makeup. The face that stared back at me when I looked into the mirror above the sink was pale and wan. And tired. So very, very tired. I had trained myself to make do with four or five hours of sleep a night. Any idiot knew that wasn't enough, but it was all I had.

A little eyeliner, dark base makeup, and blush so I wouldn't look so pale, and a swipe of lipstick later, I pulled on sweatpants and a sweatshirt and tiptoed into Mackenzie's bedroom, where I just stood for a few minutes, smiling down at her. What was it that made a sleeping kid so adorable?

With her flaxen hair fanned out in a halo around her head on the pillow, Mackenzie bore no physical resemblance to me. Our resemblance ran below what you could see on the surface.

She's been through a lot for a ten-year-old, I thought.

Like me, Mackenzie had been a "hospital child." She had spent the first eight and a half months of her life in a children's ward, where doctor after doctor tried to figure out what was wrong with the baby whose birth almost killed me. Mackenzie wouldn't eat. She couldn't eat. She didn't know how to suck. She was fed through a feeding tube directly into her stomach until she was three years old. When Mackenzie was seven—tall, thin, all arms and legs, just like I had been at that age—I learned that my only daughter had epilepsy.

Just last month, allergy doctors discovered that Mackenzie was also allergic to a boatload of everyday substances: mold, dust, mildew. Her body's reaction to them was what caused the bouts of wheezing that so terrified her—and me. The inhalant steroids and bronchial dilators to control the symptoms would cost $400 a month once the samples the doctor had given her ran out. Where we'd find the money to pay for them was anybody's guess.

Mackenzie deserves a life where she's not afraid every day that her mommy's going to die. The thought galvanized me, and I quietly turned off the multicolored nightlight DeWayne had given her for her tenth birthday, pulled up the covers she had kicked off in her sleep, and kissed her tenderly on the forehead, silently mouthing: I love you.

When I pulled the front door quietly shut behind me and stepped out into the cool, crisp darkness, I was in my zone—the emotional, psychological, and to some extent physical space from which I could accept and cope with whatever medical procedure I had to endure. It was a profoundly spiritual space, too, where I turned every element of my life over to God, and rested safe in his sovereignty.

I climbed into my silver Jeep. It had logged 160,000 miles before the odometer broke, and its exhaust system was held together with my ever versatile friend—duct tape! The Jeep had carried me downtown for my staph infection treatments every morning for so long it could just about find the hospital all by itself. As its tired engine rattled to life, I allowed myself only one thought. The usual thought. A simple prayer: *Please, let them get the needle in today—first try! Please, no digging . . . no digging*!

TWO

I don't remember anything at all about the accident that changed the course of my life and the lives of every member of my family. I was only four years old, and the trauma of what happened must have wiped my memories clean. My own recollections begin after I was released from the hospital. But for my mother, father, and sister, my grandparents and others who were there, every moment of what happened is urgently, painfully clear even after more than three decades. Over the years, I heard them tell the story so many times that I have adopted their memories as my own. Now, it's almost as if I can remember it, too, like I can recall with perfect clarity the hot, muggy May afternoon in 1973 when Mom set a pot of ribs on the stove to boil while she ran an errand.

Mom didn't intend to be gone long. Dad was selling his motorcycle, and she had to show it to a prospective buyer. Dad didn't really want to sell the bike. It was an expression of his free spirit. He was stuck in a boring, unglamorous job as a Greyhound bus driver. Every morning, he dressed in a drab, gray uniform and piloted what he called "a human cattle truck" coast to coast. That kind of lifestyle was wrapped way too tight for Dad, so he had bought the bike. Mom had been horrified. She had envisioned his mangled body smashed against a tree every time he climbed on the big Honda 1000, revved the engine, and grinned as the lion's roar of racing-bike rumble filled the air.

But Dad wasn't selling the bike because Mom was worried about him. Theirs was not that kind of relationship. He traveled; she stayed home with my sister and me. They had grown so far apart over the years that they lived virtually separate lives. The marriage was in trouble, serious trouble, and Mom knew it. But she wasn't ready to shake hands with that reality, or to do anything about it once she did.

In fact, Dad wouldn't have sold the motorcycle at all if there had been any way around it. But raising two kids on a bus driver's salary was tough. Money was tight. Something had to go. And so the bike went. Dad had placed an ad in the newspaper and a man had called that morning and asked to take a look at the bike. The motorcycle was parked in a storage building at the rear of the 360-unit apartment complex Mom managed in the northern suburbs of Memphis, Tennessee.

Mom adjusted the temperature of the burner under the pot of ribs, then called my sister and me.

"Heather! Rebel! It's time to go," she shouted out the back door at the group of children playing in the yard behind the apartment. "We have to show Daddy's bike to a man who might want to buy it. Come on!"

The two little girls who ran up to the back door were as different as night and day, midnight and noon. I was dark, with short brown hair in a permanent state of bed head. The thick lenses of my glasses magnified my green eyes, giving me a slightly Mr. Magoo look. Tall for my age, I was skinny as a rail—a bag of bones, my grandfather called me. Even at four, I already had the makings of a tomboy. I had learned to ride a two-wheeler when I was two, liked to play outside in the dirt with the neighborhood boys, and was constantly skinning a knee or scraping an elbow. I'm told that I possessed a remarkably engaging smile, and that beneath the cute little grin lay a will of iron.

Mom joked that the child psychologists who coined the phrase "strong-willed child" must have been hiding under my bed studying me. Stubborn and determined, I was always in charge even though Rebel was two years older. I was the kid the other kids followed, the organizer, the one who had a plan for everything. Like all headstrong children, I had a temper, but it was like thunder—loud, powerful, and over in a flash. And that sunny grin always came peeking through the clouds as soon as the storm was over. My mother still says that when I was a little kid, it was impossible not to like me. Even when people stopped Mom on the street to gush about her gorgeous firstborn child, they usually ended up enchanted with Rebel's ugly duckling little sister, the gangly little pixie who never met a stranger and never stopped talking.

Rebel, six, was a princess, a girly-girl who loved dolls and pretty dresses. She was a strikingly beautiful child, with long, silky blonde hair and wide green eyes—the only physical characteristic she and I shared. Quiet, reserved, and delicate, Rebel could hardly have possessed less of the character her name implied.

Mom still smiles at the memory of her obstetrician's face when he learned what she intended to name her newborn daughter. He had stormed into her hospital room and announced, "You can't do that. You can't give her a name like that—not unless you intend for her to live in the South the rest of her life!" But Mom and Dad had liked the name, just liked the sound of it, so they had stuck to their guns, consigning their firstborn to a lifetime of explanations. By the time I came along two years later, they had mellowed. Heather was a nice, normal, average name—for a child who turned out to be anything but.

A little boy named Kenny lived two doors down from us in the Memphis apartment complex. He was Rebel's age, but always came over to climb trees or build dirt fortresses with me. When Mom called us in to show Dad's bike that day, he and some other neighborhood children were playing in our backyard, too, and I pleaded with Mom to let Kenny go with us to the storage building.

"That's fine with me," Mom said. "Just get in the car, okay? I'm supposed to meet this guy in five minutes."

Mom opened the car door and the three of us climbed inside and sat down. There were no child restraint systems to buckle us into, no car seats. The two-door Dodge Charger didn't even have seat belts. Mom drove through the complex to a big building set back behind the others. The huge warehouse was located in the bottom of a shallow valley shaped like a bowl. An area directly in front of the building was flat, but the rest of the parking lot sloped gradually upward on both sides. Mom parked on the right-side slope. When she pulled into a parking space facing the building, the driver's side of the car was on the downhill side of the slope; the passenger side was on the uphill side.

Rebel, Kenny, and I piled out of the car but didn't scatter. We stuck close to Mom because the cool, shadowy warehouse was an intimidating place, filled with lawn and garden equipment—big mowers attached to even bigger grass catchers, tillers, and swimming pool supplies. Mom had a space staked out for personal items—boxes of Christmas decorations and out-of-season clothing—and that's where Dad's motorcycle was parked. It was safer there than sitting in the yard behind our apartment while Dad was gone all week.

It didn't take long for Mom to show the man the bike; it was obvious that a "crotch rocket" racing bike wasn't at all what he was looking for. He gave the big Honda a quick once-over, thanked Mom politely, and left.

"You guys go get in the car while I turn off the lights," Mom told us, and we instantly complied. We were eager to get out of the building before it was plunged into inky darkness and became a huge, black cave.

When Mom stepped out into the bright sunshine, we were already in the car waiting for her. Rebel and Kenny were in the backseat. I was on my knees in the front seat, leaning back against the car door, babbling nonstop little-girl speak. The door behind me looked like it was shut. But it wasn't. It was closed, not latched. Gravity held it snug against the door frame of the tilted car.

Mom locked the storage building, got into the car, and began to pull out of the parking space, the white noise of my chatter an endearing melody she heard but didn't really listen to.

When the back of the car swung around to the left—downhill—centrifugal force flung open the unlatched right-side door. I vanished.

It happened heartbeat fast; my life, Mom's life, and the lives and futures of every member of our family altered forever in the blink of an eye.

Mom was looking over her left shoulder as she backed out, and she didn't see me fall. But she heard Rebel scream—a piercing, shrieking cry of horror that she would hear in her head for the rest of her life. Reflexively, she hit the brake and stopped the car, even before she turned and saw the open door and the empty seat beside her.

Mom couldn't seem to get out of the car fast enough, seized by a nightmare fear so big it gobbled up all her insides in a single bite. She couldn't breathe and she didn't feel her feet touch the ground as she raced around to the front of the car.

She stopped there, immobilized by horror. The force of what she saw was a physical blow that slammed into her like a wrecking ball. I was lying faceup on the pavement with the right front tire of the Dodge Charger resting on my belly.

God, help me, help me, help me, help me! Mom shrieked inside her head as she scrambled back into the car behind the wheel.

Then she froze. Between one heartbeat and the next, nothing in the universe moved.

Forward or back?

Oh, dear God, do I drive forward or back?

The choice was agonizing—how do you decide a thing like that? Mom couldn't. But the next thing she knew, there was no decision to make. It was over and the car was no longer resting on top of me. It had been moved. Mom didn't know how. She had absolutely no memory of doing anything. When the police asked her later, "Did you drive forward or back?" Mom couldn't answer them.

In her next aware moment, she was kneeling on the pavement beside me. I was making soft, kitten-whimpering sounds as blood began to form a puddle beneath me, an ever-widening circle spreading out from my tiny body.

Rebel was still screaming. She had never stopped. She had jumped out of the car and was running around and around in crazy circles, shrieking hysterically. Kenny's face was as white as flour, his eyes huge. He had leapt out of the car behind Rebel, took one look at me, turned, and bolted for home, a wailing cry trailing after him as he ran.

What happened after that still surprises Mom. Suddenly, calm settled over her. No, more than calm. Peace. Peace enveloped her, forming a shield that fear and panic, hysteria and despair couldn't penetrate. From that moment on, she did everything right. Everything. Later, when she had time to reconstruct the events in her head, she understood. God had taken charge as she sat behind the wheel of the car with her daughter lying crushed under the front tire. From that moment on, he was running the show.

Leaning over me so close her face filled all of my view—my glasses were nowhere to be seen—Mom told me in a firm, calm voice: "Quit crying. Everything's going to be okay. You're going to be just fine. I have to go and get help."

She picked up Rebel and raced toward the back door of the nearest apartment, trying to soothe the hysterical child as she ran, pleading with her to calm down, to be quiet, to stop screaming. But Rebel continued to shriek.

Mom banged once on the first door she came to, then reached through an open window and released the latch on the screen.

She was inside the kitchen and on the telephone before the couple living in the apartment had time to get up from the table.

As totally in charge as a Marine Corps drill instructor, Mom began to bark orders. To the man: "I just ran over my daughter. Get a blanket and go cover her up." To the woman: "Take care of Rebel. Take her into the living room and quiet her down."

Into the telephone, she told the operator what had happened and where to send the ambulance. She didn't falter or stumble and she didn't waste a single word. She provided the correct address along with succinct, accurate instructions on how to weave through the apartment complex to the storage building in the back.

Then she left the receiver dangling and raced back to her baby daughter lying bleeding in the street.

With her face so close to mine our noses almost touched, Mom grabbed hold of my attention and clung to it fiercely, unwilling to let it go even for a second.

"Heather, I'm here. I'm right here," she said kindly but firmly, matter-of-factly. She didn't use the soothing tone that comforted me when I woke up frightened and disoriented in the middle of the night, the voice that lulled me back to sleep crooning the age-old mother melody—*shhhh, Mommyshere, Mommysgotcha, shhhhhh.* Mom did not want to be soothing. She wanted me awake!

"Can you see Mommy? Answer me. Can you see Mommy?"

"Uh huh," I said, nodding my head. "I can see you."

My voice was tiny, but strong. I was lucid and alert.

"Listen to me, sweetheart. You're going to be just fine, do you hear me, just fine!"

The conviction in her words was not an act. Mom honestly believed I would be okay. It wasn't just vain hope; it was certainty. She couldn't have articulated why she believed it. It certainly defied logic, given that I was lying crushed in the street in a puddle of my own blood. But Mom felt that strange peace—not shock, but peace—that she had never felt before. She knew, she *knew* that God would take care of me.

In the focused world of Mom's reality, she was aware of nothing but me, oblivious to the crowd that was gathering, standing mute in an ever-widening semicircle around the two of us, too horrified to say a word. It seemed that hours had passed before an ambulance siren finally began to wail in the distance. Mom never let go of her iron grip on my attention. And I never let go either.

"My tummy hurts," I told her, but I was not crying, just stating a fact.

"I know it does," Mom replied, "but it will be better in a little while. You'll see. In a little while, everything will be okay."

Mom did not budge from my side until an emergency medical technician gently moved her out of the way so he could tend to me. The EMTs were so careful, so tender. They eased me onto a spine board an inch at a time, taking infinite care not to injure me further. Once I was on the board, they lifted me with equal care and moved in lockstep toward the open doors of the ambulance, four big men carrying a tiny child, a tall-for-my-age, skinny little kid whose blood was dripping off the edge of the board onto their shoes as they walked.

Mom was only peripherally aware of other things going on in her environment as the EMTs prepared me for transport to the hospital. Two police officers tried to ask her questions, but she brushed them off, telling them curtly, "I don't have time for that right now."

She spoke briefly to the man who lived in the apartment where she had used the telephone to summon the ambulance. She told him to take Rebel to Kenny's house—his mom would know who to call to come and get her.

After I was loaded into the ambulance, Mom climbed into the cool, brightly lit interior and sat down beside my stretcher on a small seat in a corner, out of the way of the EMTs. She looked up as the double doors swung shut, and caught a brief glimpse of the world—and the life—she was leaving behind. Then she turned her attention back to me, and the two of us began a journey together that would never end.

. . .

Tennessee law requires ambulance attendants to ask patients where they want to be transported. The patients must pick a hospital; the attendants are forbidden to influence their decisions. But that's not what happened. One of the EMTs pointed his finger at Mom and told her firmly, "You want us to take this little girl to Methodist Hospital—don't you!" Memphis

Methodist Hospital had the finest trauma center in the state. Mom didn't know that, but the EMT did.

The ambulance took off for Methodist Hospital like a race horse out of the chute. During the siren-screaming ride, Mom focused on me and kept me talking. I told her repeatedly that my tummy hurt, but I did not cry, and I remained remarkably alert.

Orderlies were waiting with a gurney as the ambulance screeched to a stop outside the emergency room. They whisked me out of the vehicle and onto the wheeled stretcher, and Mom trotted alongside as they rushed me through the emergency room entrance. Once inside, they wheeled me into a huge treatment room, but the doorway was as far as Mom got. She couldn't go in; a nurse literally pulled a curtain shut right in her face.

Suddenly, Mom was just standing there, alone in the hallway. She could hear the furious activity going on in the room beyond the curtain, inches from her nose. But she was no longer a part of it. I was beyond her reach now, beyond the grip of her concentrated attention that had kept me conscious and calm. Beyond her care. Her daughter's fate now lay in the hands of strangers.

That's when it hit her. She had held it together as long as she'd had me to focus on. But now, standing alone in the hallway, some of the reality of what had taken place—in the last . . . how long? hours, surely—began to sink in, and the air went out of her. She started to cry. Not out loud. It hurt too badly to cry out loud. She didn't want to hear the sound of her own grief. She cried silently, tears streaming down her face and dripping off her chin.

An old orderly seemed to materialize out of nowhere. He was ancient, bent and fragile, with a face that was kind in the way that only a face that's been lived in a while can be. His eyes, buried deep inside a web of smile wrinkles, were wells of compassion, the eyes of a man who had seen lots of hurting people over the long years, and who had cared about them all.

He was either so old he could not pick his feet up off the floor or had decided it just wasn't worth the effort. So he shuffled down the hallway, taking his time, until he was right next to Mom. Then he just stood there, waiting patiently, as Mom was wracked by great, heaving sobs that didn't make a sound. Finally, she noticed him standing there. When she turned to face him, he did the most amazing thing. He reached out hands as gnarled as old tree branches and took hold of her upper arms. Then, in one sweeping motion, he lifted her up in the air like a rag doll and plopped her down on a gurney across the hall from the curtained doorway. Mom was flabbergasted.

Leaning very close, he spoke softly into her face.

"You're going to be just fine," he said. "You hear me—just fine. And your baby's going to be just fine, too!"

He picked up a blanket off the end of the gurney and wrapped it snugly around Mom's shoulders. That was the first time she realized she was shaking violently—from shock, but also from cold. She was wearing shorts and a short-sleeved shirt. It had been hot and humid when she began her day a lifetime ago. The hospital was air-conditioned so cold she was surprised her breath wasn't frosting.

The old orderly nodded and smiled reassuringly, then turned and shuffled slowly back down the hallway.

And so she sat, trembling in the blanket, watching the curtained doorway.

A short time later, the two police officers who had been at the scene of the accident approached her. They had followed the ambulance to the hospital. They gave her her purse and car keys. She had left both in the car—with the engine running. Then they wanted to know if they could ask her a few questions. They spoke softly, kindly. Mom told them what had happened. It required only a handful of words to tell the tale. Only a few words for such a monumental event. In a couple of sentences you could describe a reality that was still so huge Mom couldn't fit it into her head. I had fallen out of the car and Mom had run over me. End of story. Just saying the words granted the event substance in the swirling sense of unreality in her mind. It had happened. It really had happened. Mom wasn't going to wake up from this nightmare.

One of the officers asked if Mom wanted to call anybody, and suddenly she realized she needed to call lots of people—foremost, my father. But she had no idea how she'd locate him. A bus driver could literally be anywhere.

The policeman escorted her to a room the size of a closet, with only enough space for a small table, a chair, and a telephone. The phone was a dedicated police line, but the officers told Mom to use it to call anybody she wanted to—local, long distance, it didn't matter. She could talk as long as she liked. She called Dad's boss, her parents in Louisville, Kentucky, and her best friend, Diana. When she'd made all the calls she needed to make, a hospital staff person led her to a nearby conference room where she could wait in private for someone to come out of the room behind the closed curtain to talk to her.

Time passed. Maybe half an hour. Maybe three. Mom was aware that people had joined her in the room. My father was hours away on a charter trip, but his boss located him and he drove straight back to Memphis. In the weeks to come, he did the best he could to cope with the unthinkable.

People who lived in the apartment complex came to the hospital to comfort Mom as soon as they heard about the accident. Her best friend, Diana, came. Like a magic pitcher, the room never emptied; people left, but other people came in and took their places in an endless stream of humanity. Mom greeted them, she thanked them, it really was kind of them to come, she said. But, in truth, she was only dimly aware of their presence. Her whole being was focused on the doorway, waiting for someone to materialize there to tell her about me.

The first doctors who came out to talk to her were totally useless. They were neurologists, and they informed Mom that according to the tests they had run, I had suffered no brain damage.

Well, whoop-de-do, Mom thought. *I know she doesn't have brain damage. I didn't run over her head!* Mom thanked them and waited some more.

An orthopedic surgeon was next. He told Mom that I had suffered massive damage to my pelvis, that it was split in two right down the middle, and that the auxiliary bone structure had been pulverized.

"She will never walk again," the doctor said. "That is . . . if she survives, she will be in a wheelchair for the rest of her life."

Finally, the urologist, who was preparing to operate on my abdomen, came in to talk to Mom. He was kind, but blunt.

"I'm sorry, ma'am," he said. "I have to tell you the truth because I don't want to give you false hope. Your little girl isn't going to make it."

I would die. Another wrecking ball slammed into Mom's chest.

"I'm going to operate and do what I can, but she can't possibly survive this surgery," he continued. "There's just too much damage. All her internal organs are . . . I just don't think there's anything left for me to stitch back together."

"I want to see her," Mom said.

"I'm sorry, ma'am, but we can't let you do that. She is . . ."

Mom interrupted. "I want to see my daughter." There was no room for negotiation. "If she's not going to make it, I want to see her!"

The doctor studied her for a moment. Mom met his gaze, steady. She was upset, but not hysterical.

"Okay," he said tentatively. "But you can't cry. If you cry, we'll have to make you leave."

"I won't cry," Mom promised him. And she didn't.

The doctor led Mom to the treatment room doorway and pulled back the curtain. I was lying on the other side of the room, a tiny form on a big table.

The room looked like a war zone, like some bloody battle had just been fought—and lost—within those four walls. Pieces of my clothing, soaked with blood, lay in soggy piles on the floor. Bloody instruments, trays, and equipment were scattered about like toys in a kid's playroom. Doctors, nurses, and technicians were scurrying to and fro in a crazy dance of organized pandemonium.

I spotted my mother and tried to talk. But the oxygen mask on my nose and mouth muffled my words. Mom rushed across the room to my side.

"What did you say, honey?" Mom asked tenderly.

Again, I tried to speak, but my words were garbled.

"I'm sorry, sweetheart, I can't understand you," Mom said.

I started to speak again, then stopped, reached up, and ripped the oxygen mask off my face.

"I said, I want a drink of water!" I told her petulantly.

The strength and force behind my words was remarkable. And it occurred to Mom that I didn't look like a dying child.

Before Mom had a chance to respond, a nurse standing nearby cut in, "Oh, no, she can't have anything to drink. She's about to go into surgery."

Mom turned to relay the information to me, but I had heard for myself what the nurse said. I didn't have a clue what surgery meant, and I didn't care. All I knew was that I wasn't getting what I wanted.

"I want a drink of water. I'm thirsty!" I demanded again, and Mom could see the beginnings of a temper tantrum forming, like a thunderstorm in the distance.

"Sweetheart," Mom said soothingly. "You can't have anything to drink right now because . . ."

I wasn't buying it.

"I said I want a drink of water—now!" I shouted, temper and defiance lighting twin flames of color in my pale cheeks.

What happened next was a defining event, a seminal moment that set the tone for our relationship in this new reality, a heartbeat of time that laid the foundation for the structure of our lives from this day forward.

Mom leaned over close to my face—and shouted back at me!

"You can't have a drink of water, do you understand me!"

The room went instantly silent. The doctors, nurses, and technicians froze in place, staring in shock at a mother yelling at her dying child.

"You either do as you're told, or I'm out of here! Is that clear?"

I didn't say a word. I just glared at my mother for a few seconds, then nodded, pouting.

And Mom knew in that moment with absolute certainty that I wasn't going to die. I still had more spunk, more life in me than any of those medical professionals realized. No matter what the doctors said, I wasn't going to die.

Nurses in white starched uniforms came in a few minutes later and turned the gurney, with its accompanying forest of IV poles, toward the doorway and wheeled me out. Mom and Diana were allowed to accompany the entourage down the hall and into the elevator for the ride to the second floor, where the operating suites were located. By unspoken agreement, everyone stepped aside and left Mom alone with me for a moment before I was wheeled into surgery.

"You're going to be just fine," Mom told me confidently. "Just fine. Do you understand me?"

I nodded my head.

"I can't go in there with you," Mom said, gesturing to the swinging doors that opened into the operating suite. "So I need for you to do everything these people tell you to do. And I'll be right here waiting for you when you come out. I love you."

"I love you, too, Mommy," I said. As the nurses began to push the gurney, I called out. "I'll be a good girl, Mommy." Then the swinging doors swished shut behind me.

Mom stood for a moment, staring at the closed doors, holding tight to the image of my face, with my hair mussed up, wispy dark strands going every which way. My bed head. She smiled just a little at that thought, then turned with Diana at her side, got back into the elevator, and went down to the first floor intensive care waiting room to wait.

And to pray.

. . .

In Mom's life, prayer was so new the tag was still on it. Until recently, she and Dad had been Buddhists. Well, Dad had been a Buddhist. Mom had just gone along with it, as she'd gone along with all the other religions he'd tried. My father was constantly searching for a spirituality that always seemed to be just beyond his grasp.

But a month before the accident, Mom had gone to a revival at a little Baptist church behind the apartment complex. She went by herself. Dad wasn't interested, though they'd both been raised in traditional churches. She knew who God was, but nobody had ever told her about Jesus. She sat in the pew that night and listened to the minister deliver a simple message. Jesus Christ was the son of God. He had come to Earth to take upon himself the punishment every human being had earned by their evil behavior. He had died on a cross in their place—in *her* place. He had given his life to save the world, to save Mom. And that night, she gave her life to him.

Mom became a believer, a Christian, asked to be baptized on the spot. And even though Dad railed against her decision, she held firm. She was convinced she had found something real, something incredibly precious, and she held tight to her budding faith.

That faith was what she turned to, clung to like a drowning woman to a piece of driftwood, as she sat through the long hours in the waiting room while doctors in the surgery suite above her head tried to piece her daughter back together. She pleaded with God to spare my life, and she felt a peace, the strange peace that had enveloped her when she knelt on the pavement beside my tiny, broken body. Against all reason and logic, she was convinced that I would live. She really believed what she told me before I was wheeled into surgery—everything would be okay.

As the hours dragged by, the mix of people in the waiting room shifted and changed like the colors in a kaleidoscope.

Friends came to offer their support. Mom's mother and stepfather, Helen and Jimmy Gutermuth, drove down from Louisville, five hours to the north. Their car started acting up just outside Louisville and Jim feared a breakdown, so he pulled into the airport in Nashville and rented a car for the remainder of the trip.

More people who lived in the apartment complex arrived to offer comfort. They wanted to help, not add to Mom's burdens, so they didn't tell her about the fire.

It had started in our kitchen late that afternoon. The ribs Mom had put on the stove before she left the apartment boiled dry and caught fire, igniting the cabinets above the stove.

Kenny's mother spotted smoke coming out of our kitchen window and called the fire department.

By the time the fire was out, the kitchen had been gutted. But Mom never saw the damage. She stayed with me the whole time I was hospitalized—got friends to bring her clothes and didn't go home even once. And while she was gone, our neighbors repaired the damage the fire had done. They cleaned the kitchen, replaced the cabinets, and repainted the walls. When they were finished, there was no evidence at all that there had ever been a fire.

Seven hours after I was wheeled through the double doors of the operating room, Mom was summoned to the surgery suite. Though the operation was not yet complete, the urologist stepped out to talk to Mom while another surgeon closed my incision.

"All I could do was try to stop the bleeding," he told her. "We did the best we could, but nothing was where it should have been. It was like her internal organs exploded. They looked like ground meat."

Then he catalogued my injuries. My bladder, urethra, vaginal wall, bladder neck, and one ovary had been ripped out. Most of my small and large bowels had been destroyed and my pelvis was shattered. My reproductive organs . . . well, they couldn't find them. They were unrecognizable.

Medically, I should not have made it to the hospital alive, he said.

"Don't get your hopes up because she lived through surgery," he cautioned. "She can't possibly survive with injuries like that. I'm sorry, but you need to prepare yourself. She's not going to make it."

"Can I stay with her?" Mom asked.

"No, we're putting her in ICU where she'll be monitored every moment."

Mom's face fell.

"But you can go in and see her for a little while—once every hour."

Mom knew he only said that to be kind. He didn't believe for a minute that I would last long enough for her to make even one visit.

Once I was out of recovery and stabilized, the nurses sent for Mom. She and Grandmother went upstairs to the intensive care unit on the third floor, an open ward with nurses caring for critically ill patients in beds scattered around a single, large room.

I was lying in a bed next to the nurse's station in the center of the unit.

"How are you feeling, sweetheart?" Mom asked, kissing my cheek and brushing my hair back off my forehead. "Look, honey, Grandmother's here."

The room was noisy and full of activity. Nurses bustled from patient to patient, checking vital signs, adjusting the flow of fluids from IV bottles, giving injections, and monitoring equipment. Sick and injured people moaned and cried out. I was on edge. I jumped every time there was a loud sound, every time some machine beeped or buzzed.

Mom and Grandmother had only been by my bedside for a minute or two when a nurse motioned that it was time for them to leave.

Bending down close to me, Mom took my small hand into hers and said softly, "Say your prayers before we go and I'll come back in an hour."

That was a mistake. I only knew one prayer.

"Now I lay me down to sleep," I began in a small voice, with Mom saying the words along with me. "I pray the Lord my soul to keep . . ."

Suddenly it hit Mom what came next and she froze, the words hung in her throat and she couldn't make a sound. She tried to speak, but a sudden wave of emotion swept over her, and she knew if she opened her mouth, she would burst out sobbing.

Grandmother moved quickly. She gently shoved Mom aside, took my hand in hers, and chimed in where Mom had left off, repeating along with me . . .

". . . If I should die before I wake, I pray the Lord my soul to take."

• • •

From the moment I was wheeled out of the operating room, doctors calculated my survival chances in increments of an hour.

"If she makes it through the next hour . . ." they said. And they were certain I would not.

When I did, they stretched it to two. Then four, always convinced that the mangled organs in my little belly could not possibly hold out much longer, that soon, very soon, they would shut down and I would close my big green eyes and never open them again. They had seen my injuries; that much damage was simply not survivable. To them, I was a human clock broken beyond repair that would eventually wind down until it finally stopped ticking altogether.

It was only a matter of time, they said.

But my tiny clock kept ticking away. Against all odds it just kept ticking.

All through the night, Mom returned again and again to my bedside. Between visits, she pulled a pair of waiting room chairs together to create a makeshift bed and tried to get some rest. It was a futile effort. As soon as she began to doze off, the chairs would slide apart. By the time she had them situated again, a nurse would appear to tell her she could visit me.

Dawn painted the eastern sky pink, and to the doctors' amazement, I was still holding on, smiling weakly up at Mom when she came in to tell me that she loved me, and that everything would be okay. All through the morning, the doctors continued to issue their dire predictions and I resolutely continued to prove them wrong.

When Mom came to see me after lunch, my bed was no longer snug up against the nurse's station. I had been transferred to isolation, into a dreary, concrete-block room painted a color Mom quickly dubbed baby-diarrhea green.

Mom stood in the doorway of the room for a moment, taking it all in. I looked so tiny in the big bed. Tubes like the tentacles of some gigantic sea creature attached me to equipment that buzzed and hummed and beeped in a dissonant symphony both reassuring and maddening.

Thinking I was asleep, she eased quietly into the room, leaned over, and kissed me gently on the forehead. My eyes popped open.

"How are you doing, honey?" she asked.

I answered Mom's question with a question.

"Do you see her, Mommy?"

My voice was strong; my eyes alert. Mom was amazed at how "with it" I was so soon after such extensive surgery.

"Do I see who?" Mom asked.

"My angel," I responded. "Do you see my angel?"

Maybe I wasn't as "with it" as Mom thought. Maybe some drug they'd given me was causing hallucinations. Mom leaned closer and peered intently into my eyes. My gaze was focused and clear.

"I have an angel," I told her matter-of-factly. "She's right here on my shoulder. Don't you see her?"

"No, I don't see her," Mom said slowly. "But I believe you that you see her."

And she did. If I said I had an angel on my shoulder, then I had an angel on my shoulder. For Mom, it really was that simple.

From that moment on, I was never alone. When Mom came into the room, she would find me talking in a conspiratorial whisper, the way one little girl talks to another in bed at a slumber party, babbling away about everything and nothing in a nonstop stream of chatter. But I didn't do all the talking. Mom saw me listening, too, gazing attentively at what appeared to Mom to be empty air above my right shoulder. Sometimes, I would answer a question Mom didn't hear. Other times, I'd just smile at what I heard and say nothing at all. The angel and I carried on long conversations in the private world that included only the two of us.

I asked everyone who came into the room if they saw my angel, and eventually figured out that I was the only one who did. That didn't seem to bother or even surprise me.

"Your angel is here to stay with you when Mommy can't be here," Mom told me. "God sent the angel to take care of you, to protect you, because you are very, very precious to him."

The angel remained with me day and night the whole time I was in intensive care. As long as the angel was with me, I was calm, relaxed, and quiet. And not in pain.

That part was amazing. I should have been in excruciating pain. My pelvis was broken in half, the bones supporting it shattered, leaving the two pieces to grind together when I moved. My internal organs had been crushed—some of them totally beyond recognition. I had a gigantic incision zipping my torso shut from my sternum to my pelvic bone.

I should have been in agony. And if I had been, there would have been little the doctors could have done about it. My tiny body was much too small, my condition much too tenuous to pump me full of heavy-duty pain medication. But I didn't require it. I lay quietly in the bed talking to my angel, giggling sometimes at what Mom could only assume was an angel joke.

I had required massive blood transfusions, beginning in the emergency room and continuing throughout my surgery. The word went out among the city's emergency services personnel that a little girl had been run over and needed blood, and donors poured into the hospital—EMTs, policemen, firemen, and their families. One of Mom's neighbors, who worked at the Millington Naval Base outside Memphis, spread the word there, and hundreds of sailors showed up at the hospital, too. Within a couple of days, the hospital was so swamped with people who wanted to donate blood for me that there weren't enough nurses and technicians to accommodate the crowds, and potential donors had to be turned away.

Four days after the accident, Dad's sister, Laura, came to the hospital to give blood. Afterward, she came upstairs to the intensive care unit to see me. She walked into my ugly green room, took one look at me lying in the bed, and fainted dead away.

Mom flipped the switch and rang for the nurse.

"Please, I need help in here!" she cried, and a SWAT team of nurses and aides descended on the room, thinking the inevitable was finally happening: The little girl who had hung on for far longer than anybody believed she could was finally dying.

But the only thing wrong with me was that all the action was going on where I couldn't see it. Aunt Laura was lying on the floor with nurses scurrying around tending to her—so I sat up and leaned over the edge of the bed to watch the show.

"Heather—no!" Mom told me firmly, taking hold of my shoulders and gently easing her critically injured daughter back down on the pillow. "Honey, you have to lie down. You can't sit up!"

"But I can't see lying down!" I argued.

Mom kept me horizontal while the nurses got Aunt Laura into a sitting position and gave her a cup of orange juice. And it occurred to Mom that if she hadn't been there to stop me, I might very well have tried to get all the way out of the bed—this child the doctors were still telling her could not possibly survive.

The next day, Mom asked the friend who had been caring for Rebel to bring her to the hospital to visit me. But my older sister got only as far as the doorway of my room. She stopped cold there and refused to go any farther.

"Rebel, come on in and see Heather," Mom coaxed. Rebel stood her ground, shaking her head, but not saying a word.

"Rebel?"

Mom got up, crossed to the doorway, and took Rebel's hand to lead her up to my bedside. But Rebel wouldn't budge. She pulled away from Mom with all her strength and grabbed hold of the door frame so she couldn't even be dragged into the room.

Mom stopped trying to force her into the room and took her out into the hallway instead.

"What's the matter?" she asked, getting down on one knee so she could look Rebel square in the eyes. "Don't you want to see Heather? You're going to hurt her feelings if you don't even go in. What's wrong?"

The six-year-old's voice was very small.

"I don't want to end up like her," she whispered.

Mom's mind stumbled trying to catch the train of Rebel's thought.

"What? What do you mean you don't want to end up . . . ?" Then she got it. Rebel wasn't being defiant; she was terrified. In the twisted logic of a small child, Rebel was afraid that if she got too near, she would "catch" what I had—that the same thing that had happened to me would happen to her.

Mom reached out and pulled the frightened little girl close, hugging her daughter tight as silent tears slid down her cheeks into Rebel's flaxen hair. *Heather's not the only one who's been injured,* she thought, rocking slowly back and forth with Rebel in her arms.

Mom talked to Rebel softly, reassuring her that what had happened to me had been an accident. It wasn't contagious. Rebel was safe. After a few minutes of Mom-hugs and comfort, Rebel was willing to come into my room to visit me. I looked so small in the big bed, with tubes going every which way out of my body, and machines blinking and beeping all around me. Rebel never forgot that sight. It was the first time she had ever seen anything like it, but it wouldn't be the last.

I spent six days in intensive care. The angel on my shoulder stayed with me every minute. But when I was transferred to a private room, the angel didn't go with me.

"My angel is gone," I told Mom matter-of-factly.

"Where do you think she went?" Mom asked.

I shrugged my shoulders. I didn't know. But I wasn't scared. Everything was going to be okay.

THREE

My hospital room looked like a toy store. Colorful balloons floated in the air above my bed. There were stuffed animals in every conceivable shape and size: teddy bears—black, brown, and white ones; soft, cuddly bunny rabbits with floppy ears; puppy dogs and kitty cats. There were baby dolls, rag dolls, and dress-up dolls wearing silk gowns and high heels.

Cookies, candy, fruit—even whole cakes and pies—were delivered to the room almost every day, to be piled on top of the stacks of games and storybooks, dominoes, playing cards, coloring books, and puzzles that filled every available shelf, stacked up high on the windowsills, competing with the water pitcher for space on the bedside table.

My favorite toy among them all was a train with Mickey Mouse as the engineer. He rode in a big, noisy red locomotive with a whistle that *toot-tooted* so loud it could be heard all the way down the hall.

A few days after the accident, the hospital gave Mom a room near mine. Its bed was a bit more comfortable than the chairs pulled together in the waiting room, and it had a private bath. She remained with me 24/7, leaving only occasionally to go down to the hospital cafeteria or outside for a breath of fresh air. Days passed, and as they did, even Mom marveled at how quickly and profoundly I was improving.

By the time I was released from the intensive care unit one day shy of a week after I had been crushed under the front tire of the family's Dodge Charger, my doctors had gone from surprised to totally dumbfounded.

I shouldn't even have survived the accident, they said, shaking their heads in wonder. I should not have made it to the emergency room alive. I shouldn't have lived through the ensuing surgery. And I certainly shouldn't have kept going afterward, lying there with my bladder and most of my bowel ripped out, my pelvis crushed, and other internal organs smashed beyond recognition or repair.

The doctors shook their heads in wonder. Because I was not merely surviving, I was thriving. I was bright-eyed and alert, laughing and talking. A little wisp of a child who should have been dead, I soon refused to be confined to a hospital bed. I demanded to be up and about, and so the hospital provided a child-sized wheelchair. Mom decorated it with crepe paper streamers and balloons, transforming the small red vehicle into a chariot for a traveling ambassador.

"Hi, I'm Heather," I would declare cheerily as I wheeled myself unannounced and uninvited into one room after another up and down the long hospital corridor. "What's your name? Are you sick? What happened to you? I got run over—you wanna see my 'cision?"

Mom accompanied me on my romps through the wing, hanging in the background as I made friends with every patient in the ward—with all their family members and visitors, too—and with every nurse, aide, orderly, technician, doctor, and janitor who set foot on the floor.

She wasn't surprised by my behavior. Visits to the doctor, the optometrist or the dentist's office over the years had always been relational adventures. While Mom flipped through a magazine and Rebel sat quiet and content reading a book, I worked the room.

"Who are you?" I would inquire of the man sitting next to me. And to the woman on the other side: "I'm Heather. That sure is a big purse—what you got stuffed in there?" One after another, I would greet, interrogate, and befriend every person in the waiting room, finding out their life stories, their ailments, their problems, and particularly what kind of car they drove. I was fascinated with cars.

Mom always marveled that nobody ever seemed offended by her bespectacled little daughter's nosey curiosity. It was probably because I was so small, but spoke as clearly as a miniature grown-up. It was hard not to be charmed by the innocence of my questions, and by my tiny, grinning face framed by wispy, flyaway hair. And Mom marveled at the things people would tell me, giving me details about their upcoming surgeries, their arthritis, or their gallstones, while I listened attentively, solemn and sincere as a judge, to everyone's tale of woe.

That's why Mom didn't drop a beat when I pronounced a decree from my hospital bed two weeks after I left intensive care: Everyone who came to see me also had to visit the little boy across the hall. In making my rounds, I had observed that hardly anyone ever went to see him.

"There's this little boy, see, and he got run over by a truck," I explained patiently before I shooed my grandparents, aunts, uncles, and neighbors out the door toward his room. "But when you go in, you can't look at his . . . well, you know. Sometimes the sheet slides down and he doesn't have on any underwear. And he's a boy!"

I instructed my Aunt Nina to bake a batch of cupcakes for the little boy and bring them to the hospital.

"He can't get out of bed and tomorrow's his birthday, so you gotta bring some candles for the cupcakes, too." I told her.

The nurses were so taken with me that they drew straws to determine which one of them had to give me shots.

My recovery, however miraculous, was not unhindered by crises. My greatest struggle was against a massive infection. When my bowel was crushed, its contents were released into my abdominal cavity, and sudimonus quickly set in. The antibiotics used to fight the infection had to be injected directly into muscle—and there was precious little of that on my skinny legs. I shrieked in agony when the big needles were stabbed deep into my thighs. Often, the nurses left my room in tears.

As I improved, Mom helped keep me occupied and entertained by staging wheelchair races up and down the hospital corridor. I always won. And after a while, Mom didn't even have to let me.

Exactly three weeks to the day after the accident, I instructed Mom to assemble a group of doctors and nurses in the corridor down from my room.

"You gotta tell them to wait right there," I said, pointing to the far end of the long hallway. "I want to surprise them."

Mom did as I requested, certain that by this time most of the hospital personnel would have stood on their heads for me if I had asked them to. Dutifully the nurses stopped filling water pitchers and passing out medications, the doctors flipped their charts shut, and together half a dozen of them assembled where Mom instructed. Some of them may have suspected what was coming, but not a one of them would have believed before it happened that it was possible.

Mom wheeled me halfway down the corridor, turned me around to face my audience, and set the brake on the wheelchair.

Kneeling on one knee in front of me as I sat in the pint-sized red wheelchair, Mom put her hands on either side of my waist.

"Help me up, Mommy," I whispered fiercely, my green eyes sparkling with little-kid excitement and my face a study in determination.

Slowly, carefully, Mom lifted me out of the chair, just a few inches, just high enough. Ever so gently, she lowered me until my small, bare feet touched the cold linoleum of the hospital corridor. I swayed slightly, but she steadied me while I adjusted to supporting my own weight and got my balance.

I tottered for a moment; then I was steady.

"You can let go now," I whispered.

Mom took my arm with one hand while she gathered my IV bottle and bags in the other. Then she stepped back, still only inches away so she could catch me if I fell. And she let go.

I stood there proudly, beaming, as the doctors and nurses—including the orthopedist who had pronounced solemnly that I would be in a wheelchair for the rest of my life—burst into applause.

But I wasn't finished.

With a grin that threatened to split open my whole face, I lifted one foot and carefully took a shaky step forward.

And then another.

And another.

I didn't even limp—astonishing given that there was still an inch-wide gap between the broken halves of my pelvic bone.

The doctors and nurses began to cheer. Mom could see the looks of consternation on their faces, and she burst out laughing.

Of course, Mom had been prepared for my performance. About a week earlier, after one of our famous wheelchair races, I told Mom I wanted to get out of my chair. Mom almost said no.

But something stopped her. At the time, she didn't grasp that she was making a precedent-setting decision. Or maybe she did. She looked at my eager face and realized that the world would always try to relegate me to a nice little life in a wheelchair. Mom wanted more than that.

"Are you sure . . . ?" Mom asked.

"I can do it. I know I can," I pleaded. "I can stand up. And I can walk, too."

Surely, it will hurt if she's really doing some kind of damage to herself, Mom reasoned. *She's only four years old; if it hurts, she'll stop.*

Mom lifted me to my feet and let me bear my own weight for a few seconds. I sat back down quickly—because I was weak, not because I was in pain.

Every day, I stood beside my chair for a little while—longer each day. I took a handful of steps, too. Mom kept my accomplishment a secret so I could surprise the doctors.

. . .

Thirty-eight days after the accident, I was released from the hospital, and the first thing I wanted to do was go swimming in the apartment complex pool in my red polka-dot bikini. The doctors warned that I could not get the bandages around my incision wet, so Mom told me I could only dangle my feet in the water.

My bikini covered far less of my body than the bandages that swathed my midsection like mummy wrappings. My arms and legs were covered with needle holes, lumps, and bruises. I had a urinary bag taped to one leg with a rubber tube the size of a pencil running to the urostomy in my belly. A drain tube from my incision was attached to a bag taped to the other leg.

I sat down on the warm concrete, dipped my feet into the cool water, and began to work the crowd.

"I don't know you, what's your name? I've been in the hospital because my mommy ran over me. Did you just move in?"

As I chattered away, the other children and most of the adults gawked at my bags and bandages. But I was totally oblivious to their curious stares. Mom had noticed even before the accident that I possessed a remarkable ability to tune out anything that took my concentration off enjoying the moment.

I never made any effort to cover up my tubes or bags. But I quickly learned that not everybody accepted or even understood my condition. One summer day, Mom, Rebel, and I were in a grocery store. I had on shorts, so the bag taped to my leg was clearly visible. From the onset, I had dubbed the bag my "pee bag," and I had developed the most annoying habit of playing with it when I wasn't otherwise occupied. Standing beside my mother as she gathered a sack of apples, I was sloshing the liquid in the bag back and forth, making it foam. It was the foam the woman noticed.

She was a large woman in a print dress. Her hair was drawn severely back from her face, giving her a sort of Doberman pinscher look. She eyed me for a moment and then turned the full force of her considerable disapproval on my mother.

"You ought to be ashamed of yourself!" she hissed pompously, righteous indignation lighting pink flames behind her cheeks.

Mom actually looked around to see if the woman was addressing somebody standing behind her. She wasn't.

"Are you talking to me?" Mom asked.

"Of course I'm talking to you," the woman replied haughtily.

I was so engrossed in seeing how much foam I could produce in the bag that I didn't even notice her until she jabbed her finger in my direction and continued.

"Giving beer to a child to play with! What kind of mother are you?"

Mom was so stunned she was speechless. But I wasn't.

"Here," I said, holding out the bag toward the woman. "You can have a drink of it if you want. Mommy says I'm s'posed to share."

That line brought the house down. Mom, Rebel, and I burst into hysterical laughter, holding our sides as we roared. I was laughing so hard I would have wet my pants if I'd been able to.

The woman's face flushed redder than the apples in Mom's sack.

When I caught my breath, I put my hand on my hip and informed her: "It's not beer, it's pee! You know, wee wee . . . tinkle . . . winky-tink . . . *urine!*"

At that, the woman wheeled around and, with as much dignity as she could muster, marched out of the store with our delighted laughter ringing in her ears.

. . .

As the years passed, I orbited in and out of the hospital with the regularity of a weather satellite. Every few months, I required some sort of surgical procedure. I was incontinent because my bladder had been blown apart and the urethra torn away. In the first operation after the accident, the surgeon repaired as much damage as he could, but my injuries were so extensive that more surgeries were necessary. Then fistulas—holes—began to appear in the patched-together tissue; nothing ever remained fixed for very long. Painful adhesions—thick, hard scar tissue from repeated surgeries—began to build up in my abdomen. Before long, performing surgery on my belly was like blasting through concrete.

When I was six, Mom and Dad divorced, and Mom moved back to Louisville, her hometown, where both sets of my grandparents lived.

I was something of a celebrity in elementary school. The other students were curious about my bag and tubes, and I was more than willing to explain all about it—in infinite detail. I was never in school more than a few months at a time between surgeries, and when I returned to school in a wheelchair, the other children fought over who got to push me down the hall, sharpen my pencils, or bring me a tray in the lunchroom.

During each of the growing list of surgical procedures—they numbered in the dozens before I was ten years old—there were certain constants. I required an ever-growing amount of anesthesia to put me to sleep; I rebounded amazingly fast, healed quickly, and endured pain better than adults five times my age; and I always found fun, laughter, and joy in even the most dreary circumstances.

And I had a talk with God before every surgery.

Mom took Rebel and me every Sunday to a little church called Southeast Christian, located in the growing east end of Louisville on Hikes Lane. The congregation was warm and friendly and welcomed our little family—even me, with all my problems. Mom had grown up observing her mother's and grandparents' faith, but at Southeast I did more than just observe. I developed a faith of my own. I discovered that I could speak to God anytime I wanted. That was huge, because there was nothing in life I liked better than talking.

"God," I would whisper quietly, as I lay on the cold, hard surface of an operating table, so nobody but God could hear. "I need you to make sure I wake up. And I don't want to throw up because it hurts to throw up when you have stitches. Amen."

Even as a very small child, I could sense God's presence. He was always there. I don't remember any time when I didn't know God was with me, only a whisper away.

. . .

The older I got, the more I longed to be "regular"—normal, just like all the other kids. I wanted that more than anything else in the world. And if you wanted to be regular, you had to act regular. So I figured out fast how to fall, how to cover my urostomy with my arms like a football player holding a ball as he runs down the field. I played baseball with neighborhood boys much older than I was, many of whom hung around our house because they had a crush on Rebel. I slid into bases, played dodgeball and kickball during field day at school, fell off my bike and skinned my knees.

One of my favorite activities was climbing trees. There was a particularly good climbing tree in the backyard of the house where my father's parents lived in Shively, a suburb in south Louisville. The tree was a tall, stately oak with thick, strong limbs and a sturdy trunk more than three feet in diameter.

One hot summer day when I was seven, Rebel and I were visiting Mamaw and Poppy, playing in the sprinkler and knocking wooden balls through the wire hoops in our grandparents' backyard croquet court. I had convinced my grandfather to make a tire swing. I had also convinced him to allow me to climb up into the tree to throw the rope for the swing over a low-hanging limb.

I scampered up onto the limb with the ease and grace of a spider monkey, and sat there waiting while Poppy went into the garage to get the tire. But patience was not one of my virtues. I quickly tired of sitting on the limb, and decided to venture a little higher up into the tree. Then a little higher. And a little higher still.

Finding handholds and footholds almost as easily as climbing a ladder, I clambered up into the very top of the tree where the leaves blinked light and dark green in the dappled sunlight.

I hid there among the leaves, keeping very quiet, watching Rebel and my grandparents search for me in the yard. Finally my grandfather spotted me.

"Why, Heather, that's the highest you've ever climbed!" he shouted up at me.

"You come down out of there right this minute before you fall and break your neck," Mamaw said.

When I didn't budge, Mamaw played her ace.

"Rebel, you come on in the house, sugar, and get cleaned up," she said. "And we'll go out and get some ice cream."

That built a fire under me. But as I began to descend, I discovered that climbing down wasn't nearly as easy as climbing up had been. The leaves got in my way and I couldn't see where to place my feet. Finally, I gave up trying to climb down as I had climbed up, and simply grabbed hold of the tree trunk like a fire pole and slid down. When I got near the large lower limb, I put my foot out tentatively, feeling for the branch—and slipped. My shoe slid off the smooth bark. I lost my balance and tumbled out of the tree to the ground.

I scratched my leg and banged my head on the way down, and landed flat on my back in the dirt with a resounding *plunk* that knocked the wind out of me.

My grandfather burst out laughing, and my grandmother rushed to my side, absolutely certain that I had killed myself.

"I'm okay, Mamaw," I told her, breathlessly. "I just bonked my head a little is all. I'll be fine as soon as . . ."

That's when I saw it. Dangling on a limb high above the ground was my pee bag, swaying gently in the breeze. The tubing had obviously gotten caught on something when I was shinnying down the tree trunk and got stuck there when I fell.

My grandmother followed my gaze, saw the bag and tube hanging high above our heads, and went immediately into panic mode, fluttering around me in a dither of concern.

"Oh, my . . . oh, my goodness!" was all she could say. "Poppy, would you look at that! Heather's pee bag is up in the tree!"

My grandmother rushed into the house to call Mom, and I got up, dusted myself off, and climbed quickly up into the tree to retrieve the bag. Then I followed my grandmother into the house. I knew Mom would want to talk to me. Mom always asked to speak to me when there was a problem. She could tell by my voice if there was really anything to be alarmed about.

"Is she going to bleed to death?" Mamaw was asking Mom

when I came into the room, dangling my pee bag by the tubing. My grandmother listened for a moment, let out a sigh of relief, then handed the receiver to me.

"Well, what did you do?" Mom asked.

"I fell out of the tree and my pee bag got caught and I had to climb back up there and get it," I replied.

"Are you hurt?"

"No."

"Tell your grandmother I'll be right there."

Mom arrived in time to reinsert the tubing before the hole in my side closed up. She stretched me out on the living room floor, lifted my shirt, and forced the end of the tube back into the opening. But a few more minutes and I would have swapped a short visit to the ice-cream store for a much longer stay in an emergency room, where doctors would have inserted forceps into my side to stretch the opening enough to reinsert the tube. That hurt! I knew precisely how bad it hurt because that wasn't the first time—and it wouldn't be the last—that I accidentally parted company with my pee bag.

. . .

Things like that happened sometimes when you were regular. But not even regular kids—real regular kids—ever had as magical a summer as the one I had at age eight.

After my parents divorced, both my mother and father re-married. Mom married Jim Robertson, a Christian man she had known only two weeks. Rebel and I were stunned. Shell-shocked. One minute we had Mom all to ourselves and the next we were sharing her with some guy we hardly knew. It was years before I grew to appreciate the tall, quiet man with the gentle smile who had stolen my mother's heart. I watched Jim take Mom in his arms and waltz slowly around the kitchen so many times while I was growing up that I would one day define love as dancing when there isn't any music.

My father and his new wife, Millie, lived on a ranch in Montana, and when Rebel was ten and I was eight, we spent our summer there.

Neither of us had ever seen a horse, at least not up close where you could touch it. Dad had three—Angel, Hoho, and Snooper. The first time I saw them, I stood transfixed, mesmerized, hypnotized by their size and grandeur. I was absolutely certain I had never seen anything in my life as beautiful as those animals.

"Do you want to ride?" Dad asked when he saw the look of adoration on my face. I was so awestruck I was actually speechless. But I could nod, and I almost broke my neck fervently nodding my head.

Dad saddled up Angel, a gentle, chocolate brown mare with white socks and a black mane and tail. All he had was a grown-up saddle—big enough for three kids my size—but I felt totally comfortable the minute he lifted me up and sat me in it. I felt like I had spent every waking moment of my life seated on top of a horse. And somehow I knew—instinctively—that I needed the stirrups shortened.

Pointing out that my legs were dangling free on both sides of the saddle, I told my dad, "I want my feet in those things, 'cause I might want to go fast!"

Dad laughed and adjusted the stirrups so they fit me perfectly, making certain I could stand up in them with a couple of inches of clearance. He showed me how to control the horse, how to urge the animal forward with my heels, pull the reins in the direction I wanted to go, and back when I wanted to stop.

"She'll be comfortable and relaxed if she thinks you know what you're doing," he said. "Don't let her see you're afraid."

"I'm not afraid, Daddy!" I said. And I wasn't.

As my father saddled up Snooper for himself and Hoho for Millie, I leaned over and stroked Angel's neck, reveling in her smell and the softness of her skin, crooning to the big animal softly: "I'm Heather. You sure are beautiful, yes, you are. So beautiful. Your mane is so soft. Do you like apples? I heard all horses like apples . . ."

When my father mounted Snooper and turned the big bay toward the gravel road in front of the house, I whispered: "I sure hope your name's Angel because you're sweet. You may not know it, but I've never done this before. And I gotta figure it out quick 'cause you're a whole lot bigger than I am."

"Are you ready?" Dad asked, but didn't even wait for a reply before he headed down the road. Hoho and Angel followed.

The long, straight road led to a wheat field, and when Dad reached it, he walked the horses part of the way around it, then asked if I wanted to "canter."

"That's faster than a trot and slower than a run," he said.

I urged Angel forward until she broke into a slow gallop, her hooves hitting the ground in a smooth *ka-plop, ka-plop, ka-plop* rhythm. The fluid motion was like gliding up and down over gentle swells in the ocean.

When Dad reached the far corner of the wheat field, he turned Snooper back toward the road, stopped, and waved. Then he urged the big horse into a dead run across the field. I watched the two of them fly across the ground, saw how Dad leaned forward in the saddle and let the reins hang loose.

I took a deep breath, reached up and plucked off my glasses, and dropped them down the front of my shirt. Then I turned Angel toward the field and loosened the reins, just like I'd seen Dad do with Snooper. Grabbing the saddle horn in one hand and Angel's mane in the other, I leaned forward and kicked with my heels as hard as I could, shouting at the big horse beneath me, "Angel, please don't kill me!"

And we were off!

Angel flew out across the field with me on her back. The wheat slapped at her legs as she ran, and I instinctively stood up in the stirrups for balance. The sun beat down on my back, the wind whipped my hair in my face, the hooves of the big animal beneath me thundered on the ground. I had never felt so alive!

I turned Angel at the edge of the field and pounded down the road behind my father. When he saw me closing in on him, he urged Snooper forward, and the two horses raced for the barn, crossing the front yard and rounding the side of the house with the dogs barking at their heels and the other children squealing as they passed.

Angel came to a skidding halt at the fence line, almost dislodging me from the saddle.

"Are you okay?" Dad asked. "Are you hurt?"

I finally found my voice.

"Can I go again?" I begged.

I repeated the journey down the gravel road and across the wheat field five more times before it got too dark to see where I was going. Angel quickly figured out the drill and grew more and more excited each time we reached the high end of the field and turned back toward the house. When Dad finally lifted me out of the saddle to the ground, I actually felt odd for a moment without the horse beneath me, like some important part of me wasn't there anymore.

I spent every day of that summer with Angel. I learned how to care for the mare, how to groom her and clean her hooves. I discovered that the big chocolate horse had a sweet tooth, and I always carried peppermints in my pockets.

On our last day in Montana before we returned home to Kentucky, I took Angel out for a ride alone. I moved as one with the huge animal as it loped across the field, and I understood things I was still way too young to tack words onto. There weren't many times that I felt in charge of my life. I had no say over what happened to my body when I lay on an operating table with some doctor cutting into my belly. But I was in control when I rode Angel, and with that control came a feeling of exhilaration that was so sweet it was almost painful.

On top of a horse, I was in charge. And I was free.

FOUR

I piloted my wheelchair down the hospital corridor past the nurses' station to the cubicle where Dr. Bertoloni was filling out charts, and pulled to a stop in front of him.

"Is Tony gonna die?" I asked.

Dr. Bertoloni was a pediatric oncologist and Tony was his patient, a high school football player with leukemia. I had spotted the teenager, whose buzz cut failed to hide his thinning hair, when he moved into the room across the hall from me earlier in the week. I always knew when somebody new was brought into the ward. And I'd been hospitalized that time for so long I not only knew the names, but the entire life stories of every patient, nurse, nurse's aide, and orderly on the 3A wing of Norton Children's Hospital. Most of the doctors, too.

I also was on a first-name basis with the Domino's Pizza delivery boy. Supreme, no peppers or olives, extra-extra cheese. I was a ten-year-old pizza freak.

I had a particularly good view of Tony's room because it was directly across the hall, and when his door was open, I could look in without even having to get out of bed. I saw all his visitors. Several groups of big, husky football players had shown up the day he moved in, laughing and cutting up in the hallway outside his room, shoving each other and playing hat keep-away. But when they came back out of his room, they weren't laughing anymore. They walked out in silence, heads down. I even thought some of them were crying. None of those boys had come back to visit a second time.

I watched Tony's room as closely as a police surveillance team, scrutinized every person who went in or out. It wasn't just that I didn't have anything better to do, which I didn't. Or that I was nosey, though nobody ever accused me of being a mind-your-own-business kind of kid. I studied the humanity all around me because people fascinated me. I was unashamedly a pint-sized busybody, and I never once entertained the notion that people might not want to share all their physical ailments or personal problems. My life—and most of my internal organs—had been open for public inspection for as long as I could remember. I assumed everybody else's life was, too.

I had been on my way to introduce myself to Tony before his backside got his sheets warm the day he moved in. But the nurses stopped me. They told me he wasn't having any visitors, that he didn't want to see anybody.

I was scheduled for surgery the next morning, and I was anxious to make friends with the newcomer across the hallway. Having a stranger within wheelchair range of my room was like an itch, a mosquito bite. I had to scratch it.

Dr. Bertoloni looked up at me and smiled. He wasn't my doctor, but he was friends with my doctor. And everybody knew me. He came in and said hi to me every morning when he made rounds. I called him Dr. B.

"Have you met Tony?" he asked, instead of answering my question.

"No, not yet. I'm not s'posed to go in there because he doesn't want visitors."

"He needs to meet you," Dr. B said.

"How come?"

"Tony doesn't have enough hope in his heart to make it," Dr. B said. "You have more hope than he does in your little finger. You need to go meet him."

"But the nurses say I'm not s'posed to bother him."

Dr. B cocked his head to one side and looked at me, a tousle-haired little munchkin peering at him through thick glasses.

"Since when did that ever stop you?" he asked. "He'll probably tell you to go away, but don't."

"Okay!"

I had my marching orders. I spun my wheelchair around and rolled down the hallway to my room, where my grandmother was sitting in the recliner with her feet up, reading a newspaper. Mom had gone to get things in order at home so she could be back early in the morning for my surgery.

I considered ditching the wheelchair. I could walk just fine, but my surgeon wanted me off my feet, so I had to stay in the chair whenever anybody was looking. Then I thought better of walking into Tony's room unannounced; it occurred to me that a big football player wouldn't hit a little kid in a wheelchair.

"Grandmother, I'm going across the hall to meet Tony," I announced. "And even if he yells at me, don't come!" Without waiting for a response, I wheeled around and shot across the hall. I didn't knock, just pushed the door open and rolled in. The young man on the bed looked up as I wheeled into the room.

And I stopped cold, like my chair had slammed into an invisible brick wall.

Tony had the biggest blue eyes I had ever seen! Piercing blue eyes. Get-lost-in-them blue eyes. Swim-around-in-them-doing-the-backstroke blue eyes.

If there is such a thing as love at first sight, there must be such a thing as crush at first sight, too. I had a crush on Tony two heartbeats after I met him.

"What do you want?" he demanded in a surly voice.

I just stared at him.

"Hello? Knock, knock. Anybody home? I said, 'What do you want?' "

I finally found my voice.

"So, are you scared you're gonna die?" I asked.

Tony was dumbfounded.

"Get out of here!" he roared.

I didn't budge.

"I know you've got leukemia. Well, you don't have to die just because you've got leukemia."

"Do you have cancer?" Tony asked sarcastically.

"No, but . . ."

"Then you don't know anything about it."

"I don't know anything about cancer," I shot back, "but I do know what it's like to be in the hospital all the time. And I know what it's like to have surgery and it hurts and you can't get out of bed and you get an infection and get shots in your legs. And I know if you fight, you've got a better chance of beating this. You gotta fight. You don't have to die if you don't want to!"

"Just get out of here! What are you doing in here, anyway? I didn't invite you to come into my room. Get out!"

"Okay," I said, reluctantly. Then I added, "I'm having surgery tomorrow morning, so I'll come see you after it's over."

"I don't want you to come see me tomorrow. I don't want you to come see me ever! Now, get out."

I turned my wheelchair around and called over my shoulder, cheerful as a sunflower, ". . . so I'll see you tomorrow. I hope you sleep good tonight . . ."

"And I hope you die in surgery tomorrow!" he yelled as the door swung shut behind me.

Dr. B was standing in the hallway just outside the door. He had been there listening to the whole conversation, and his eyes were moist. He took hold of the handles of my wheelchair and pushed me back into my room. Then he got down on his knees in front of me and gave me a big hug.

"That's a start," he told me. "You hang tough in that surgery tomorrow, and go see Tony when you're feeling better. He needs a true friend."

An orderly came to get me the next morning about 6 A.M. As he rolled my gurney out into the hallway, I asked him to push open the door to Tony's room so I could tell him good-bye. I didn't really expect him to be up that early, but he was. He was sitting on the side of his bed sobbing.

"You need to suck it up, you big baby," I told him.

Tony was embarrassed and furious!

"I hope you die on the operating table!" he yelled at me.

I responded happily, "I'll see you tonight!" Then the orderly pushed the gurney down the hallway to the elevator.

Yeah, Tony needed to suck it up, all right, I thought as the elevator carried me up to the surgery floor where the OR suites were located. *Just suck it up and go on.*

Those seven words were printed on page one of the owner's manual of my life. Mom made it clear from the moment I woke up from my first surgery that self-pity was not an option, and Mom's wasn't the only voice singing that song. Growing up in medical facilities, I learned lessons before I could do long division that many grown-ups never figured out. The hospital became my College of Life. I started out studying suffering, but I quickly changed my major to gratitude.

Every time I was hospitalized, there was discussion about where to put me. I wasn't sick; I hadn't just suffered some traumatic injury. Since there wasn't a ward for "repair work," I was slotted into a room wherever there was an empty bed.

Usually, I landed in a med-surge ward. But over the years, I also spent months in cancer wards where I was the only healthy child there. I was even placed in the burn unit once or twice when no other beds were available.

The reality of life in those wards shaped my view of the world and of my own circumstances. I grew up with kids who had no hair, pale children who didn't have the energy to play. Often, when I returned to the hospital for additional surgery, every child who had been my friend in the cancer ward was dead. I lay awake at night listening to children in the burn unit screaming in agony as their burns were scrubbed clean every four hours. I hung out with kids in wheelchairs who weren't ever going to get up out of them and walk.

Hospital life taught me a simple, profound lesson: There were a whole lot of people worse off than I was. My view of my own condition was just as simple: I was a healthy little kid with a lot of scars and a pee bag. In the grand scheme of things, I didn't have anything to complain about. So I just sucked it up and went on.

When the elevator doors opened that morning and I spotted my mom, the first words out of my mouth had absolutely nothing to do with my impending surgery.

"Mom, that guy Tony across the hall is so cute!" I gushed. Mom just shook her head and laughed. Then the family gathered around and the ritual began.

The presurgery routine—doing the same things the same way every time—was to me what Linus's blanket was to the little boy with his thumb in his mouth in my favorite comic strip.

"When you're gonna have surgery, you gotta do three things," I would explain to anybody who asked—and to everybody else who happened to be within earshot. "You pray hard, you kiss everybody you love, and you hold the doctor's hand while you go to sleep."

The routine called for a circle of prayer around me in the holding area in front of the surgery suite doors. My family—Mom, Jim, and Rebel, assorted grandparents, cousins, and Aunt Laura—and ministers from my church gathered around my bed, held hands, and prayed for me. The doctors, nurses, technicians, and anesthesiologists were always invited to participate, and they always stopped what they were doing and bowed their heads.

I closed out the prayer that day: ". . . and God bless Tony. Amen."

Then I hugged and kissed my family, and told every one of them that I loved them. I didn't say good-bye, and none of them said good-bye either. Nobody ever said good-bye! They all said, "See you in a little while."

Everyone stood and waved at me as my gurney was wheeled into the operating room. The doors closed behind me and I was in that squeaky-clean world of shiny stainless steel, bright lights, and the smell of disinfectant. Nurses lifted me onto the operating table. One nurse strapped my arms down while the other nurse fastened a Velcro band across my chest.

It was all so familiar that it wasn't scary anymore. That didn't mean I liked it. I never liked being in that room, with all the nurses and doctors in those green gown things, so covered up you could only see their eyes. It was always cold in there, and I knew what was coming. It wouldn't hurt at first, of course. It would feel good to get sleepy—like I was all wrapped up in warm cotton. But it wouldn't feel good when I woke up. Then I would feel like throwing up; usually I did throw up. My throat would be raw from the breathing tube. And the incision . . . that would hurt. That would really hurt!

I didn't allow myself to think about those things as I lay on the hard surface of the operating table wishing somebody would give me a blanket. I didn't dwell on the future; I stayed in the present, lived in the moment. There would be plenty of time for crying and pain later. And I'd get through it. I always did. You just had to suck it up and go on, that's all.

It wasn't time to go to sleep yet. The music hadn't started. Every doctor had his own music. Some were into Mozart, others liked Journey or Chicago. My favorite instrumental was from the movie where this kinda ugly, kinda good-looking guy named Sylvester Stallone played a boxer. But not many doctors wanted the *Rocky* theme song blasting out in the operating room during surgery.

I turned to Marge Fitzgerald, the anesthesiologist, who was sitting on a stool near the head of the operating table with her assistant, Carol Gowan, standing behind her.

"What did you guys have for dinner last night?" I asked.

They looked at me, a little surprised.

"I had fried chicken," Marge replied.

"Meatloaf for me," said Carol.

"I like fried chicken," I told them. "I like mashed potatoes, too, but they have to be real mashed potatoes. Instant mashed potatoes taste yucky."

"Well, I had mashed potatoes," Marge said. "And they weren't instant."

"What kind of car do you drive?" I wanted to know. I had more questions than a game show host. I was determined to be "real" to medical professionals who cared for an assembly line of patients every day, and the way you were a real person was to ask real-person questions.

Marge and I hadn't yet reached an agreement on whether a Ford Mustang or a Corvette was the totally coolest car on the road when Dr. Howerton came in and told me, "Time to go to sleep now."

Dr. Howerton and I were good friends. He smiled at me. I couldn't see his mouth but I could tell he was smiling by the way his eyes crinkled up, and he reached over and took my hand. He knew the drill: I wouldn't go to sleep unless the doctor was holding my hand.

The music started. Debby Boone began to croon, "You light up my life . . ."

"Okay, sweetheart, I need you to count backward from one hundred . . ." Marge said.

I drifted off to sleep, secure in the knowledge that my mother would be there in the recovery room when I woke up. I could depend on that. And I could always count on my mother to tell me the truth with the husk still on it. If a doctor dropped a scalpel during surgery and perforated my bowel, my mother didn't pussyfoot around it. Medical personnel learned quickly that Mom was my calming force. If I woke up and my mother wasn't there, I had been known, on occasion, to go berserk, throwing whatever I could get my hands on at the nurses and pulling out all my tubes and IV lines. But I was as serene as a nun on Valium with my mother at my side.

. . .

When I was wheeled back into my room that afternoon, I was still pretty dopey, but not so spaced out that I missed the NO VISITORS sign on Tony's door. I was in a lot of pain, crying as a nurse helped me into my bed and Mom tried to make me comfortable. Nurses hung bags of antibiotics on my IV pole to drain down the clear tube into my little arm, and they left a blood pressure cuff on the other arm so they could check it every fifteen minutes, a process I found as annoying as having a fly buzzing around my head.

As soon as I was settled, the entourage came to visit: Jim, Rebel, my grandparents, Aunt Laura, and assorted cousins. They all hugged me carefully, and planted gentle kisses on my cheek or forehead.

When a nurse appeared to pump up the gray band around my arm, I mentioned that I was going to see Tony later in the day.

The nurse laughed.

"Honey, you're not going anywhere today!" she said. "You're not getting out of that bed."

She saw my face fall.

"You can go see him tomorrow. Maybe. Maybe you'll feel like getting up for a few minutes tomorrow. Anyway, Dr. Bertoloni is getting ready to do a bone marrow transplant on Tony, so he's in isolation. He can't be around anybody's germs. Even if you could go see him, you couldn't do anything but stand at the door and wave."

My pain medication finally kicked in and I drifted off to sleep. When I woke up, it was late in the evening. I'd slept through dinner, and Mom offered to go get me something to eat. But I wasn't hungry; I never was hungry after surgery.

I had rested well. I felt good. There wasn't any reason that I could see why I couldn't go visit Tony. But I knew my mother and the nurses would never allow me to do it if I asked them. So I didn't ask.

I lay quietly, thinking. It didn't take me long to come up with a plan. The first thing I had to do was make sure the IV pole and all my drains and bags were on the same side of the bed as the door. Not a problem.

"Mommy, I'm tired of lying on my back," I said. "I want to roll over on my side."

I rolled over facing the door, and Mom moved the equipment to that side of the bed. I asked her to turn on the television, said I didn't want to watch it, just listen to it. Could she please turn the sound up? Oh, and it's hot in here. How about opening the door to let in some fresh air?

Then I relaxed and waited. I knew Mom was exhausted. It wasn't long before she came over to kiss me good night. She prayed with me, told me she loved me, then collapsed on the cot near the window. I knew she'd be out cold in no time.

And she was.

Of course, I had to make sure.

I raised up on my elbow, picked a piece of peppermint candy off the bedside table, and tossed it at her. No response. I lobbed another couple of pieces. All of them hit their mark; none of them got a rise out of Mom.

It was time.

Slowly, quietly, I sat up and hung my legs over the side of the bed. Then I slid carefully off the edge until my bare feet touched the cold tile floor. When I let my weight down and stood, the world went black for a moment. I was sure I was going to collapse and fall in a heap on the floor. But the blackness passed and I steadied myself. My wheelchair was parked by the bathroom door, but I wouldn't be using it. I couldn't manage all the bags and the IV pole and operate a wheelchair, too. I'd have to make this journey under my own steam.

I held on to the bed for support and moved slowly, inching along. From the bed to the night table. From the night table to the chair next to the bed. The chair had wheels on the bottom, and I had already scoped it out as the perfect chariot. I reached over and unhooked the bags from the side of the bed and hooked them to the bottom rung of the chair. Then I used the chair like an old lady's walker and scooted slowly toward the doorway, dragging my IV pole along after me.

I was in pain. It hurt to be up walking around, pulling on the stitches and the staples. But I sucked it up and kept moving. When I peeped around the corner of my doorway, I saw nurses standing at the station just down the hall. I sank down into the chair and waited. A few minutes later, I looked again and the hallway was empty.

I moved as fast as I could across the expanse of green linoleum to Tony's door; if a nurse spotted me in the open hallway, I'd be busted. Sitting beside the door was a cart with sterilization equipment. Gloves, masks, gowns. Everybody entering Tony's room had to be completely covered head to toe. I just stared at it, overwhelmed. I couldn't possibly put all that stuff on.

"I've got antibiotics coming out of this bag and dripping right into my arm," I reasoned. "With all that stuff in me, there's no way I could make anybody sick."

So I grabbed a mask and held it in front of my nose, pushed open the door, and scooted my chair in front of me.

The room was lit by the flickering light from the television mounted near the ceiling. On the screen, Tattoo was shouting, ". . . Zee plane . . . zee plane . . ." Tony heard me come in.

"What are you doing here?" he snarled.

"I told you I'd come to visit you tonight."

"And I told you I don't feel like having visitors." He turned back to *Fantasy Island* and ignored me.

"I think what you feel is sorry for yourself," I said. "You know, for a football player, you sure are a big baby."

"I'm not a football player," he said. "I can't play football anymore. I'm gonna die."

"You don't have to die if you don't want to. My mother ran over me and I didn't die."

"Yeah, right," Tony said sarcastically.

"She did, too," I said. "Look!"

I lifted my hospital gown and showed him the bandages that swathed my midsection above my little pink panties. Drainage tubes poked out through the bottom portion of the layers of white and slithered down to the bags hung on the chair. A larger tube snaked out of my side and dumped its contents into the pee bag taped to my leg. I described the accident and gave him a quick summary of my injuries, rattling off medical terms as fast as an auctioneer selling tobacco, and told him how I wasn't supposed to make it to the hospital alive, or survive the first surgery, how I should have died a bunch of times during the four dozen or so surgeries I'd had in the last six years.

Tony stared at me in disbelief.

"I told you I was coming to visit you and here I am," I said, and in spite of myself I winced in pain. "Can I sit down in your chair?"

Tony hopped out of the bed, helped me into the chair, and flipped up the footrest so I could lean back and get comfortable.

Then we started talking. Tony told me about his family, about playing football, about how upset everybody was when they learned he was sick. He said he had the worst, least curable form of leukemia, and that his family wasn't handling the diagnosis very well.

"Dr. Bertoloni says there's a chance I can beat this," Tony said. "But I don't think my parents believe I will."

"I believe you will," I said.

Tony smiled.

I smiled, too, then realized Tony couldn't see me smile because I was holding that stupid mask.

"This mask stinks," I said. "Do I have to wear it?"

"No, take it off," he replied. "I can't see your face with it on."

I liked that! I tossed the mask into the trash basket, and began to tell Tony about my life and family. We were in a deep discussion about my father's horses in Montana when the door suddenly opened and in marched a nurse, decked out in scrubs from head to toe. She was the nurse who had told me earlier that I couldn't possibly get out of bed today, and she was so surprised to see me sitting there with my feet propped up in Tony's room that she froze, unable to say a thing.

When Tony and I saw the look on her face, we locked eyes with each other and burst out laughing.

The nurse quickly found her voice. "You're not supposed to be in here!" she said to me. "Didn't you see the NO VISITORS sign on his door?"

Then she launched into a lecture about isolation, what it meant, why Tony needed to be kept away from people with germs, what would happen to him if he weren't kept away from people with germs, etc., etc., etc. As she waxed eloquent about microbes and bone marrow, a small crowd gathered outside the door: two nurses, an aide, and a respiratory therapist who happened to be passing by. You could hear the nurse's sermonette all the way down the hall.

"You don't even have a mask on!" she scolded. "Didn't you see the scrub cart? Didn't you assume it was there for a reason?"

"I figured I was taking so much medicine I didn't have any more cooties than he did," I replied.

The crowd outside the door tried, and failed, to strangle their laughter. Everyone thought my "cooties" remark was funny except the nurse who had caught Tony and me dead to rights.

"Up and out of here you go," she said. I got up slowly, in pain, and headed for the door.

"I'll see you tomorrow," I said to Tony as I pushed my chair out into the hallway.

Tony nodded. He didn't say yes, but he didn't say no, either.

Back in my room, the nurse settled me in the bed—quietly, so we wouldn't disturb Mom. She had been gone only a few minutes when Mom rolled over and noticed I was awake.

"Are you okay, sweetheart?" she asked. "Do you need something?"

"I went to see Tony tonight," I told her.

"You did not!" Mom said.

"I did, too," I responded. "His mommy and daddy think he's gonna die, so he thinks he's gonna die. But I don't think so. I think he's gonna beat this!"

Tony and I became fast friends. Tony told everybody that I was "his girl"; I fairly glowed. Both of us cycled in and out of the hospital for the better part of a year. I was released for five or six weeks at a time to recover sufficiently for my next surgery, and then I'd be back in the hospital for another month or two. Tony went home occasionally, too, but he didn't do well at home and was soon hospitalized again.

Every time I saw Tony, he was weaker than he had been before. Slowly, the hulking football player vanished and was replaced by a frail, emaciated boy. But I clung fervently to the belief that he could beat the leukemia, and I wanted desperately for him to believe it, too.

Tony repeatedly underwent chemotherapy and radiation treatments that required the whole isolation routine. Although there was a playroom at the end of the hallway, Tony was only allowed to go there once in the morning and once at night because all the other children had to leave when he was there.

The nurses would walk him down the hall wrapped up like a mummy, swathed in surgery scrubs, shoes, and gloves. A surgical cap covered his bald head, and a mask obscured his whole face. The only thing that showed were his eyes. Tony hated the mummy suit, and every time I saw him in it, I hollered out, "Hey, good lookin'!" I thought that made him smile, but I couldn't tell for sure.

One day, as he was being transported down the hallway ensconced in his mummy suit, Tony managed to whisper to me that he was going to request a late-night playroom time and that I should meet him there. I sweet-talked one of the volunteers into hiding me in the closet in the playroom, totally decked out in isolation gear myself: scrubs, mask, and gloves. I even had a sheet draped like a tent over my omnipresent IV pole.

When Tony got to the playroom that night, he shooed out all the nurses, said he wanted to be alone. Then he whispered, "Heather? Heather, are you in here?"

I flung open the closet door with a flourish.

"Ta-da!" I proclaimed, showing off my isolation garb with an exaggerated bow. Tony smiled, a real smile, and proceeded to teach me how to play pool, foosball, and air hockey. Eventually, the nurses heard us giggling and were about to evict me when Dr. B intervened.

"Tony and Heather are fine," he said. "Leave them alone."

. . .

A week later, Tony placed a big, hand-lettered NO VISITORS! sign on his door. He told his family to stay away, wouldn't even see me. It was his birthday, and he was devastated to be turning sixteen in a hospital.

I was determined to cheer up Tony. So was Dr. B, and he came to my room to brainstorm ideas. He told me he'd buy me a pizza if I could figure out a way to get Tony to smile.

"You know . . ." I said, ". . . my mom taught me once how to use syringes as water guns. How mad do you think Tony would be if we got him wet?" I asked.

"Let's find out," Dr. B said.

When Dr. B came back to my room a few minutes later, he had snared two 250 cc syringes, the biggest syringes in the hospital, and filled them full of water. He had also found two long, thin cardboard boxes full of the plastic tubing that fits on the ends of thermometers. We dumped out the tubing, and I stuck an arm down into each one of the boxes. They were a perfect fit. The boxes stretched from my shoulders past the tips of my fingers so you couldn't see the water-gun syringes in my hands.

Dr. B had to open the door to Tony's room for me. Tony was sitting on the edge of his bed, staring at the floor. Before he had a chance to say anything, I squealed, "Happy Birthday, Tony!" lifted my arms like twin cannons, and fired, squirting streams of water like two fire hoses right into Tony's face.

Mom, Dr. B, and the nurses gathered in the hallway outside Tony's room burst out laughing.

Tony reached for a pitcher of water.

I turned tail and ran.

Down the hallway I flew, holding my cardboard cannon arms straight out to the side like wings. Hot on my heels came a barefoot Tony with a pitcher of water, wearing nothing but his Joe Boxer black pants covered in bright yellow smiley faces.

I would never have made it as far as the playroom if Tony had been the runner he once was. But he caught up with me when my wing/arms snagged on the doorway, grabbed the back of my shirt, and pulled me up short. Then he poured the whole pitcher full of water—ice water—over my head. I shrieked as the frigid water ran down my neck. Then I wriggled free, ditched the boxes, reloaded my syringes at the water fountain, and went gunning for Tony. The water fight quickly escalated into war; both sides lost. Within minutes, Tony and I were drenched from head to toe.

The nurses quietly shooed the other children out of the playroom and left it to the two of us. After we dried off, we spent the rest of the afternoon together playing air hockey, pool, and foosball.

At dinnertime, Dr. B's pizza payment arrived. Tony and I were preparing to go back to my room to divvy up the spoils when Tony suddenly gave me a big, long hug and kissed me on the cheek. Even though I was only the kiss*ee* and not a participating kiss*er*, I maintained for the rest of my life that Tony's was my "first kiss."

Somebody broke a candle off a table arrangement in the waiting room and set it in the middle of the pizza. Everyone on the floor gathered around and sang "Happy Birthday." Tony made a wish and blew out the candle.

After that day, Tony informed his parents and everybody else in his life that he wasn't going to die. He was going to beat the leukemia. He was going to get well. He was going to pull one out of a hat just like I had done so many times.

I was released from the hospital a few days later and didn't return for several months. As soon as I was readmitted, I dodged the nurses intent on drawing blood for pre-op testing and went looking for Tony.

He wasn't in his usual room. I was disappointed that he was home while I was in the hospital. But this was a big surgery; I'd likely be here for a while. He'd be back before I left. I turned to go offer up my arm for a blood sacrifice when I spotted Dr. B in the hallway.

"Hey Dr. B, what's cookin'?" I called out. Dr. B finished his conversation with a nurse and came to give me a big hug.

"When's Tony coming back?" I asked in mid-hug. Dr. B got very still. I didn't like that.

He released me from the hug, put his hands on my shoulders, and looked into my face.

"Heather, I need to tell you something," he said.

A big hole opened up in the middle of my belly.

"Did he die?" I asked. Dr. B started to respond, but he didn't need to. I knew. "He did, didn't he? He died! Didn't he? Didn't he?"

"Yes, Heather, Tony died," he said.

I didn't cry. It hurt too bad to cry yet.

"He fought a good fight," Dr. B continued. "And he fought because you gave him something his doctors and his parents couldn't give him. You gave him hope. But it was an aggressive cancer and it was too much for him."

My eyes filled with tears, but I still didn't cry.

"I'm so sorry, Heather," he said. "Everybody knows you loved him very much. And he loved you, too."

I turned without saying a word and walked away, an unspoken question ringing in my ears. If everybody knew I loved him, why hadn't somebody called me? Why hadn't anybody believed I was important enough in his life to give me a call when he died? I didn't even get to go to his funeral.

Over the years, I continued to make friends whenever I was hospitalized. I had buddies I played cards and board games with. A few of them even knew their way around a pool table. And every now and then God placed another Tony in my life—to keep me real, to remind me that there was always somebody who was worse off than I was.

FIVE

The big man who smelled of oil and grease and sweat opened the drawer and showed me its contents: a loaded .45-caliber revolver with a clip of bullets beside it, a smaller silver pistol, a pair of handcuffs, and several knives. He picked up one of the knives—the biggest one, the hunting knife—pulled it out of the green leather scabbard, and stuck the sharp point of it under my chin.

"Special friends keep special secrets," he told me in a hushed, menacing whisper, jabbing the point of the knife just deep enough into my skin to draw a drop of blood. "And we're going to be special friends."

He leaned closer, so close the rotten smell of his breath almost made me gag, and dropped the next words one at a time, like individual rocks into a glassy pond. "Very. Special. Friends."

. . .

I was eight years old, riding my Green Machine down the sidewalk across the street from my house on the hot summer day in 1976 when I first met Mr. Jennings. I had been practicing the fine art of spinning out on the low-slung tricycle—pedaling as fast as I could and then pegging the oversized front wheel all the way right, throwing the back of the bike into a sliding whirl that sometimes spun me completely around in a circle.

It was a maneuver that set me apart from the dozen or so children who lived in neat white houses along a tree-lined street in the northern part of Louisville. Oh sure, most of the boys could do it. But none of the girls could. None of them except me.

I pulled into the driveway of my friend Kate's house just as she stepped out onto the porch. Kate was a beautiful child, older than I was—ten, maybe eleven. But she looked even older because she had already started to "fill out," as my mother put it.

Kate's yard was separated by a chain-link fence from a house with a four-bay garage in the back, and I noticed a man standing on the other side of the fence. He was a big man, well over six feet, with thick glasses, a big nose, and salt-and-pepper hair. He had on dark blue coveralls, the kind mechanics wore, that were stained with grease and oil.

"Katy-Katy," the man called out in a singsong voice. "Would you like a treat? I've got something sweet for you to eat."

Kate had been walking down the driveway toward me when she heard his voice, and she froze, like she was playing sling-the-statue. She answered without turning toward him or looking at him.

"No, thank you, Mr. Jennings," she said.

But Mr. Jennings went right on talking as if he hadn't heard her. He said he had candy that was dandy and made other rhymes I thought were stupid—all the while urging, and in some odd way, almost threatening Kate to entice her over to the fence where he was standing.

Finally, Kate caved in. It was like the man had some power over her she couldn't resist. But before she turned toward him, she reached out and grabbed my hand and literally dragged me off the Green Machine. Then she held on tight and pulled me along with her as she crossed the yard to the fence.

Mr. Jennings smiled broadly, but the smile never reached his eyes. He held out his hand—it was oil-stained and his fingernails were black—and lying in his greasy palm was a collection of Jolly Ranchers and Blow Pops.

"Pick what you want," he said, but when Kate reached for a Jolly Rancher, he pulled his hand back.

"Take a Blow Pop," he told her. "I want to watch you suck on it." And he let out a strange little giggle.

I looked at the man as if he'd lost his mind.

"Who sucks on a Blow Pop?" I asked incredulously. "You're s'posed to bite into it so you can get to the bubble gum."

The man turned his gaze away from Kate toward me, as if he were seeing me for the first time.

"I know a little girl who needs to be taught patience," he told me. Then he stepped back and eyed me from head to toe. "You look like a little boy," he said. "But you've got pretty-little-girl potential . . . yes, pretty-little-girl potential."

I had absolutely no idea what the word "potential" meant. I did know that I'd never been anybody's definition of a "pretty little girl." That was Rebel. I was tall and skinny, hair cropped short, glasses, scabs on my elbows and knees—with a tube in my side and a bag taped to my leg.

Before I had a chance to ask him what he meant, I heard my mother's voice.

"Heather!" Mom called. "Come on home. It's time for supper."

I turned to leave and Kate turned with me, still clinging tightly to my hand.

"My mother's not home," Kate whispered.

"Oh . . . well, do you want to come eat at our house?" I asked. "My mommy won't care." My house was the neighborhood hangout. Mom never knew on any given night who might show up at the supper table.

Kate nodded her head vigorously. "Yes!"

Without so much as a word to Mr. Jennings, we crossed the yard to my Green Machine in lockstep. But when we reached it, Kate grabbed it in her free hand before I had a chance to climb on board, and she dragged it along beside us all the way across the street and down the sidewalk to my house. She dropped the tricycle in front of the porch steps, and only then did she release her grip on my hand.

"You don't ever hold my hand, Kate," I said, looking at her quizzically. "What's wrong with you?"

Kate just stood there for a moment. When she finally replied, she looked into my eyes with an intensity that made me uncomfortable.

"Mr. Jennings is a very bad man," Kate said, and there was a quality in her voice I had never heard before. It was a long time before I understood what it was. It was terror. "Don't *ever* go play at his house!"

I never forgot the warning. Or the sound of Kate's voice when she issued it. The words were always there in the back of my mind every time I saw Mr. Jennings. But I spent most of the rest of the summer at my father's ranch in Montana, and in the fall I was hospitalized for months at Norton Children's Hospital for a series of surgeries. As time passed, the urgency of Kate's warning began to fade. Mr. Jennings always waved at me and smiled whenever he saw me riding my bike or playing in someone's yard. Sometimes he'd cross the street and give me candy. I watched the other adults on the street, too, the parents of my friends. They all stopped to talk to him, took their cars to him to repair when the vehicles wouldn't start or were making some kind of funny noise. In fact, Jim took our family car across the street to Mr. Jennings's garage for a tune-up.

Surely if he was a bad man, the grown-ups would know, I reasoned. And after a while, Mr. Jennings didn't seem all that dangerous anymore.

The next summer, I was playing on the tire swing in Kate's backyard when I noticed Mr. Jennings standing at the fence. There was a hole cut in the chain-link next to the side door of Mr. Jennings's garage. As soon as Kate saw him, she gathered up her little sister, Sue, and headed for the back door of her house.

When he called out to me, I climbed down off the tire swing and went to the fence where he was standing. He gave me candy, then made me an offer.

"I'll give you a dollar a day to hand me tools while I work on cars," he said.

Kate shouted a warning from the safety of her back porch. "You should go home, Heather!" she cried. "You should go home right now!"

But a dollar was a lot of money to a nine-year-old, so I climbed through the hole in the fence and took my first innocent steps into the world of unspeakable depravity that lay behind the black plastic on the windows at the far end of the garage.

There were four big garage doors on the building. That day, two of the doors were raised. Sitting inside one of the open bays was a blue car with the hood up. It looked like the car my grandfather drove.

Mr. Jennings took me into the building to the cluttered work space in front of the car. Tools were scattered on the greasy metal surface of a tool bench that stretched the length of the back wall of the building or hung up on a Peg-Board above it.

"This is a Phillips head and this is a flat head," he said, pointing to the two different kinds of screwdrivers. "This is a ratchet, this is an Allen wrench, these are sockets . . ."

As he spoke, he stretched out to point to the tools hooked on the Peg-Board, and before I noticed it, he had moved behind me and had placed his hands on the bench on both sides of me so that I was trapped within the width of his arms.

That's when I noticed his smell: an ugly, rancid, oily stench, a combination of sweat and grease and something else I couldn't identify—a sweet, cloying odor. As I stood there, he took a step toward me and began to rub my back.

"Now, tell me what tools you already know," he said.

"Well, that's a hammer, and that's a pair of pliers and . . ."

He reached up and began to stroke the back of my head.

"My, your hair is soft," he said. "And your sister, Rebel—she's got beautiful hair, so long and pretty. I bet it's smooth and silky to touch . . ."

As he spoke, he pushed against me, pinning me against the workbench.

"Your sister is blossoming, yes, she is, that Rebel is blossoming . . ."

I didn't like how he was saying Rebel's name. I didn't know what "blossoming" meant, but by the way he said it, I thought it must be something . . . well, dirty.

As a matter of fact, I didn't like being there at all, with him pushing me up against the workbench and hanging over me so close the stink of him filled my nostrils.

I sure didn't like him rubbing against my back, and I couldn't turn around or I'd be facing his chest and that would be even worse.

Finally, I couldn't stand it any longer. I ducked down and darted out from under one of his arms and headed for the door.

"Wait a minute," he called after me. I stopped and turned back toward him.

"You forgot your dollar," he said, and handed me a crisp one-dollar bill.

"Tomorrow when you come, you mustn't tell your mother about it," he said. "Your parents wouldn't like for me to be paying you. You're not supposed to pay children. If they knew, they wouldn't let you keep the money. This is just between you and me. It's our secret."

I didn't say anything. I just turned and left. When I climbed back through the hole in the fence, Kate came running out of her house.

"Are you okay?" Kate asked. "What did he do to you?"

"Nothing," I said. "He just gave me a dollar."

Kate didn't believe me.

"What did he do to you?" she demanded.

"Nothing! He didn't do anything."

I turned and ran for home. I didn't want to talk to Kate anymore because I didn't want to hear any more of her dire warnings. The truth was, I wanted to go back to Mr. Jennings's garage. Oh, he smelled bad and acted weird, but he'd given me a dollar. I felt the bill I'd shoved deep into my pocket. I wanted more. My mind instantly conjured up fantasies about all the things I could buy with a dollar, or two dollars . . . or five! Why, if I worked for him long enough, and did a really good job, I could earn . . . well . . . maybe even ten dollars! And what's so awful about having a secret, anyway? I reasoned. My mother knew Mr. Jennings. If there was anything wrong with the man, she wouldn't be so nice to him.

The next day, when I went to visit Mr. Jennings, I didn't go through the hole in Kate's fence. I walked right down his driveway. The man in the dirty blue coveralls was working under the hood of a small, white car. When he lifted his head and spotted me, he smiled a big, satisfied smile. He stepped away from the car and wiped his hands on a filthy rag. Then he picked up an RC cola that was sitting on the workbench, put it to his lips, and drank it almost dry in one long gulp.

"So," he said. "Are you ready to be my special helper?"

I said yes and followed him into the garage to the tool bench. That day, only one of the four garage doors was open. As soon as I was inside, Mr. Jennings closed it.

A little tickle of fear crawled up the back of my neck.

"I hope you've been practicing and know all your tools today," he said. But he didn't ask me to name any. He just motioned me over to the far end of the bench.

"This is a special drawer," he told me.

"What's special about it?" I asked.

"There are special things in it," he replied. "And nobody knows it's here."

With that, he pulled the drawer open and showed me the guns and knives and handcuffs inside.

I had never seen a gun up close. The ones on television didn't look as big as the one lying there beside its clip of bullets. They didn't look as scary, either. The pistol that Dan-o pulled on the bad guys on *Hawaii Five-O* looked like a toy compared to the ugly black thing lying in the drawer. I didn't like Mr. Jennings's gun; it frightened me.

Mr. Jennings took the hunting knife out of the sheath, held it under my chin, and told me the two of us were going to be very special friends. I was so terrified I couldn't seem to breathe. I was genuinely surprised that my knees didn't fold up and dump me on a heap on the floor.

Then Mr. Jennings reached up and started opening the front of his coveralls.

He put the gun down, took my hand, and forced me to touch him. I was sobbing silently, tears streaming down my cheeks, but

Mr. Jennings didn't notice or care. His head was thrown back, his eyes closed, lost in his own world of perverse pleasure.

I squeezed my eyes shut, wanting this to end. Then he called my name. I kept my head down, my eyes downcast, refusing to look at him. But he took my chin in his hand, forced my head up, and glared full into my face.

"If you're not back here on Monday . . ." he said, then reached over and picked up the huge black gun and put the barrel against my temple. "If you don't show up, I'll blow your mother's brains out. And your sister's brains out. Don't you think for a minute I won't do it! They'll be dead and it'll be . . ."—he leaned close and hammered the next words into my heart like nails into a coffin lid—". . . *all your fault!*"

Then he turned away, ignoring me completely, as if I weren't there. I turned on my heel, and bolted out the side door of the garage, and raced every step of the way home as fast as my long legs would carry me.

When I burst into the house, Mom was setting the table for supper. I just stood there, looking at her, not saying a word.

"Don't I get a hug?" Mom asked.

I launched myself into my mother's arms and squeezed her with all the strength in my skinny arms.

"Whoa, what's that about?" Mom asked. She pulled away and looked down at me inquiringly. "Are you okay? Is something wrong?"

And there it was, right there in front of me. Escape. All I had to do was open my mouth and pour out my terror, disgust, and pain. All I had to do was say something—anything. A handful of words and Mommy would know, and I wouldn't have to go back there on Monday. I started to speak . . .

. . . *all your fault!*

"Nothing's wrong," I said. "I'm fine."

Then I went into the bathroom, tore my clothes off, and got into a tub of water so hot it turned me as red as Rebel and I were the day we went swimming and stayed out in the sun too long. I scrubbed and scrubbed and scrubbed, trying to get that awful stink off my skin.

But no matter how hard I scrubbed, I still could smell it. As I lay awake in my bed that night, silent tears running off the sides of my face and into my hair, I could still smell Mr. Jennings's rancid, dirty stench. The odor filled my nostrils and ignited nightmares that kept me awake all night long.

I went back on Monday—I had to. I was afraid of what he'd do, not to me, but to Rebel and Mom if I didn't show up.

The fourth garage door on Mr. Jennings's shop building did not open onto a garage at all. The windows on the door were covered with black plastic, and the space within had been converted into a room where Mr. Jennings took his "special friends."

The room was dim, lit only by a yellowish bulb in the ceiling, and it was stifling hot. The summer sun beat down on the metal walls and roof, turning the interior into an oven. It was sparsely furnished. A couple of chairs, a stool, and an army cot.

The first time Mr. Jennings took me into the room, he sat me on a stool and taught me how to load the pistol, made me hold it and put bullets one at a time into the chamber. Then he told me to put the gun to my head. Reluctantly, I lifted the heavy black pistol and held the barrel to my left temple, my hand trembling violently.

Mr. Jennings leaned over inches from my ear.

"Bang!" he whispered softly.

I flinched and Mr. Jennings smiled the smile that never reached his eyes.

"That's what's going to happen to your mommy and your sister if you ever say a word to anybody about our special friendship."

Mr. Jennings did terrible things to me in that room. He touched me and he hurt me.

And he took lots of pictures. So did his buddies. He often brought men to see the "special friends" he assembled in the room: boys, girls, some older than I, some younger, most of them children I knew who lived on other streets in the neighborhood. He forced us to do perverse things with each other and took pictures.

Sometimes, one of Mr. Jennings's customers would come to pick up a car while he was entertaining special friends in his secret room. Mr. Jennings would leave us behind in the room while he chatted casually with some neighbor just outside the door.

At those times, I was tortured by an almost uncontrollable desire to scream. I yearned to start shrieking and not stop until Mr. Jennings's customer heard me and came to see what was wrong, and took me and the other children away where Mr. Jennings couldn't hurt us anymore. But I didn't. Neither did any of the other children. As if by some mutual agreement, we all remained mute, not daring to move or make a sound, not even speaking to each other. After a few minutes, Mr. Jennings would come back into the room and take up where he had left off as if there had been no interruption at all.

There were so many times I wanted to tell, so many times I was right on the edge of spilling the whole, ugly story. When my mother tucked me into bed at night, kissed me, and told me how much she loved me, the words were on the tip of my tongue. But I didn't say them. I didn't dare say them.

When Rebel leaned over out of the top bunk, her long hair a waterfall of blond, and asked why I cried myself to sleep night after night, I ached to blurt out the truth. But I couldn't.

. . .

I adored my fourth- and fifth-grade teachers. Both women showered me with love, tenderness, and acceptance, and I wanted so desperately to unload all my fear, pain, and anger on them. I planned out just what I would say and how I would say it. Every morning, I promised myself that today would be the day, today would mark the end of the hiding and the sneaking and the lying, the end of Mr. Jennings's hands on me and the stink of him all around me. I went to school day after day, convinced that today I would tell. But I always walked out the door at the end of my last class with the dirty little secret still locked up tight inside me.

No matter how badly I wanted to unburden myself, I just couldn't. I had to protect Mommy and Rebel. Period. No matter how awful it was, I had to keep my mouth shut or Mr. Jennings would kill them, shoot them with the big black gun. I hadn't been totally convinced he'd actually do a thing like that at first, but it wasn't long before I had absolutely no doubt. As the months of abuse stacked up one on top of another, I learned the depths of the man's soullessness, found out just how pitiless and depraved he was. Mr. Jennings was capable of any horror, any brutality. He would put that gun to Mommy's head and blow her brains out without a moment's hesitation. He would hurt Rebel. And when he did, it would be my fault.

Every night before I went to sleep, I talked to God about Mr. Jennings. I never asked God to make Mr. Jennings go away, just like I never asked God to make the pain go away when I had surgery. I knew God loved me as surely as I knew that Mommy and Daddy and Rebel loved me, but my concept of God was deeper and more profound than the average child's. I didn't see God as Santa Claus, a nice old man with a white beard who gave you what you asked for if you were good enough. My God was bigger than that. I never believed it was God's job to get rid of the bad stuff in my life; it was God's job to help me cope with the bad stuff, whatever it was. It was God's job to comfort me and grant me peace even when bad stuff was happening. It was God's job to be there with me all the time, to give me strength to do whatever I had to do, to help me suck it up and go on.

"Help me be a big girl and not cry," I whispered into the darkness as I lay in bed at night, my pillow soaked with tears. "Help me not be afraid, God, 'cause I'm so scared. Please take care of Mommy and Rebel. Please don't let Mr. Jennings hurt them."

The only time I ever felt any peace at all was when I talked to God. Contrary to all my rational understanding, when I prayed, I believed everything would be okay.

SIX

During the time when the shadow of Mr. Jennings stalked my every waking moment, I actually looked forward to surgery. Operations took me out of my everyday life and deposited me in another world. Oh, sure, I suffered in that other world, too, but that was a pain I understood. In that world, only my body hurt, not my heart. I yearned to lie in a hospital bed on clean white sheets, with the whisper of nurses' shoes up and down the hallway at night, and the comforting *beep, beep, beep* of the monitors lulling me to sleep. I longed for quiet and solace and people taking care of me. I ached to feel safe.

Over time, I learned to disassociate from the horror. I functioned normally, went to school, to my grandparents' house, and to the hospital—where I worked the floor, making friends with every patient, visitor, doctor, nurse, and orderly. Like countless other victims of abuse, I taught myself to tune out and turn off. I locked the nightmare up tight in a solitary room deep down in some dark corridor of my mind. With practice, I learned how to stop any thought that attempted to go there. I learned how to live in the moment, in the world of light, and to block out the anguish born in the world of darkness.

Until one Sunday morning when my whole family was in the car on the way to church.

I hadn't planned to say anything. In fact, I didn't even realize I was talking until I heard my own voice.

"Mr. Jennings touches me!"

Did I say that out loud? Did everybody hear me say that?

There were two, maybe three heartbeats of absolute silence in the car. I couldn't breathe.

"Touches you?" Jim asked. "Touches you . . . where?"

"Everywhere!" I heard myself blurt out, and with that one word the dam broke and I couldn't hold on to any of it anymore. It all gushed out in one great tidal wave of emotion that threatened to wash me away in a sea of tears.

Suddenly I was bawling, pointing down into my lap. "There! He touches me there!" I cried, then managed a strangled: "Mr. Jennings is a very bad man! He's going to kill Rebel and he's going to kill Mommy and . . . and . . . and I don't want him to touch me anymore!" I couldn't say anything else after that. All I could do was sob in great heaving, wrenching gulps.

"We're going home," Jim announced, his voice trembling. Mom and Rebel were crying, too. "And that man is never going to hurt you again! Do you hear me—never again! Why didn't you tell me?"

I didn't answer. I just cried and cried and cried.

That afternoon, I watched from my front porch as the police arrested Mr. Jennings, put him into a cruiser in handcuffs, and took him away to jail.

That nightmare was over. But another one was just beginning.

The police found boxes full of physical evidence in Mr. Jennings's special friends' room, stacks of kiddie porn, and hundreds of pictures he and his buddies had taken of children. But the parents of almost all the kids in the pictures refused to allow their children to testify against him. They believed their kids had been wounded enough by the experience, and they wanted to spare them the further trauma of having to describe the abuse—in gruesome detail—to a roomful of strangers.

I was angry that the others kids wouldn't stand up and tell the truth about it. I felt isolated and alone. My parents wanted me to testify because it was the right thing to do.

In the end, only one little boy and I ever took the stand to tell the world what Mr. Jennings had done to us all.

A few days after he was arrested, I had to go to the police station downtown to tell my story. Mom was not allowed to accompany me when I was taken to a room where two detectives—both men—were waiting with a tape recorder. As soon as I was seated in a big chair at the end of the table, the questioning began.

"Tell us what happened to you," said the first detective, the tall one. "Start at the beginning, and we'll stop you if we want to know more."

I tried. But I didn't like having to describe what Mr. Jennings had done. I didn't even like to think about it, much less tack words onto the awful images and say it out loud to two people, two strangers—two *men*—I didn't know.

So I hesitated, and the silence quickly grew uncomfortable. When I finally got started, I stumbled trying to find the right words. I couldn't look at them as I spoke, fixing my eyes instead on the black tape recorder sitting in the middle of the table with a tape turning slowly around and around inside.

I did as good a job as I could of describing what happened that first day in Mr. Jennings's garage, the day he put the knife under my chin. When I stopped talking, the second detective—the one with the big nose—spoke for the first time.

"That didn't really happen, now did it," he said softly. "You're just teasing, aren't you?"

I was horrified.

"It did, too!" I cried, looking both men full in the face. They smiled condescending smiles and told me to go on with my story.

Now, I was really rattled. I tried to continue, but they kept interrupting me, asking me questions that didn't make any sense to me. Didn't anybody care what had happened to me? I was angry, and I was beginning to be afraid, with both men asking me questions that I couldn't seem to answer to suit them. I wanted my mother and I wanted to go home! It finally occurred to me that the less I said, the sooner they would take me out of that horrid room. So I clammed up and refused to talk to them at all.

"You know, you're going to have to go to court and tell your story," the tall one warned me ominously as he turned off the tape recorder and took out the tape. "And that man, Mr. Jennings, he'll be in the room when you do."

Mr. Jennings would be there? In the same room? The prospect of seeing him, of looking into his eyes, scared me to death.

. . .

The day of the trial, Mom dressed me in my best Sunday dress, complete with white socks, folded down neatly, and black patent leather shoes. I had to wait outside in the hallway with a social worker for my turn to testify. Swinging my feet back and forth under the bench where I sat, my gaze was fixed on the big double doors of the courtroom. I knew what I had to do. It had all been explained to me over and over again. I had to go into that room and sit down in a big chair beside the judge and tell him what Mr. Jennings had done to me. When I was finished, I could leave. I could go home with my mommy and daddy. It would be over, all over.

One of the doors suddenly opened and a man came out and called my name. The social worker escorted me across the marble floor, my heels *click, click, clicking* as I walked, and held the door open for me as I stepped inside. The courtroom was huge, the biggest room I had ever seen. I spotted my mother and stepfather quickly, and they waved and smiled at me reassuringly.

Then, I fixed my gaze on my feet and walked down the aisle toward the raised podium where a man in a black robe sat behind a big desk. My heart was pounding in my chest like a jackhammer.

The judge smiled and said, "Hi." I said, "Hi," back in a voice so tiny the room instantly swallowed it up.

The bailiff got up from his seat and came around to where I was standing. He got down on one knee before me and held out a Bible.

"Put your left hand here," he said, indicating the big black book. "Raise your right hand and repeat after me."

I got my hands confused momentarily and the bailiff waited until I got it right.

"I—state your name—do solemnly swear . . ." the bailiff began.

I didn't understand.

"State your name, you know . . . Heather. I, Heather . . ." he prompted.

"Oh, I'm sorry," I said. I was having trouble concentrating. I knew Mr. Jennings was in that room somewhere. I hadn't seen him yet, but I knew he was there. I could feel his eyes on me.

". . . do solemnly swear . . ."

". . . do solemnly swear . . ." I repeated.

". . . that the testimony I am about to give . . ."

I parroted the phrase after him.

Where was he? Where was Mr. Jennings?

". . . is the truth, the whole truth, and nothing but the truth, so help me God."

I swore I'd tell the truth, though nobody except my parents had been very interested in hearing it so far. Then the bailiff got up off his knee and showed me the steps that led to a big chair right up beside the judge. I sat down in it and looked out over the vast courtroom.

There he was! Mr. Jennings was sitting at a table not twenty feet away. He wasn't in dirty overalls, though. He was all scrubbed up clean in a suit and tie. But I could smell him. I could still smell that stink. Or at least I imagined I could. I was suddenly nauseous.

Then I heard his voice, that husky voice that haunted my dreams.

"Don't you tell!" he hissed at me.

And nobody in the courtroom said a thing to him! I was dumbfounded. Nobody told him to shut up and not talk to me! The judge was in a deep discussion with two men standing in front of his big desk. Either he didn't hear or he chose to ignore the whole thing.

"Don't you say a word, do you hear me, not a word!"

I stared at my tormentor. I heard him talking, but I didn't see his mouth move. Didn't anyone else hear him?

The judge finally broke the spell.

"Heather . . ." he said, and when I turned to him, I saw that his face was kind. He spoke to me quietly, gently. Oh, he asked me some of the same dumb questions the policemen had asked, but mostly he was nice and he let me talk. When I was finished, he thanked me and told me I could go, and I hopped down out of the chair and raced across the courtroom into my mother's arms.

. . .

Mr. Jennings was convicted. Mom told me that he had admitted doing lots of awful things to other children, but she didn't say what. She didn't want to talk about it. She didn't want to talk about what he had done to me, either. Nobody did. I ached to cry out my pain and anger and disgust, but nobody wanted to hear it. So I was silent, bottled everything up inside, never brought the subject up. And our whole family went on with life like nothing at all had happened, like everything was just like it was before the day I walked down the long driveway into Mr. Jennings's garage. Only it wasn't the same. And I wasn't the same little girl, either, though I was too young to understand how profoundly different I was.

But there was one reality I could acknowledge, and I clung to it fiercely. It was over! He was gone, that's all that really mattered—right? Mr. Jennings was gone and out of my life!

Three months later, Mr. Jennings was back in his garage down the street from my house.

Mom and Jim had been consulted about his sentence. He could be sentenced to five years in prison, they were told, or he could serve ninety days in jail and five years of probation—with mandatory twice-a-week counseling. My parents agonized over the choice. Eventually, they picked probation. They reasoned that without some kind of intervention, Mr. Jennings would come out of prison a greater danger than when he went in. But if he were forced to get counseling for five years, surely he would get better. Surely, five years of therapy would heal his twisted mind and he'd be able to overcome his perverted behavior. Mom and Jim picked probation because they believed in their hearts it was the best way to ensure the safety of other children, so no other child ever had to suffer what I did.

Over time, the neighborhood changed. Families whose children had been abused moved away. My family had to stay. The cost of my medical care had so impoverished us we couldn't afford to move. I never went anywhere near Mr. Jennings's garage again. For years, I wouldn't even allow my parents to drive past his house; I made them go around the block. But I saw him from time to time nonetheless. And every time he saw me, Mr. Jennings smiled and waved. And blew me kisses.

The day I turned sixteen, I got my driver's license, and I borrowed my father's car to go for a spin. In my excitement, I didn't think where I was going, and I headed down the street toward

Mr. Jennings's house. As I passed, I saw children walking down the driveway to his garage.

But I didn't even flinch. I had buried my pain so deep inside that I didn't even acknowledge its existence anymore. And it stayed buried for years, until tragedy dug it all back up again.

SEVEN

Shortly before I turned twelve years old, Dr. Howerton told Mom there was nothing more he could do for me, that Louisville didn't have the facilities necessary to perform the kind of reconstructive surgery on my urinary system it would take to make me continent. He suggested that Mom needed to explore other options.

One of them was the Mayo Clinic. Dr. Howerton said that a urological surgeon there named Dr. Barrett had developed an innovative procedure using an artificial sphincter muscle that might be just what I needed.

Mom talked it over with me, thought and prayed about it, and finally agreed. Dr. Howerton's office made all the arrangements, and a few months later, Mom took me to one of the most famous medical facilities in the country. I was bouncing off the walls with little-kid excitement. I had never been away from home for a surgery, and even though Rochester, Minnesota, wasn't exactly a tour bus destination, going somewhere new and different sounded to me like a grand adventure.

My first look at the medical complex left me dumbfounded, gawking at building upon building, stretching block after block as far as I could see. It was bigger, more imposing, more sophisticated and more intimidating than any hospital I could have conjured up in my wildest flights of fancy. But it wasn't long before my awe was replaced with a growing distaste, and after a week of being poked and prodded by the best and the brightest medical masterminds in the country, I described the world-famous Mayo Clinic to Rebel over the phone with only six words: Take a ticket, take a seat.

When Mom and I showed up the first morning to begin the rounds of tests that were necessary to determine if Dr. Barrett's surgery would work for me, the atmosphere was something less than warm and cuddly. An unsmiling nurse wordlessly handed Mom my testing schedule. It read like the assembly instructions for a nuclear reactor.

For the rest of the day, we dashed from one appointment to the next at a dead run—a CT scan in one building, a chest X-ray in another, lab work in a third, all scheduled back to back, *bam, bam, bam*. For hours, we bounced from one end of the huge medical complex to the other.

Through it all, I was keenly aware of the complex's clinical sterility. I was accustomed to the kid-friendly atmosphere of Norton Hospital's pediatric wing. I was used to getting to know my nurses and doctors. But at the Mayo Clinic, I felt like a bug on a pin, like I was merely on display for them to study. My smiling, chattering friendliness was greeted with cold reserve. The staff wasn't interested in making a relationship investment in a twelve-year-old kid from Kentucky. They were all business, stiff, starched, detached, institutional.

After what seemed like endless days of testing, Mom and I finally met Dr. Barrett. Nothing in my experience at the clinic—or with the dozens of other physicians I'd seen over the years for that matter—prepared me for the man who came striding into the examining room that morning with a big smile and a warm hello. Tall, with salt-and-pepper hair and the chiseled face of a male model, the world-famous surgeon, who might hold the key to my whole future in his hands, was what my prepubescent friends and I would have dubbed—in giggling awe—"drop-dead gorgeous."

But it was not just his looks, striking as they were, that I responded to. I felt the same instant connection to him that I had felt to Dr. Howerton years before. When I look back now, I know what happened that morning. I felt the presence of God in the room. I felt a peace like what my mom felt the day of the accident. I knew God was in charge, that this was a divine appointment, and I was secure in Dr. Barrett's care, I was absolutely certain that no matter what happened during his medical treatment of me, Dr. Barrett would keep me safe.

Even though the warmth of his smile raised the room temperature ten degrees, he didn't bring good news. The testing had revealed that I was not a candidate for the artificial sphincter muscle procedure. In order for the procedure to be successful, a patient had to have some residual muscle control. I had none.

Once he had explained why that procedure wouldn't work, he proposed another one. He had devised a plan to rid me of my leg bag by building me a reservoir for urine and connecting it to a tiny opening what little remained of my urethra. To empty the reservoir, I would have to catheterize myself every few hours by inserting a tube into the opening.

Dr. Barrett had designed the procedure specifically for me; he had never done anything like it before. But he believed it would give me a shot at being continent, and I would take any chance, endure any pain, to be rid of my pee bag.

As a small child, I had either ignored the bag or lifted my dress to show it to everybody I met. Those days were long gone. As soon as I was old enough to grasp that the bag set me apart from other kids, I was no longer indifferent to its presence. The older I got, the more the bag embarrassed me. I hated it. I would do anything to be rid of it.

Even if I had to endure the pain of surgery and stitches, the isolation and loneliness of hospitalization, and months upon months in bed recuperating to become a "regular" kid, I was in.

It was my determination to be free of my leg bag that had compelled Mom to search the country for any doctor who might be able to help me. Mom agreed with my assessment of Dr. Barrett: He might just be what we'd been looking for.

. . .

On the day of my surgery, Dr. Barrett was happy to pray with me and my mother, and to chat with me and hold my hand as I went to sleep. He pulled up a stool and sat down beside me, asked me about my life and my family and told me about his. When I began counting backward from one hundred, I was relaxed. I felt safe. Dr. Barrett's warmth more than made up for the cold, clinical atmosphere of the hospital.

For the first few days after surgery, I was in a lot of pain. As that eased up, the discomfort of lying absolutely flat on my back took its place. I could not sit up, even when I used the bedpan.

The walls of my room were papered with get-well cards, and I talked on the phone to friends and family members often. My grampa called me every day, and always wanted specifics about my condition—was I running a temperature, was I constipated?

"Honey, if you can't poop, then you need to pass gas," he told me solemnly. "That'll make your belly feel better!"

The novelty of a grand adventure in a new place wore off quickly. As the days turned into weeks, I grew more and more lonely. I had been running a slight fever and they hadn't been able to track down the cause, but other than that, I was progressing remarkably well. And I wanted to go home.

Finally, Dr. Barrett agreed that I could complete the healing process in Louisville, but I needed to get out of bed and walk around a little first. I had been flat on my back for weeks.

The day I was scheduled to check out of the hospital, two nurses came to help me gather my belongings so I'd be ready to leave when Mom got there to pick me up. As the nurses busied themselves straightening up the room, I remembered Dr. Barrett's stipulation that I had to walk before I could go home. I sat up for the first time since my surgery, shifted position so my legs were dangling off the edge of the bed, and slid down onto the floor.

I stood for a moment, a little shaky, then took a step. That's when it happened. Without warning, my incision started to burst open from the top down, like unzipping a jacket!

I felt it give way, a little at first, then all in a *whoosh.* When I looked down and saw what was happening—and smelled the stench!—I started screaming. I was terrified, certain that this time, I really was going to die.

My belly was ripping open! And I was trying to hold it shut, trying to keep it from opening up all the way, trying to keep my insides from . . . from spilling out!

I had never been so scared. But there was nothing I could do except scream. And scream and scream and scream . . . as a foul-smelling brown liquid soaked through the bandages and the front of my gown and began to drip onto the floor.

The nurses grabbed me and lifted me back up onto the bed, and suddenly Mom was there, holding me down, trying to calm me.

"Heather . . . Heather, listen to me . . . *listen . . . to . . . me*," Mom said firmly. Her voice sounded perfectly calm. Whether she really was or not, I don't know, but she always sounded totally in control. Always.

"Stop freaking out, do you hear me, stop it! Calm down!" she said, but I was hysterical, wailing in terror, and Mom could do nothing to soothe me.

One of the nurses who'd been in my room tracked down Dr. Barrett in surgery and told him what had happened. He immediately turned the patient over to another surgeon and raced upstairs to my room in his scrubs. He could hear my screams all the way down the hallway.

"We've got to clean this out—now!" he said when he saw—and smelled—the infection in the open wound on my belly. And right there on my bed, he opened up the rest of my incision and began to flush out the whole area with sterile solution.

Mom held one of my arms, a nurse held the other, and two additional nurses held my legs.

"You've got to be quiet," Mom told me. "You've got to stop crying and be still."

I continued to struggle and shriek, though I was more frightened and traumatized than in pain, freaked out by the sight of the open cavity in my belly.

Finally, Mom got right in my face, inches from my nose.

"Heather, shut up!" she yelled at me. "Do you hear me, I said, 'Shut up!' "

The verbal slap in the face shocked me into silence. But inside my head, I was still screaming—screaming at my mother: *You shut up! This hurts! It hurts! Why won't you let me cry, Mommy? Why won't you ever let me cry?*

The doctor and nurses flushed out my belly with sterile solution over and over and over again, cleaning out the infection that had caused my fever, that had been there, building up pressure until it burst open the stitches.

Once the wound was clean and sterile, it had to be allowed to heal from the inside out. That meant the open area—the gaping hole in my belly from my sternum to my pelvis—had to be packed with sterile gauze and then bandaged.

As soon as the wound was finally taped shut, the crisis was over. Obviously, I wasn't going anywhere; home was out of the question. Dr. Barrett spoke softly to me for a little while, trying to reassure me, then he and the nurses left. Mom and I were alone in the room. Both of us were emotionally spent.

As Mom sat in the chair beside my bed, staring with unseeing eyes out the window at the street below, I just knew the tired old phrase was echoing in her head: *This many bad things can't possibly happen to one person!*

How many times over the years had we heard somebody say that about me? Every time yet another ghastly thing occurred, we could count on fielding that comment from someone.

And how many times had Mom looked somebody in the eye and responded, "Well, guess what—that many bad things do happen, and keep happening, to Heather!"

The reality of my life offered the only possible explanation. By age twelve, I'd had more than seventy-five surgeries. When you've gone under the knife that many times, you come under the official jurisdiction of Murphy's Law—if something can go wrong, it usually will.

Like the surgery in Louisville to repair fistulas—holes—in the mesh lining in my belly. Afterward, I had to lie flat on my back. I couldn't move, couldn't even roll over, for weeks. To prevent the bed sores that such prolonged inactivity often causes, I was placed in a Stryker bed. The bed consists of a canvas "mattress" stretched on a frame, and an apparatus to flip the frame over. To turn me from looking at the ceiling to looking at the floor, the frame had to be unscrewed and opened, and a second piece of canvas hooked into it on top of me. With the frame bolted shut, a machine slowly turned it over, leaving me on my stomach on the second piece of canvas—until it was time to flip me on my back again.

One afternoon, a nurse's aide came in to turn me from my stomach to my back. She was a sweet girl, one of my favorites because she was cheerful and talkative and always took the time to stay for a little while in my room chatting. That day, she must have gotten too involved in her conversation with me to pay attention to what she was doing. She got careless and forgot to refasten the screws before she turned the machine on to flip the bed. When the bed turned up on its side, the frame came open and I spilled out in a heap onto the floor, ripping out tubes and drains and IV lines.

The aide was so horrified, she turned and bolted. Mom didn't wait to use the call light. Two men—two strangers—were walking past the doorway, and Mom screamed at them.

"I need help in here! Now!"

The two men rushed to my aid. I was a mess, lying on the floor bleeding. They lifted me up and helped Mom get me back into bed. Remarkably, I suffered no great harm from the fall. But I was traumatized, nonetheless, as I had been traumatized the day I woke up in the recovery room and discovered that no surgery had been performed.

I had been wheeled into the operating room early that morning, and Mom had just gotten settled in an uncomfortable chair with a good book. Passing time was a skill she had mastered so well she could have snared gold on the U.S. Olympic Waiting Team.

Suddenly, the surgeon came striding into the room, still in his scrubs.

"I cut the wrong thing," he told Mom bluntly, as he peeled off his gloves. "Bring Heather back in three weeks and we'll try again."

At least that time, Mom was able to gather me up and take me home. She wouldn't be taking me home from the Mayo Clinic after the disaster there. The infection, the gaping wound in my belly, and the packing and bandages guaranteed that I would be hospitalized for another week, maybe more.

And I had so been looking forward to going home.

Mom leaned over my bed and patted my hand.

"I'm sorry, sweetheart," she said. "I know how homesick you are."

"I want my daddy!" I said, still sniffling.

"Honey, you know your father's not going to come to see you way up here in Minnesota!" Mom replied. After my parents' divorce, my father almost never came to visit me during my surgical procedures. I had real abandonment issues over that; I didn't have a daddy like the other kids did. And I had needed one so badly so many times.

Mom had been divorced only two years when she married Jim—after she had dated him for just two weeks! The aftershocks of that rocked the house for years. Mom, Rebel, and I had been a close team after my father left; we were tight. Then, suddenly, a man showed up in our lives, a man Rebel and I didn't pick, a man we hardly knew. He moved in, and stepbrothers and stepsisters did, too, on visitation days.

In truth, I didn't have anything against Jim except his presence. But that was enough to build a wall between us.

So when I told Mom that day at the Mayo Clinic that I wanted my daddy, Mom was stunned and confused. Why on Earth would I think my father would show up there, when he had never come to any of my other surgeries—operations that were conducted much closer to where he lived than upstate Minnesota?

But Mom had misunderstood what I meant.

"I don't mean Daddy," I said. "I mean Daddy Jim. I want Daddy Jim to come to see me."

I'm still not sure what prompted my sudden need to see Jim. I just felt so alone. I was freaked out by what had happened and devastated that I had been packed up and ready to leave and suddenly couldn't go home at all. I suppose I was just grasping at straws.

"Jim?" Mom said. "You want Jim to come here?"

I nodded my head. So Mom called her husband and put me on the line.

"I want you to come here!" I blurted out as soon as I heard Jim's voice. "It's been horrible and I want you to come!"

"But aren't you coming home?" he asked.

"No," I wailed, and started to cry. Through my tears, I told him what had happened, that I had been getting ready to go home when my incision burst open. That I would have to stay in that cold, unfriendly hospital for another week.

"Will you come . . . please?" I begged.

Jim stammered and stumbled. He couldn't just drop everything and travel from Louisville, Kentucky, to Rochester,

Minnesota. He had a job. He had Rebel to take care of, and his own son, who was living with Jim and Mom at the time. They were both teenagers; he couldn't leave them home alone.

"Honey . . . I'd love to come," he said. "But I just don't see how I can. I'll try . . . but I don't think there's any way."

I hung up the phone and cried.

I had trouble going to sleep that night so I was given medication to sedate me. I didn't wake up until almost noon the next day. When I opened my eyes, Jim was sitting beside my bed.

"I'm sorry it took me so long to get here," he said. "I had to drive."

He had driven all the previous afternoon, all night, and all that morning—650 miles, nonstop!

I sat up, threw my arms around him, and began to cry. The tears spoke of many things. It was like the tumblers in a lock all fell together and a door opened. Seeing Jim sitting there put all the pieces together. I did have a daddy! I had had one for years.

As Jim held me, a movie rolled in my head, the familiar scenes colored with new meaning and understanding: Jim making supper and bringing it to the hospital for Mom and me, night after night after night. Jim working two, sometimes three jobs so he could afford medical benefits. Jim driving an old car and giving up vacations to pay for the out-of-pocket expenses of my care. Jim, quiet and calm, always in the background, always there at every surgery, always just *there* for his family. I didn't see a single image of him complaining. Jim never told Rebel and me to call him "Dad." He just acted like one.

Jim wasn't a man who found it easy to say, "I love you." But I realized his actions had been shouting that at me for years. That day, I took the "step" off the front of my relationship with Jim. I never again referred to him as my stepfather. He was my daddy.

Mom had been working all morning to spring me from the hospital. She knew her little girl needed a break, that I had to get out of that environment for a while even if I couldn't go anywhere or do anything. Finally, Mom talked Dr. Barrett into allowing me to go with her and Jim to their hotel room across the street from the hospital. But first, Mom had to learn how to care for my wound; the packing had to be changed every four hours around the clock.

That evening, Jim and Mom checked me out of the hospital and moved me with them into a 15' × 15' hotel room with two beds, a tiny bathroom, and a black-and-white television. Since I couldn't get out of bed, there was nothing for the three of us to do but play games and watch television. For three days, that's what we did. We played cards, Monopoly, Scrabble, Yahtzee, and watched reruns of *Gilligan's Island*, *General Hospital*—my grampa's favorite soap opera—*The Price Is Right*, *Battlestar Galactica*, and *The Mary Tyler Moore Show*. It should have been an awful time. But it wasn't. I have always treasured that memory as one of the best times I ever spent with my parents . . . my mother and my father.

EIGHT

Almost every night for years, I dreamed that the other kids noticed, stopped to stare, and pointed and laughed at me.

Sometimes, what they noticed was the bulge in my jeans where I had crammed three maxipads between my legs. Only in my dreams, it wasn't just a lump that nobody but me paid any attention to. In my dreams, the bulge was huge, like I had a pillow stuffed down my pants. It was so big, I had trouble walking, and everyone I passed in the hallway gawked at me, pointed at me, and laughed.

Sometimes, I dreamed that I wet myself, that suddenly I was soaked in pee. I was always standing in front of a class of faceless kids at school when it happened, and the whole class saw my wet pants and roared with laughter.

I woke up from nightmares like that in a cold sweat, my heart pounding. Then the sick feeling would dissolve into joy as I realized I was at home in my own room—that nothing that horrifying had really happened. It was only a dream.

That's what I wanted so desperately to do that day in Mrs. Barnett's class in sixth grade. I wanted to wake up from the nightmare, to open my eyes and discover I was safe at home in my own bed. But that day, I couldn't wake up because I wasn't asleep. And it wasn't a dream. That day, my worst nightmare really happened.

. . .

The first day I set foot in Barrett Middle School, I rounded a corner in the hallway and ran smack into Mr. Bradley, an African-American counselor so menacing he could break up a fight or put a bully in his place with nothing more than a stern look. But underneath his intentionally intimidating exterior was a giant teddy bear of a man who took an instant liking to the skinny, dark-haired little girl with the vacant, deer-in-the-headlights look in her eyes. Mr. Bradley became my champion; his office was my safe place. And I often needed one.

After the surgery at the Mayo Clinic, where Dr. Barrett had created a reservoir for urine in my abdomen, I had to catheterize myself every three or four hours. I even had to set an alarm so I could empty the reservoir in the middle of the night.

The procedure appeared to work at first. But the success was short-lived. Within weeks of the surgery, I was wetting the bed again. I had no muscle structure, so there was nothing to keep the hole that led to the reservoir sealed. Once the swelling in the adjacent tissue went down, the opening began to leak. The leak quickly became a flood. Even sleeping in a Depend diaper didn't keep me dry. I still woke up with my underwear, T-shirt, and sheets soaked in urine.

Every morning before I went to school, I stripped my bed and put the soaked sheets in the washer. If I forgot, the whole downstairs of the house smelled like a toilet. Then I took a bath, slathered myself in baby powder, and put on two, sometimes three maxipads. The bulge they made in my jeans was all the more noticeable because I was so skinny.

The students and teachers at Field Elementary School had known my medical history. I hadn't had to explain my long absences. Everybody had understood.

But middle school was a new game on a new field with new players. Several elementary schools fed students into Barrett. I didn't know the kids from the other schools, and they didn't know me—or my issues. There were cliques in middle school, too. Athletes. Band kids. Science Club. Cheerleaders. I had to figure out where I fit among the different groups, and I feared I didn't fit anywhere at all.

I kept extra maxipads and several changes of clothing "just in case" in the health room at school, and spent most days in a state of self-imposed dehydration. I drank as little as possible so I wouldn't produce any urine, then lied to Mom—who worked as a volunteer in the health room—about my liquid intake, assuring her that I'd had plenty to drink.

I was absolutely paranoid about what my fellow students might notice: the pants bulge, that I smelled funny—like pee or baby powder—even that I sometimes changed clothes twice a day. Certainly, middle school was puberty with the training wheels still on, but even then we all fully understood the Cardinal Rule of Adolescence: Thou Shalt Not Be Different.

My favorite class was Mrs. Barnett's sixth-grade English class, room 210. Mrs. Barnett was a neat woman in her fifties with pewter-gray hair and clothes that were always coordinated—including socks to match every outfit. I loved her because she encouraged her students to write about reality, about events and feelings that didn't have to be "nice." You could write about anger and despair. You could be real.

One afternoon, I was sitting at my desk in her class daydreaming about Sean Mattingly instead of working on the sonnet that was due at the end of the period. I had an impassioned crush on Sean, who had long blond hair, piercingly blue eyes—and was madly in love with Rebel, just like every other boy with a pulse within a ten-mile radius. Sean was seated on one side of me, Janene Jacobs, my best friend, was in the row of desks on the other side, and Ricky Therman was in front of me.

I had been thirsty all morning. Usually, I didn't give in, but in an uncharacteristic binge, I had downed three chocolate milks at lunch. Mrs. Barnett's was the first class after lunch, and as I sat there imagining what I would say if Sean asked me to go steady, I suddenly felt a warm gush between my legs. I looked down in horror, watching my light blue jeans turn darker and darker. I hadn't wet just a little; I had completely soaked my pants all the way through.

What was I going to do? I gritted my teeth to stifle a wave of paralyzing panic. Think. *Think!* I had to get to the health room—without everybody noticing that my pants were soaked! Okay, how? I looked around frantically. Janene! Leaning across the aisle, I whispered desperately.

"Can I borrow your jacket? And will you walk behind me when I get up? I peed all over myself."

Janene had been my friend for years. She knew instantly what had happened, and understood how mortified I would be if anybody noticed.

Wordlessly, she handed me her jacket, and prepared to get up when I did and walk behind me, as if we both were on our way to the pencil sharpener by the door. I wrapped the jacket around my waist and tied the arms in the front so the jacket would drape down over my soaked jeans. Then I poked Ricky in the back.

"I leaked all over myself," I told him, near tears. "Please help! Walk with me so nobody will see."

Ricky was an old friend, too.

We all looked at each other and timed it just right. The three of us got up in unison. Ricky draped his arm around my shoulders and walked close to me. Janene was right behind me.

I almost made it to the door. We were only a few steps away when Mrs. Barnett looked up.

"Heather," she said, "if you're going to the bathroom, will you stop by the office and see if there's any mail in my mailbox?"

I turned and said, "Yes, ma'am." That's when it happened. The knot I had tied in the arms of Janene's jacket came undone, and the jacket fell to the floor—leaving me standing in front of the whole class, my jeans soaked in pee. The kids who had glanced up when I spoke spotted my wet pants and began to laugh, poking their neighbors and pointing at me. Within seconds, the whole class was laughing.

Janene looked at me, her eyes crying out, "I'm so sorry!" and I bolted—out the door, through the hallway to the stairs, and down the stairs to the very bottom. Then I collapsed on the last step and burst into tears.

Janene bolted, too—straight to Mr. Bradley's office to tell him what had happened. He found me at the bottom of the stairwell, sat down beside me, put his big, burly arm around my skinny shoulders, and pulled me close.

"They . . . laughed . . . at me!" I cried, my words coming out in the jerky, hitching rhythm of my sobs. "They all saw me and they laughed." The final "laughed" trailed off in a pitiful wail, and then I sobbed even harder.

"Now, sweetheart, don't you let that get to you," Mr. Bradley said. "We're going to go back to that class right now—together, you and me—and have a good, long talk with those kids!"

Mr. Bradley got me to my feet and we climbed the stairs and walked down the big, empty hallway side by side. I was still crying when I passed Rebel's classroom. My sister saw me and ran out to see what was wrong.

"What happened, Heather?" Rebel asked. "What's the matter?"

"I peed all over myself in front of the whole class and they laughed at me!" I blurted out, then turned before Rebel could say a word, and continued down the hallway.

When I rounded a corner, I saw Mom. Someone had told my mother that I had run out of class, and she had come looking for me. When Mom saw me, she knew instantly what must have happened . . . and she burst out laughing. Not exactly a typical response, but I wasn't surprised.

"Honey," Mom said, mirth in her voice, "you've been so worried about something like this happening and now it has. Well, guess what? You lived through it. You're fine."

I wasn't shocked at Mom's apparent lack of sympathy. If my mother ever felt sorry for me, she rarely showed it, and she never allowed me to feel sorry for myself. That was hard at the time, but looking back, I realize my mother's attitude taught me to laugh in the face of pain and kept me from becoming a very bitter woman.

Mom took me to the health room and helped me change clothes—dousing me in baby powder to hide the smell. By the time I was redressed, it was about five minutes before the bell signaling a change of classes. The three of us went back to my class together. Mr. Bradley and Mom on either side and me, small and miserable, in the middle. I walked as slow as I could, praying the bell would ring before I got back to the room. It didn't.

We all stopped at the door.

"You go first," Mr. Bradley said to me.

"No, you go first," I said.

"Will that make you go in—if I go first?"

I nodded.

Mr. Bradley opened the door and stepped into my classroom. Janene saw him.

"Is Heather okay?" she asked.

"She's right behind me, see for yourself," he said.

When Janene spotted me, she ran up and threw her arms around me in a huge hug.

Then she pulled back and looked at me. "How did you change clothes so fast?" she asked. "I didn't know you were Houdini."

That got a smile out of me. It was a small smile, but it was better than nothing.

Mrs. Barnett took over from there.

"Heather, what happened to you, sweetie?" she asked. The class was listening more attentively than they'd listened to a thing the woman had said all year.

"My last surgery didn't work," I replied.

Mrs. Barnett turned to the class.

"I know you don't understand what's wrong with Heather," she said. "So ask her. Ask her any questions you'd like."

The class was as silent as a pharaoh's tomb. Finally, somebody had the courage to ask what everybody else in the room wanted to know.

"Why did you pee on yourself?"

I squared my shoulders and started to talk.

"I got run over when I was four years old," I said. "The tire of the car crushed my belly and destroyed some of my internal organs. One of them was my bladder, so I can't hold pee like you can. I don't have a bladder to hold it in."

The more I talked, the more I relaxed.

"For a long time, I had a bag that was taped to my leg, with a tube that went into my side and into my kidneys. The pee drained into the bag and then I emptied the bag. But I hated the bag. I didn't want to wear it. I didn't want to be different. I wanted to be like you and everybody else in school. So I had surgery to fix me so I wouldn't have to wear a bag. But the surgery didn't work."

The room was silent for a second or two.

"Where did you get those clean clothes?" somebody asked. It was a lighthearted enough question that it released some of the tension in the room.

"I keep a change of clothes here at school, so if something like this happens, I won't have to walk around for the rest of the day wet," I said.

More silence.

"So . . . it's not your fault that you peed yourself," somebody said, voicing the dawning of understanding in the room. "You can't help it."

"No," I said. "I can't help it."

From that day forward, the students in Mrs. Barnett's class were my staunchest supporters. When word got out about what had happened, they explained to other kids why. But I was only a real person to the kids who had witnessed my embarrassment and pain firsthand. The rest of the students in the school didn't care. The next day in the lunchroom, I heard if for the first time.

"Hey, Miss *Peabody*," somebody called out. Then the other kids standing nearby snickered.

That became my nickname. A nickname I loathed. Years later, when I was a young adult, I ran into a former classmate in a store.

"Hey, how you doin', Peabody," he said.

I wasn't a kid anymore.

"I don't like that name, and I don't ever want to hear it again," I said firmly.

The young man was stunned at the force behind my words.

"Well, okay . . . sorry. I didn't mean . . . why not?" he said.

"Do you know why the other kids called me Peabody?"

"No, I just supposed it was your nickname . . . you know, like some kids are Dufus or Bubba or Butch."

He thought it was just a nickname, an innocent nickname. He didn't even know where I got it. I shook my head and sighed, remembering all the pain that "innocent nickname" had caused, how it shadowed me everywhere I went from the day I first heard it in the lunchroom in the sixth grade. I had hoped I'd be able to leave it behind when I left middle school. But it stuck to me tighter than sour on pickles all the way into high school.

. . .

I was more frightened the first day of high school than I had ever been approaching a twenty-hour surgery. Being a lowly freshman at Atherton High School was far scarier than the prospect of dying on the operating table. I might not have made it through the day if Janene hadn't turned up in my homeroom. Janene was just as terrified as I was, but misery loves company.

About midmorning, as I was swimming upstream against the flow of students in a frantic search for my locker, desperate to get my books and get to my next class on time, somebody spoke to me.

"Hi, Heather," the boy said as he approached me. Two words. That's all. But they were possibly the two most important words I had ever heard in my whole life. He knew my name! And he was a guy—a good-looking guy! An upperclassman!

As he passed me, he turned to the friend walking with him. "That's Heather, Rebel's little sister," he said.

From that moment on, I was "in." Rebel had put the word out: "Keep an eye on my little sister." If Rebel had asked for the Hope diamond or the Holy Grail, twenty drooling high school boys would willingly have laid down their lives to get it for her. Rebel was beautiful and popular and I was her little sister. It would be hard to come by any better credentials than that.

Soon, I was hanging out with Rebel's friends—juniors! I knew all the hot guys—upperclassmen guys. My stock went up quickly among the other lowly freshmen.

In October, the student body cast ballots for homecoming queen. The queen had to be a senior girl. But each of the other classes voted for a princess. I didn't even know I'd been nominated for freshman class princess until it was announced over the intercom to the whole school that I had won.

Mom bought me a beautiful dress—knee-length, with copper, brown, tan, and burgundy stripes—to wear the night of the homecoming game. I got to sit in the backseat of a Corvette convertible and wave at the crowd as the other princesses and I were driven one lap around the field. Then the other girls and I were each escorted to midfield for the queen-crowning ceremony.

My escort was a boy named Zach. As we were standing on the fifty-yard line, he asked me to go steady with him, and slipped a silver and gold heart ring on my finger.

After that, he walked me to each of my classes, and held my hand in the hallway. Mom had strict rules about dating. Only group dates. No exceptions. She would haul four or five girls and an equal number of boys to the mall and come back a few hours later to get us. Same rules for movies, eating out, or school functions—lots of kids and Mom driving.

When basketball season rolled around, I represented the freshman class as the basketball homecoming princess as well. Two titles in one year was unprecedented; my canoe had finally come splashing down out of the rapids and was sliding across smooth, clear water.

Zach and I were an item through our freshman year and we "dated" all the next summer. But a little over a month into our sophomore year, I had to go to Boston for a major surgery. Zach promised he would wait for me. He promised he would write and call. And he did. For a while. He probably meant to remain faithful until I got back.

But the months dragged on. Other girls thought he was cute; other girls flirted with him. Other girls right there in Louisville. Slowly, the letters and the phone calls stopped.

The Boston surgery cost me my boyfriend. It also killed me.

NINE

The nurse's face turned as white as her uniform.

"You don't understand," she stammered. It was obvious to her that this sixteen-year-old girl lying on the examining table didn't realize who she was dealing with. "Dr. Hardy Hendren is the head of the whole surgery department," she said. "He's a very busy man. He doesn't meet with patients before he operates on them."

"No, ma'am, *you* don't understand," I told the woman. I was polite, but firm. Very firm. "Either he comes in here and talks to me or there isn't going to *be* any operation."

I had a single rule that applied to every surgery, from the simplest diagnostic procedure to the most complicated eighteen-hour operation. I didn't go to sleep unless the doctor was holding my hand.

It was about being real. Mom has often said that she didn't know when or how I came by an understanding of such a profound human dynamic. It seemed to her that I'd always known it. Maybe I had. Maybe my need to be a real person to my doctors was intuitive, instinctive. It certainly manifested itself at an early age.

Mom, Rebel, and I had moved to Louisville when I was seven, and Mom had to find a doctor there willing to take on the responsibility of caring for a child who would likely require repeated surgeries for years. We met with several surgeons and urologists, but in the end, I made the final selection.

Dr. Lonnie Howerton was the hands-down winner thirty seconds after I met him. Dr. Howerton didn't talk to Mom as if I weren't even in the room, or treat me like I was too dumb to answer questions about my own body. That's what most doctors did. Dr. Howerton talked to *me*. He got down on one knee so he could look me in the eye, and discussed my medical situation with me like . . . well, like I was a real person.

That was huge. That was everything. Even as a small child, I grasped the significance of not being just another body that needed repair work—like a television set with little wavy lines on the screen or a toaster that burned the bread. At the time, I probably couldn't have tacked words onto my fear of becoming anonymous, but as I grew older, I learned to articulate my needs in simple, blunt terms nobody could misunderstand.

"If I'm going to plop my backside on an operating table and let some doctor cut my belly open, he's going to know who I am," I informed every medical professional who crossed my path, "he's going to know me, and I'm going to know him."

So when the nurse at Boston Children's Hospital informed me that my surgeon was too busy to see me, Mom winced. She knew the woman dressed in white had just pulled the pin out of a hand grenade.

"I've never even met this man!" I said, drilling my words into the pale nurse like stickpins into a bulletin board. "Until I do, he's not touching me."

I looked over at Mom, who nodded her head in support.

"You don't have to do this if you don't want to," Mom told me—saying it more for the nurse's benefit than for mine. I knew my mother would never force me to allow some stranger to use a scalpel on me.

This particular procedure didn't involve cutting, but it did involve being put to sleep, so it amounted to the same thing in my mind. This was a pre-op examination before the big surgery that was scheduled five days later. The world-famous surgeon wanted to take a look for himself at the mangled labyrinth of missing and damaged organs he'd read about in my medical charts.

The pre-op procedure was the surgeon's opportunity to scope out the lay of the land, to see for himself the damage a wide, black tire had done to my body a dozen years before.

Dr. Hendren had designed a bold plan to do more than simply repair that damage; he intended to completely rebuild my urinary system using skin grafts from my hips and bowel.

The accident had left me with kidneys and ureters but no bladder. Dr. Hendren intended to build me one. He planned to use about a foot of bowel to create a reservoir for urine, and a long, slender piece of bowel—cored out—to make a urethra and a bladder neck. The most innovative part of the surgeon's design was his plan to restore the vaginal wall that was destroyed in the accident. Not only would he replace what was missing, he intended to provide a big enough blood supply to the replacement tissue to nourish nerves so there would be feeling in the area. To do that, he intended to cut a flap of skin off my buttocks—leaving one end attached—and flip that flap of skin down and into my vagina. He would then create from that flap of tissue something like a glove, with blood supplied through the intact vessels where the skin remained connected to my body.

Nothing even remotely like this surgery had ever been performed anywhere. I was the perfect candidate for such an innovative procedure for several reasons. I was young. Other than the injuries I had suffered in the accident, I had always been healthy. I had just the right pieces of organs remaining. And I had spunk.

Dr. Hendren had proposed the surgery to Mom in a telephone conversation after a colleague told him about my case. Mom was skeptical; Dr. Hendren was determined.

"I can fix her!" he had said.

"How do you know you can?"

"Because I'm the best there is," he had replied.

Mom hung up the phone after their conversation thinking: *That man's ego wouldn't fit in this room.* But she had to admire his confidence. He was convinced he could do it, and because he was so certain, she tried to be confident, too.

But the surgery wasn't going to happen if I didn't get to meet Dr. Hendren first. I sat up and started to get off the table.

"Wait!" the nurse said. There was something like panic in her voice when she realized I wasn't bluffing. "Don't . . . I mean, you can't just . . . please, stay here and I'll go . . . well, I'll just go tell him . . . you know . . . tell him what you want."

It was soon obvious that Dr. Hendren didn't take the news well.

Mom and I were in a small examining room outside the OR, which was an open area with swinging doors separating each surgery suite from the next. We could hear the doctor coming.

Bam! A distant set of swinging doors slammed open.

Bam! The next set gave way.

Bam! He was getting closer.

Bam! Nurses, orderlies, and technicians scattered out of his path like the parting of the Red Sea.

Suddenly, there he was in the doorway, a small, balding, singularly unimpressive man made huge by his arrogance—and his anger.

Outrage rendered him temporarily mute, and he just stood there, staring at Mom and me, a slender blond woman and a dark-haired teenager. He quickly found his voice.

"Who in the hell do you think you are?" he snarled in a tone that would have curdled new milk.

I didn't flinch.

"I'm Heather," I replied pleasantly. "Who are you?"

"I'm Dr. Hardy Hendren, head of the surgery department," he announced with a pompous grandiosity that under any other circumstances would have been comical.

"Oh . . ." I said, "then you're not God."

He couldn't believe his ears.

"What did you say?"

"I said, 'You're not God!' " I replied.

Holding himself under tight control, he continued through clenched teeth, "I don't have time for this. I don't operate this way."

"Well, you're not going to operate at all, not on me anyway, unless you sit down here and talk to me," I said. "I don't let anybody put me to sleep that I don't know."

A range of emotions washed across the little man's face so quickly that no single one was discernible. Then the air hissed out of his outrage and his demeanor changed between heartbeats. Resignation sat unquietly on his shoulders. He didn't become anybody's definition of affable, but he was at least polite.

"All right," he said with a sigh. He pulled up a stool and sat down. "What do you want to talk about?"

"What kind of car do you drive?" I asked. I had something of a fetish for cars. I believed you could tell a lot about a person by the car he drove.

"A Mercedes," Dr. Hendren replied.

"Why?"

"Because it's the safest car on the road."

"Yeah, but they're expensive. I can't afford one."

"What do you drive?" he asked.

"All I've got is my mom's old Honda," I said, and the stiff doctor actually smiled.

So it went.

"Do you have any kids?"

"Yes, a boy and a girl."

"Tell me about them."

"Well, my daughter has had to have lots of surgeries—just like you."

"What's the matter with her?"

"She has a birth defect."

He began to describe his daughter's medical condition, and the difficulty she faced in life because of it, and in spite of himself, humanity crept into his voice.

I changed the subject.

"Where did you have dinner last night?" I asked.

The doctor cringed.

"I went to an Italian restaurant."

"Don't you like Italian?"

"Not particularly, but I was in surgery until ten o'clock, and it was the only place around here that was still open."

I was quiet after that, so he asked, "Is there anything else you can think of that you want to know?"

"No, I guess not."

"So . . . is it okay to go to surgery now?"

I eyed him for a moment.

"Yeah, I guess so," I said.

Dr. Hendren turned to Mom.

"You've really got something on your hands with this one," he said, shaking his head.

Mom nodded.

"Heather's real, and she wants everybody else to be real, too," Mom said. "Doctors . . . well, *some* doctors, have very big egos. Heather just doesn't want to get lost in the shuffle."

Dr. Hendren took my hand and helped me down off the examining table. But instead of putting me on a gurney, he hooked my arm in his and walked with me—pushing my IV pole—into the surgery suite. I climbed up on the operating table, turned to my mother, and the ritual began. First came the prayer. Mom invited Dr. Hendren to join in. He bowed his head while Mom asked God to watch over me and keep me safe.

Then came the hug, the kiss, the "I love you," and the "See you in a little while" instead of "good-bye." Mom left the room, and Dr. Hendren held my hand as the anesthesiologist put me to sleep.

• • •

I had to undergo several days of testing before the operation on January 2. Since I didn't have to be hospitalized until the night before surgery, Mom rented a room for the two of us in a bed-and-breakfast not far from the hospital. We stayed in the beautiful old brownstone in Brookline from the day after Christmas until the evening of New Year's Day.

I had never seen anything like the huge old home, with its high ceilings, wide doorways, sweeping staircases, beautiful hardwood floors, and intricately carved crown molding. All the guests ate meals together on a big dining room table covered in a starched white linen tablecloth. The food was served on fine china, and shiny silver cutlery rested on cloth napkins beside each place setting. Almost everyone staying at the bed-and-breakfast was caring for a child hospitalized at Boston Children's Hospital, and over time we bonded together and became a family. Every night, the guests from all across America gathered in the parlor and played games—Monopoly, Yahtzee, and Parcheesi. Afterward, Mom and I sat up in bed late into the night—me journaling and Mom reading a book—in a room so cold we were dressed in sweatsuits. We piled our winter coats on top of the bedspread when we went to sleep.

On New Year's Day, Mom decided to go shopping. Back home in Louisville, the big department stores always staged huge New Year's Day sales. It would be a shame to be in such a big city and not snare some bargains in Macy's or Saks Fifth Avenue. Besides, neither Mom nor I had ever ridden a subway. It would be an adventure.

We probably should have figured out that something wasn't right as soon as we stepped onto the train. Sure, this was our first subway ride. But we had at least seen pictures of subways and scenes in subways in movies. And in all those pictures and movie scenes there was a single common characteristic—people. Subways were supposed to be jammed with people. The train we were riding had two passengers—Mom and me.

When the train pulled into a downtown station, the platform there was equally deserted—so totally devoid of humanity it was almost spooky. Had the city been evacuated last night while we were sleeping?

"I wonder why there's nobody here," I said, looking around the cavernous lobby on the other side of the empty turnstiles.

"Maybe everybody's nursing a hangover," Mom joked. She had no idea how close she was to the truth. She didn't know that Boston closed up shop on New Year's Day so its citizens could stay home and recover from the city's New Year's Eve festival.

Of course, some of its citizens had no homes to recover in.

We crossed the lobby, the clicking of our heels on the stone floor echoing in the empty silence. The only person we saw was a homeless man asleep on a bench, shopping bags full of his belongings stacked on top of him to keep him warm.

It was a bitterly cold day, with the sun shining out of an achingly blue, cloudless sky. When we came up out of the subway station, it took our eyes a moment or two to adjust to the bright light. Then we just stood there, looking around in wonder. We weren't amazed at what we saw; we were stunned into silence by what we didn't see.

There were no crowds. No shoppers carrying bulging sacks. No laughing families, with kids bundled up against the cold. No strolling couples. No groups of teenagers. The sidewalks were deserted—except for street people, some drunks, and a couple of prostitutes. Homeless people were pushing shopping baskets loaded down with everything they owned in the world; a few men lay sleeping or unconscious in doorways.

Mom seemed very nervous.

"Heather!" she hissed through her teeth as I stared unashamedly at the people and the buildings. "Don't look so conspicuous."

Mom told me to take off my jewelry and put it in my pocket, as she unclipped her own earrings and unhooked her pearl necklace. The pearls weren't real, of course, but I doubted that the people staring at them could tell the difference.

"Put your purse inside your coat and zip your coat up," Mom said. I looked at her. There was a beat or two of absolute silence, and then both of us burst out laughing.

Mom was the first to regain her composure.

"We've got to get serious here," she said, struggling mightily to do just that. "Don't make eye contact with anybody and just keep walking."

Mom linked her arm through mine and off we went in search of a store and a half-price sale, walking purposefully. We walked for blocks, passing one closed business after another. Mom spotted a McDonald's open on a corner, and we sat down at a table by a window while Mom tried to figure out what to do.

Sitting at the next table was a woman with wild hair and even wilder eyes. Suddenly, the woman began to flail her arms around in the air above her head as if she were shooing off an attacking horde of killer bees. She stopped just as suddenly, looked Mom in the face, and told her solemnly, "It's cold and dreary out today," as if she were the Dalai Lama imparting a profound truth of incalculable worth. Then she began to shriek: "Eeeeek-Eeeeek! Eeeeek-Eeeeek! Eeeeeeeek!"

Mom glared at me, her look shouting: "Don't you dare laugh!"

But I couldn't hold it in. I put my hands over my mouth and tried to sound like I was coughing, or choking, while my body shook and tears filled my eyes. Once I started laughing, I couldn't stop. I was sixteen years old and I had the giggles, and nothing short of a jolt from a cattle prod was likely to shut me up.

"You quit laughing right now!" Mom warned me sternly, but the sense of urgency in my mother's voice and the grim look on her face struck me as immensely humorous, and I laughed even harder. I put my head down and slid down in the plastic seat. A squeak or two escaped now and then as the only evidence that I was cackling soundlessly.

"We have to get out of here!" Mom whispered. She grabbed my arm and dragged me along beside her. Then she walked as fast as she could, without breaking into a dead run, out the door of the McDonald's, across the street, and down the concrete steps into the subway.

We stopped there for a moment to catch our breath, looked at each other, and sailed off again into hysterical laughter, our voices echoing in merriment off the cavernous walls.

My giggling didn't wind down until I was sitting in the train and we were speeding along under the streets in the darkness. When I finally sobered and thought about what I had just seen, I realized there wasn't anything at all to laugh about. Derelicts. Prostitutes. Junkies. People who had nothing and nobody. The saddest part wasn't even that some of them were pushing everything they owned around with them in shopping carts. The saddest part was their isolation.

They were all so alone. They didn't huddle together in groups. They didn't even walk along the street two by two. They were all singles, each a captive in his own private hell, a prison that locked him in and everybody else out.

"Those people don't have anything at all and I have so much!" I thought with such a sudden, profound sense of gratitude I was afraid I might start crying. "I have God—who never leaves me, who is as close to me as my next breath—who protects me and takes care of me. I have a mother and a father who love me. I have a sister and grandparents and friends. I live in a nice house and I have warm clothes to wear and enough to eat. Those people have nothing and I have everything that matters."

I never looked at the world the same way again.

In the months to come, I thought often about that time, that day when I realized how fortunate I was. And after what happened to me during the surgery that followed it, I sometimes wondered if God orchestrated my adventure for a purpose. Maybe God wanted me to see the suffering of other people to put my own suffering into perspective.

TEN

I checked into the hospital the night before my surgery. The next morning I was unusually teary. Dr. Hendren had blocked out a whole day to do the surgery. Teams of anesthesiologists were scheduled to cover fourteen- to sixteen-hour shifts. The surgeon intended to perform ten different procedures in one operation. Even though I was a veteran of more than one hundred surgeries already, I knew that this time I was really in for it. And I was scared.

Part of my anxiety was simple homesickness. This hospital environment was so foreign to me. I was used to having what the doctors in Louisville called my "entourage" with me when I had surgery. My parents, sister, grandparents, Aunt Laura, and assorted friends were always there. One or two—sometimes more—ministers from my church always showed up. The group prayed with me and for me, and kept me laughing until I was wheeled into the OR.

This time, it was just Mom and me.

When Dr. Hendren came into the room, he announced cheerfully, "Well, I'm here!", making the point that he had, indeed, shown up to hold my hand while I went to sleep. He got up on the gurney beside me and asked if I understood what was about to happen.

I knew, but he described it for me again anyway, and it seemed even more horrendous than when I'd heard it the first time.

During the first part of the surgery, I would be suspended from the ceiling. A strap around my midsection would hold me up with my backside in the air and my legs spread apart.

Yeah, there would be people watching. Lots of people. Boston Children's Hospital was a teaching facility, and the gallery in the glassed-in seats above the operating table would be jammed with doctors who wanted to see Dr. Hendren's landmark operation.

"While you are hanging in the air, I'll cut the flap of skin from your hips and flip it inside your vagina to rebuild the vaginal wall," he said. "Then we'll take you down and lay you on your back and open you up, sternum to pelvic bone. I'll take out the bowel pieces I need and build you a bladder and urethra."

The surgeon explained the whole procedure so matter-of-factly you'd think he had done it hundreds of times, when in fact nothing like this surgery had ever been attempted by anyone, anywhere.

Dr. Hendren prayed with Mom and me before surgery, stood back as we performed our ritual farewell, then linked his arm in mine and walked with me into the surgical suite. The doctors and nurses there and in the gallery above openly gawked at the two of us, whispering among themselves that "Dr. Hendren never does that!"

I climbed up on the table and Dr. Hendren held my hand as medication coursed through my veins and put me to sleep—very light sleep. Because it would be such a long procedure, the anesthesiologist gave me the lowest possible dose of anesthesia. Then he put Vaseline on my eyelids, placed sterile sponges over them, and taped them shut so they wouldn't open automatically and dry out. As I slipped into the foggy, surreal world of unconsciousness, I could hear the music playing in the surgery suite. As blackness enveloped me, I had time to think one final coherent thought: "When I wake up, it will all be over."

But that's not what happened.

Six hours into the surgery, Dr. Hendren accidentally cut an artery in my hip and I lost fourteen pints of blood in a matter of minutes. My heart stopped beating and I died.

It happened while I was hanging suspended from the ceiling. The surgeon was removing the flap of skin from my hips that he planned to use to rebuild my missing vaginal wall. It was a slow, tedious process, inching along, taking infinite care not to damage the blood vessels or nerve tissue. Suddenly, Dr. Hendren's scalpel sliced through an artery that wasn't supposed to be there, and blood spurted out like a leak in a fire hose, spraying the doctor's face and soaking the front of his scrubs.

Chaos erupted in the operating room.

"Blood! I need blood stat!" Dr. Hendren cried, and nurses scrambled to mount bags on my IV poles.

Blood spewed out of my body in a pulsing torrent as the surgeon tried frantically to close off the spurting artery.

"Heather needs more blood!" he cried. "Give her more!" The nurses squeezed the bags to force the blood into my veins faster. But the bright red liquid was squirting out of my body quicker than they could replace it.

Blood was everywhere, cascading down my legs and puddling on the floor, spraying the doctors and nurses, drenching their green surgery suits, splattering on instruments and equipment.

"She's bleeding out!" someone cried.

A minute later, my heart stopped beating.

Dr. Hendren ordered me lowered out of the sling and onto the table so he could turn me on my back and use paddles to restart my heart. The anesthesiologist unhooked the anesthesia while the doctors and nurses flipped my body, then reconnected it to the tracheotomy tube down my throat once I was lying flat.

That's when I woke up.

I floated up out of the dark waters of unconsciousness and bobbed to the surface of awareness.

But I wasn't in the recovery room, my mother's face hovering near, the comforting smell of her coffee breath announcing that I had made it.

My eyes were still taped shut so I couldn't see. But I could hear. And I could feel. Warm liquid was pouring over me. I could feel it running down my legs and dripping off my feet.

Reality was blurred and I struggled to focus it, straining to bring it into crisp definition like an image in a camera lens. But clarity brought with it the growing sense that something was wrong.

Voices. Frantic voices.

". . . we still don't have a heartbeat . . . !"

". . . hook it up . . . charge the paddles . . . !"

I could distinguish Dr. Hendren's voice out of the pandemonium.

"Don't let her die," he cried. "Don't you let this little girl die!"

Then I felt cold metal on my chest. Dr. Hendren shouted, "Clear!" And the most excruciating pain I had ever experienced shot through my body like a lightning bolt. I shrieked in agony in my head, but no sound came out of my mouth.

How can this hurt if I'm dead? How do I feel this if I don't have a heartbeat?

"Shock her again!"

I felt the cold metal on my chest a second time. *No! No, no! Please! Don't . . .*

A lightning bolt burned a trail of agony through my body.

"There . . . I think we've got it!" someone said.

"We've got a heart rate!" came another voice.

"More blood, get me more blood!" said Dr. Hendren.

Suddenly, soft words drowned out the panic and brought an instant hush to the room.

"I think she can hear us," the anesthesiologist said.

The room was suddenly quiet. No one moved.

"Heather, if you can hear me, squeeze my hand," he told me.

I squeezed his hand with all the strength in my body.

There was a moment or two of absolute silence. Perhaps the anesthesiologist mouthed something or communicated with hand motions, but he didn't say another word until he spoke to me again.

"Heather, if you're mad at me, squeeze my hand," he said.

I tried to break the bones in his fingers.

"Sweetheart, you're fine, you're doing good," he told me soothingly. "You're going to go back to sleep now. I need you to relax, just relax . . ."

A world of puffy white cotton enveloped me again.

. . .

For more than an hour, the surgical team continued to pour blood into me before Dr. Hendren believed it was safe to continue the surgery. Then he took up where he had left off, and the hours ticked by.

Every three or four hours, Dr. Hendren left the operating room for a few minutes. He ate a piece of fruit, went to the bathroom, and then completely rescrubbed and went back to work.

Twenty-seven hours after Dr. Hendren held my hand as I went to sleep, I was wheeled out of the operating room and into the ICU. When I finally opened my eyes, Mom was sitting in a chair beside me, reading a book resting against my side.

"Well, hi, sweetheart," she said when she noticed I was awake. I was hardly recognizable. The fluids forced into my body had made my face swell up as big as a volleyball.

Mom stood and planted a kiss on my forehead, and I smelled the aroma of my mother's coffee breath—just like I always did after surgery. It was a comforting smell. It meant I'd made it.

I tried to speak, to tell my mother what had happened, but I had a respiratory tube down my throat connecting me to a ventilator, and an NG tube down my nose.

"Honey, don't talk, don't try to talk!" Mom said.

But I was determined. I had no voice, so I mouthed the words: *I woke up!*

At first, Mom couldn't tell what I was trying to say. I had to repeat it two or three times. Then recognition dawned on my mother's face.

"Are you saying, 'I woke up?' " she asked.

I nodded my head yes.

Then I put my free hand, the one not connected to an IV line, on my chest and patted it. Mom lifted my gown and saw the paddle burns on my skin.

No one had told Mom that I had awakened during surgery or that I had coded.

"I understand what you're saying. I get it. Now you just rest. You're going to be just fine. You made it. You beat it."

As I drifted back to sleep, I heard my mother's voice speaking to someone else. "I want to see Hardy Hendren in this room—now!"

. . .

The next time I opened my eyes, Dr. Hendren, a nurse, the anesthesiologist, and my mother were conducting a powwow at the foot of my bed.

". . . and hopefully once she gets out of ICU she won't remember a thing," the anesthesiologist was saying.

"Why didn't you tell me she coded?" Mom asked.

This time it was Dr. Hendren who spoke.

"Because we got her back and the surgery went on."

"How many?" Mom asked.

"How many what?" he responded.

"How many times did you have to shock her back?"

There was a moment or two of uncomfortable silence.

"Three," Dr. Hendren said.

I went back to sleep.

. . .

When I opened my eyes again, the anesthesiologist was sitting beside my bed stroking my hand.

. . .

The next time I woke up it was night. I was still in ICU. Dr. Hendren was there with me, but he wasn't examining me. He was down on his knees beside my bed praying.

When I was finally moved out of the ICU into a private room, I had only the vaguest notion what the surgery had done to my body. I was as swathed in bandages as a mummy. Oh, I knew there would be some swelling. There was always swelling after surgery. But I assumed that when I was finally able to see what had been done, I would find things, well, normal—that between my legs would look like it always had; the changes would be inside my body where I couldn't see them.

I spent six weeks in the hospital. The walls of my room gradually vanished, covered up with get-well cards from the folks back home. Flower arrangements jockeyed for space with bouquets of balloons and a menagerie of stuffed animals on the tables and windowsills.

About a month after the surgery, Dr. Hendren came into my room to remove the bandages and packing. Perhaps he did it the way he did because he thought it would hurt less. Or maybe he was just in a hurry. I never knew which. What I did know was that instead of removing the bandages one by one, layer by layer, and then taking out the packing from my vagina and rectum in pieces, he removed the whole thing in one gigantic yank.

It hurt almost as bad as being shocked back to life. I cried out in agony, unable to breathe. It felt like he had ripped me apart. But it was done, and I could finally see the results. Scooting up a little in bed, I leaned over to take a look.

What I saw was a purple ball of swollen tissue between my legs extending six inches down toward my knees. I felt like I had a football between my legs. I looked like an alien.

I was devastated. From the onset, all I knew was that this famous doctor was going to rebuild my internal organs, with the key word in that sentence being "internal." Nobody warned me about the thousands of stitches, the bruising, or the swelling. Nobody told me I'd look like a freak.

That sight sent me into an emotional tailspin, and I realized just how homesick I was. It had been coming on for some time. Six weeks was a long time to be away from home for surgery. I missed my family. I missed my friends. I missed Louisville. I missed my own room and my own bed. I wanted to go home.

The only bright spot in the darkness of my despondency was a nurse named Trisha. She and I became instant friends. Trisha worked extra shifts to look after me when I had to undergo some special procedure. Trisha stayed after her shift was over sometimes just to watch a movie with me, and she sneaked me hamburgers and milkshakes after visiting hours.

Trisha was engaged to a tall, good-looking young man. He was also very hairy, a significant detail in the story Trisha told me the morning after the couple's bachelor/bachelorette parties.

She swore me to secrecy, then described what had happened to her fiancé the night before at the party thrown by his friends.

"You're not going to believe what they did," Trisha said.

"What? Tell me what!" I begged.

"Well, you are absolutely not going to believe it," Trisha said. She came closer to my bed so she could speak more softly. The last thing she wanted was for the rest of the shift nurses to find out what had happened.

"Don't tell anyone," she continued, "but they stripped off all his clothes . . . and duct-taped him to a freeway exit sign!"

I laughed so hard I was afraid I would blow out every one of Dr. Hendren's thousands of meticulously placed stitches.

But Trisha wasn't finished. As soon as I caught my breath, the nurse continued. The exit sign was next to the off ramp Trisha took on her way to work.

"I saw this guy getting arrested as I drove by this morning, but I didn't know who it was until he called me to come get him out of jail."

Much later, when Trisha's fiancé came with her to visit me, Trisha made him show me the tape burns, great swaths of bare skin where the police had ripped the duct tape off his body—taking all the hair and a layer of skin with it.

. . .

Trisha wasn't the only one trying to cheer me up. Mom noticed my failing spirits, too. She had always managed to elicit a smile from me by performing her world-famous chicken dance. It wasn't exactly a marketable skill, but my mother could look just like a chicken. She pulled her arms up close to her body for wings, stuck her head out on her long neck, and strutted around my room making "*. . . pock . . . pock . . . pock*" sounds and scratching at the linoleum floor with her shoe.

When that failed to get a rise out of me, Mom resorted to Plan B. One night, she went with some friends she'd made during the long stay in Boston to the Cheers bar, the one where the television show was filmed each week. She had one glass of wine there, but that's all it took to make her loopy.

My room had windows all across the side that looked out onto the hospital corridor. When Mom came back to the hospital that night, she didn't go directly to my room. In fact, the next time I saw my mother was in sections. First I saw her head. Then I saw her feet. Then her head. Then her feet. Head, feet. Head, feet. Head, feet. Mom was doing cartwheels down the hospital corridor.

When I was finally allowed to go home to Louisville, I was bedridden for months. It was my worst hospital trauma, but for me all the misery was worth it. I was willing to pay any price to be continent. I would suffer any discomfort not to smell like urine all the time, not to have to wear super-strength maxipads to staunch the leaking. I would do just about anything to be like everybody else.

It took months for the swelling to go down enough for me to determine how well the newly created organs inside my body were functioning. Only then did I discover that they weren't functioning at all, that they never would function, that the operation that cost me so much in so many ways was a failure. The never-before-attempted surgery, the grand scheme to rebuild my urinary system was a total flop. It didn't work.

Mom, Rebel, and I are cuddling on the couch two years before my accident. I was two years old; Rebel was four.

About a year before the accident, Rebel and I posed for the camera, giving our brightest smiles. I was three and she was five.

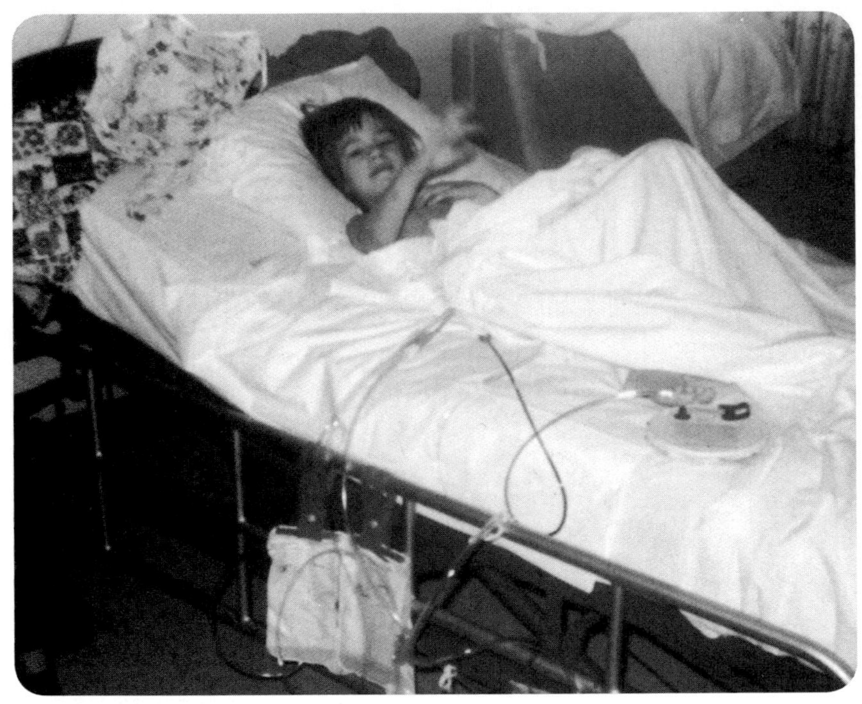

I had just been moved out of the intensive care unit to a private room after I had my accident. The angel who was on my shoulder the whole time I was in intensive care did not go with me when I left the ICU.

About six months after the accident, I was resting on the couch watching television.

When I was in Montana visiting my father, I played in the sprinkler in my bikini and then jumped on Angel's back for a ride.

Grandmother was with me by the pool when I was twelve years old. It was the first time I had been allowed to go swimming since the accident. For eight years, I had only dangled my feet in the water for fear I would get an infection around my bag. As it turns out, the chlorine in the water would have prevented an infection. I could have been swimming all along!

Mom, Rebel, and I have gone through a lot together. Over the years, their support has given me the strength to keep going.

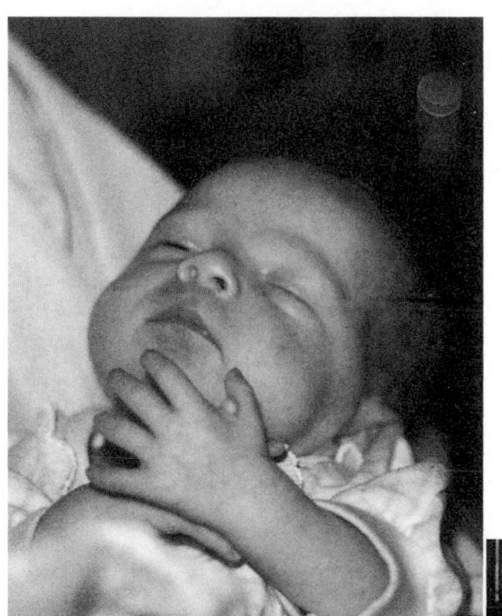

At birth, Mackenzie looked like the picture of health. But the doctors soon discovered massive medical problems, and they predicted she wouldn't survive. She proved them all wrong; Mackenzie has her own miracle story.

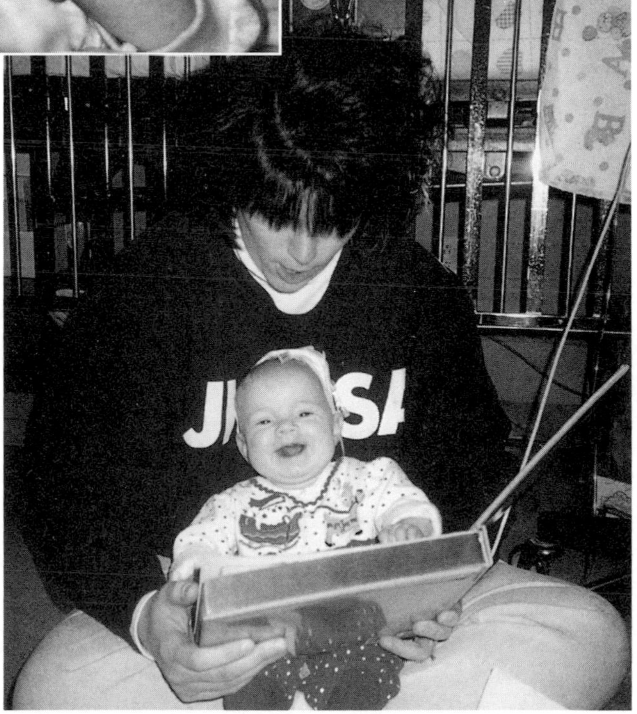

Mackenzie was seven months old on her first Christmas, and she was still in the hospital. She was finally allowed to go home a month later.

Even after Mackenzie was released from the hospital, she spent a lot of time there with me, as I had one operation after another.

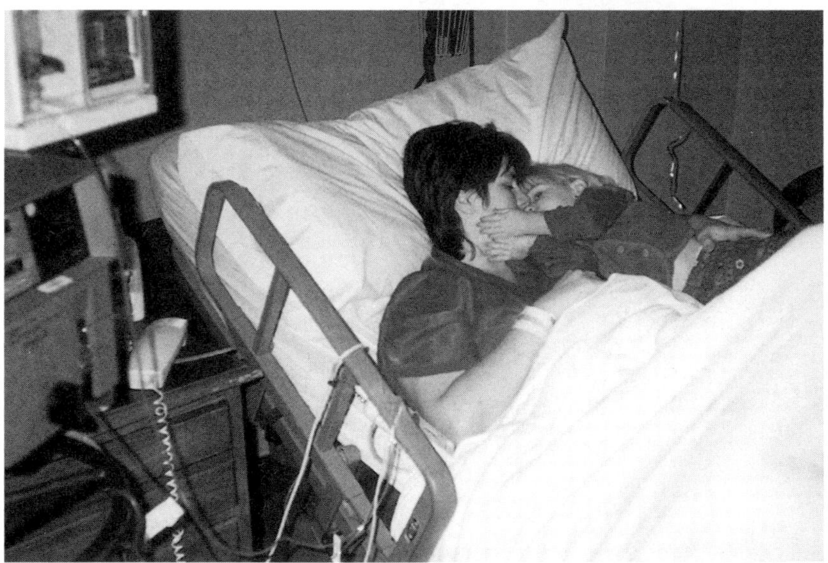

I had seventeen surgeries during the first four years of Mackenzie's life, so she often came to the hospital to visit me, as she did here when she was two and a half.

When I was growing up, I often saw Dad take Mom into his arms and dance her around the room—even when there was no music playing. Their marriage was an example of what a good marriage should be, and I defined love as: dancing when there isn't any music.

DeWayne and I had our wedding reception six months after we got married. We couldn't afford to have one any sooner.

God has given me gifts of joy every day of my life. The greatest gifts he has ever given me are DeWayne and Mackenzie. They are the brightest stars in my life.

ELEVEN

Bowel tissue constantly contracts. That was the problem. That was why the Boston surgery was a failure. Dr. Hendren had believed—mistakenly, as it turns out—that he could use pieces of bowel to create a bladder for me, and the tissue would eventually stop contracting. That's not what happened. The bladder he created in my belly constantly spasmed. It didn't just leak urine, it squirted urine. All the time.

I was angry and fed up. I had endured pain, looking like a freak, and months of recovery believing that finally I would be normal. That I would go to school like my friends, date, have boyfriends, go to the prom, do all the things other regular teenagers did. Instead, I was home with a tutor, back to wearing maxipads because I was yet again incontinent.

When one of the ministers from my church showed up for a visit after I returned from Boston, I unloaded my frustration, and it landed on him like a ten-ton gorilla.

The church where I was baptized when I was nine years old had grown over the years. By the time I was in high school, Southeast Christian had well over 1,000 members and a large youth group. I was active in the group and close to Greg Allen, one of the ministers. He visited me every time I was in the hospital, and prayed for me with the rest of my entourage before my surgeries.

"Why did God do this to me?" I demanded to know, as soon as Greg walked into the room. "What have I done to deserve this? Will you tell me that! What have I done?"

"Well, hello, Greg, how are you?" Greg said. "Oh, I'm fine, Heather. And how are you?"

I didn't think he was funny. Greg sighed.

"Is that what you think?" he said, answering my question with a question. "You think God is punishing you for something?"

"He must be! If he's not mad at me, why does he keep doing this to me? I just want to be normal, that's all. Is that too much to ask—normal? I just want to be like everybody else. Every time I have surgery, I pray and pray and pray that God will heal me this time, that everything will be all right *this time.* But it never is. No matter how hard I pray, it never is!"

"And that makes you mad," Greg said—not a question, a statement. He was right, of course, only I wasn't quite ready to go there. But I was close.

"Why won't he give me what I want?" I asked, crying now. "He gives other people what they want. Why not me? What's wrong with *me*? Why won't he answer *my* prayers? Why not, Greg? Why not?"

Before Greg had a chance to answer, the dam started to crumble.

"He could fix everything, you know. But he won't! He could help me—snap his fingers and I would be just fine, completely healed. He does miracles all the time. That's his job. But he won't. Why *not*? I am so mad . . . soooo mad . . ."

Finally the dam broke, and the flood waters carried me away.

". . . at God!" There, I'd said it. I had finally said it. I had finally owned my rage.

"I'm mad at God, Greg," I cried. "I am so mad at *God!*"

"Have you told him that?" Greg asked.

"Told who what? Told . . . God?"

"Yeah, God. Have you told God you're mad at him?" That wasn't the response I was expecting. "You need to tell him you're mad at him, Heather, and tell him why. Be real. Don't decide that a 'good Christian girl' wouldn't be mad at God and then pretend you aren't. If you're mad, say so. God can handle it."

It was the first time I ever considered telling the God of the universe that I didn't like the way he was running it.

"God loves you, and there is nothing you can ever say or do that will change that," Greg said. "He's not doing what you want him to do right now and I don't know why. I wish I could tell you why. I wish I could give you an answer that would explain everything, make sense of all of it. But I can't because I don't know. What I do know is that God is here and he's not going anywhere. He's not going to bail on you just because you're mad at him."

Nobody had ever told me it was okay to be mad at God, or advised me to tell God how I felt about him. It was the first time anybody had ever suggested such a thing, but it wouldn't be the last.

Like every other Christian, eventually I had to wrestle with the unexplainable. I had to make sense out of pain and suffering. Why would God allow this to happen to me? Why had he allowed all the other pain in my life? If he loved me, why did he let me get run over in the first place? Those questions raged like an angry storm in my soul for months, and I never found satisfactory answers to any of them. But in the end, nothing could change the reality of my relationship with Jesus Christ. He was there—profoundly, personally there in my life.

He was my peace. He was the source of my strength—of my whole family's strength. But God didn't just do the heavy lifting. Every day, he gave me joy, little gifts of joy.

Like that day in Boston: tests, poking, prodding, pain, needles—and then that baby. I had been lying on a gurney waiting for a CT scan, alone and miserable, telling God how unhappy I was. And suddenly that baby had come toddling around the corner. She was a chubby little Asian girl with a big red bow in her black hair, barely able to walk unaided. But she'd seen an open hallway and made a break for it, toddling away from her mommy as fast as her stubby little legs would carry her. And she was squealing in delight, a lilting, infectious, bubbling giggle! She waddled up to my gurney and stopped, swaying, barely holding her balance. She stared up at me with huge black eyes, then she smiled and blew me a kiss! Moments later, her mother scooped her up and carried her away, but she looked over her mother's shoulder and waved bye-bye at me until she was out of sight.

It was like there was a golden glow around that child, like she sparkled, like God had wrapped her up in light, placed that red bow on her head and said, "Here, Heather. Enjoy! This is how adorable you are to me."

Once I was able to admit my anger, God's gifts of joy were more readily evident to me. These gifts of joy taught me to live in the moment, to treasure what was beautiful and good.

A few months after the failed surgery, God presented me a special delivery package straight from heaven in the form of a horse named Zack. Zack belonged to Paula Benson, a friend from the youth group at church. When she learned that I loved horses, she invited me to ride Zack "anytime you need to get away." I took Paula up on her offer as often as I could manage it. Zack became my refuge, my solace. Sometimes I spent the whole day on his back, riding across fields, down trails in the woods, through meadows, and up streambeds. The rhythm of his movement beneath me was soothing. I always found a peace in the saddle I found nowhere else on earth. When I was riding Zack, I was glad to be alive—no matter what difficulties I was facing in my life.

And I *was* facing difficulties. Additional surgeries were necessary to undo the failed attempt at rebuilding my urinary system. I was homeschooled the beginning of my junior year, but finally returned to Atherton High School in a wheelchair.

The world I found there was not the one I had left behind in the middle of my sophomore year. When I went to Boston for the surgery to end all surgeries, I had been on top of my game. I was popular—and not just with my peers. Because of Rebel's influence as a senior, I was several rungs higher on the social ladder than the rest of my classmates. I had been president of the pep club. I had been on the student council. I'd had a boyfriend who promised to wait for me.

When I returned to school as a junior, things had changed. In the survival-of-the-fittest adolescent culture, I never had a chance.

Rebel had graduated, taking with her all the upperclassmen who knew and liked me. My boyfriend had found greener pastures while I was gone, and was going steady with another girl. Even my friends, for the most part, had fallen away.

They had promised to visit while I was home recovering. And they did. For a while. But nobody kept it up for very long. They had lives to live, dates and proms to get ready for, classes to attend. It wasn't much fun hanging out with someone who wasn't doing any of the things they were doing. Pretty soon there just wasn't anything to talk about anymore.

A handful of friends were loyal and faithful—Grover, Kenny, Mary, and Janene—but eventually all the others went on with their lives without me. I was left sitting on the bank, watching the river of life flow past. By the time I got back into the water, everybody else was too far downstream to care about me anymore. I wasn't in the in-crowd; in fact, I didn't seem to fit anywhere.

For one thing, there were the rumors. The kids who didn't know why I had been out of school for so long made up a reason. Word got around that I had gotten pregnant and had gone away somewhere to have the baby—and then gave it up for adoption. My friends knew that wasn't true. It was, in fact, a physical impossibility. But that didn't stop the talk.

And I was peeing on myself again, back to wearing thick maxipads everywhere I went, changing in the bathroom, and wearing two or three outfits in the course of any school day. I smelled like urine. At least I thought I did, and that's all that really mattered.

I yo-yoed in and out of school my junior year, having surgery just often enough to keep me in social and educational limbo. I'd be making progress in the teen scene and then I'd be gone again. I had to have a tutor in order to keep up with my schoolwork, and I always seemed to be behind and scrambling—on all fronts.

But the summer before my senior year in high school, my life finally took a turn for the better.

I was visiting Aunt Patsy, my mother's sister, and hanging out in the front yard with my cousins, Stacy, Gigi, and Stevie. The four of us were playing "truth or dare." Gigi dared me to strike up a conversation with the young man working on his car in a driveway down the street.

I took the dare.

I ambled down the sidewalk, trying to figure out what to say to the young man and how to get his attention. He looked like a rock star, like Jon Bon Jovi, with long blond hair and brown eyes. He was buried up to his elbows in the guts of the car and took no notice of me at all. At least he didn't appear to.

When I couldn't think of anything to say, I chickened out at the last minute and just kept walking, right past the car. Now what was I going to do? I couldn't very well go strolling past him a second time. But there wasn't any other way to get back to my aunt's house.

As I drew even with his car on the return orbit to my cousins, he looked up from the engine and smiled.

"Aren't you Heather?" he asked. Hmmm . . . he must have seen me sometime at my aunt's house and asked who I was. I liked that!

"Yeah," I said. "I'm Heather." Now there was a singularly original and clever comeback! But that was the best I could do. I found myself strangely tongue-tied around this guy—and I was never at a loss for words.

The conversation, however stumbling and halting at first, finally got off the ground. We talked about school and music—and cars! I loved cars. Within fifteen minutes, Jamey had asked me for a date. He wanted to take me to the fair.

The Kentucky State Fair was held every August in the exhibit halls and show barns at the Louisville fairgrounds. It was a mammoth event, featuring all the elements of a traditional county fair—barns full of prize pigs, cows, lambs, sheep, goats, chickens, and rabbits, and exhibit halls bursting at the seams with homemade jams and jellies, biscuits, cakes, pies, pickles, and quilts.

Hordes of people strolled past carneys on the midway, plunking down their money to toss a ring around a milk bottle, sink a three-pointer at a basketball hoop, burst balloons with darts, or nail the metal ducks in a shooting gallery—spending five dollars in quarters to win a two-dollar stuffed animal.

The bright lights of amusement park rides lit up the muggy, velvet darkness, where the adventurous screamed their way up, down, and around the twists and turns of the rollercoaster and shrieked as they were whirled, spun, and flung through the air.

Jamey and I wandered up and down the midway. He won me a teddy bear at the ring-toss booth. We ate corndogs and cheese fries, cotton candy, popcorn, funnel cakes, and corn on the cob. We rode the rides, too—particularly the Tilt-a-Whirl, where we were pressed snug against each other by centrifugal force. But by then, both of us were aware that a force greater than physics was drawing us together. Jamey kissed me when he took me home, and asked me for a date the next weekend.

Soon, Jamey and I were going steady, and I looked forward to my last year of school, sure I was going to have a senior year to treasure, certain it would be the best year of my life. It wasn't. Two hammer blows in quick succession spoiled it all.

The first blow fell in the hall at Atherton on a dreary winter day right after Christmas.

I had just come out of the lunchroom, on my way to gather up my books before my next class. When I rounded a corner, I saw a crowd of students gathered at the other end of the hall. At first, I thought it must be a fight. The group of students huddled at the far end of the hallway by my locker must be watching a couple of guys—or maybe even girls!—slug it out.

I started to hurry. I certainly didn't want to miss a good fight.

But the crowd didn't have that feel to it. Nobody was cheering anybody on, nobody was pushing and shoving to get a better view of the action. In fact, nobody was saying anything at all. Nobody was moving. They were all just standing there, quiet.

What were they looking at?

Suddenly, I felt a sense of dread in the pit of my stomach, like you feel when you know something bad has happened, but you don't know what it is yet. Like you feel in a dream, when you can't seem to walk fast enough, when distances are elongated and the place you want to go to keeps getting farther and farther away.

It took way too long to get to the edge of the crowd. When I did, they parted to let me through. Some were giggling nervously, others just looked uncomfortable.

Then I saw it. My locker! What had they done to my locker?

Someone had "decorated" it. Dangling all over the locker like ornaments on a Christmas tree were fifteen or twenty maxipads smeared with mustard. Scrawled in mustard on the locker door was a single word: "Peabody."

I never found out why it happened—or who orchestrated the event. But in the grand scheme of things it really didn't matter who or why. It had happened. The desecration of my locker demonstrated how the other teenagers viewed me. I was different. I was a freak. I was Peabody.

After that, I had no desire to be normal, to be regular, to be like everybody else. I knew I'd never fit in and there really wasn't anything to be gained by trying.

Then the second hammer blow fell. Halfway through my senior year, my high school guidance counselor called me into his office to deliver devastating news. I was not going to graduate with my class.

Orbiting in and out of school, taking classes at home with a private tutor, always playing catch-up—somehow I had dropped a ball somewhere. I lacked three credits of electives to graduate.

After all I had gone through to be just like everybody else, I wasn't even going to walk across the stage and get my diploma "like everybody else." In a fit of rage, I dropped out of school and got a job.

I went to work in the Southeast Christian Church Day Care Center, taking care of twenty-two two-year-olds. At night, I attended class at the Jefferson County Public School Extension. I got the credits I needed and graduated at nineteen—with a ceremony and a cap and gown, but not with my classmates. Not like a regular kid.

As soon as I graduated, I enrolled in night school at Jefferson Community College. I had a clear view of my future career. It was a natural. I wanted to be a nurse. In fact, my nursing vision was even more specific. I wanted to be a liaison nurse in the surgery department—a nurse who observes surgical procedures and then goes out and reports to the family what's going on, keeping them informed, helping them get through an awful time. It was a job I knew I could do.

Jamey was in the Speed School of Engineering at the University of Louisville and worked nights "throwing boxes" at the United Parcel Service hub in Louisville, loading and unloading the huge brown airplanes that landed and took off every sixty seconds.

While I was studying nights at JCC, I changed my daytime job and became a nanny for the single parent of one of the two-year-olds in the day care center. Steve Sample had three children—eight-month-old Brian, two-year-old Brent, and three-year-old Jenna, and I became a member of the family.

Being a nanny showed me how much I wanted to be a mother, because that's what I was to those three children. I arrived at the Samples' house at 7:30 in the morning, and didn't leave until 6:30 at night. Sometimes I worked weekends, too. I fixed the children's breakfast, lunch, and sometimes their dinner. I kissed their skinned knees, listened to their silly songs, and loved them as if they were my own.

I even potty-trained Brian. I didn't have a clue what I was doing, but what I lacked in knowledge I made up for in enthusiasm. Since the little boy was too short to stand in front of the toilet, I taught him how to climb up on the toilet seat and sit down—facing backward. His father wasn't particularly taken by my technique.

"What do you think you're doing?" Steve asked incredulously. "Get him a step stool for Pete's sake! Don't teach my son to pee like a girl!"

Steve always sent flowers, and he and the kids visited me faithfully whenever I was in the hospital.

Jamey and I had been dating steadily for three and a half years when we decided to get married. Mom and Jim thought it was a really bad idea and tried desperately to talk us out of it.

What my parents recognized that Jamey and I didn't was the incredible financial and emotional strain my medical problems would put on our relationship. They sat us down and tried to make us understand what it would be like—the hospital and doctor and medicine expenses, thousands and thousands and thousands of dollars out of pocket all the time. They pointed out that they had—willingly!—made huge sacrifices over the years to pay for my medical care. Where were two people in their early twenties going to find the resources to pay bills like that? Did we have any idea how hard it would be?

We said we did. But we didn't. We were young and in love and that was all that mattered. Jamey and I were married on June 2, 1990, and moved into a little starter home in Okolona, a suburb of Louisville.

I believed that as a married woman, I would finally be normal. I would be regular. I would be just like everybody else.

TWELVE

I would not have been more surprised if my gynecologist had told me I was about to sprout feathers and squawk like a chicken.

"What do you mean, I've had a *miscarriage*?" I asked him incredulously. "How could I possibly have had a miscarriage?"

It had never entered my head that the heavy bleeding I had experienced was anything more than yet another malfunction of one of my damaged organs. Now my doctor was telling me I'd had a . . . that I had been . . .

I literally had to force my mind to go there, had to consciously walk my thought processes through the implications of what the doctor was saying.

I have had a miscarriage, I told myself slowly, deliberately. *Which means . . . I was pregnant. I was pregnant!*

If ever there were a time in my life when I didn't know whether to laugh or cry, this was it. Never before had I felt two polar-opposite emotions with equal intensity at the same time.

I was devastated. And I was ecstatic. I had lost a baby. But that meant I could conceive . . . I could get pregnant!

As a teenager, I had earned enough money to buy my own car by babysitting. What my customers never knew was that they really didn't have to pay me at all. I'd have looked after their kids for free: I adored children. I loved playing mommy to Steve Sample's kids—loved their little munchkin faces, their innocence and trust, and the way they looked at the world brand-new every morning, like God had just colored the sky blue and the paint was still wet.

But I had always understood that bearing my own children was a card that had been permanently removed from my life's deck the day I fell beneath the right front tire of a black Dodge Charger. I had come to terms with that reality by the time I was in elementary school. And the possibility that I could conceive had never been in the playbook of any doctor who had ever examined me. The surgeons who operated on me right after my accident told Mom they couldn't even find my reproductive organs. I didn't bother to go on the pill when I got married: I figured I needed birth control like a blind man needed sunglasses.

And now . . . a miscarriage?

How could I possibly have functioning fallopian tubes when every other organ in the same zip code had been ripped out?

How could the tubes have remained attached to my ovaries—unnoticed!—through more than 150 surgeries? How could any of my reproductive plumbing operate normally in the tangled maze of scar tissue in my belly? How could . . . ?

There wasn't a how. There was only a Who. God. Getting pregnant was a medical impossibility. But it had happened. It was a miracle. And I enjoyed an intimate, personal relationship with the only being in the universe with "perform miracles" on his job description.

The doctor was still talking, telling me that I would need a D & C to clean my uterus of any remaining tissue from the miscarriage, explaining how the procedure would be performed and what it entailed. I was only focusing on his words with about 3 percent of my attention. The other 97 percent of my mind was throwing the mother of all celebration bashes. I could get pregnant! I could have a baby! Wait 'til I told Jamey!

Jamey's reaction was predictable. He was elated. Mom's reaction was just as predictable. She wasn't.

"You'll just have to start taking birth control pills," Mom told me after she recovered from her own shock. Then she eyed me suspiciously. I was positively beaming.

"You're not planning . . . you couldn't possibly be thinking . . ." Mom began. "Heather, honey, you couldn't carry a baby to term! Your body is way too fragile, there is too much scar tissue, and . . ."

Mom kept talking and I tried to listen, I really did. It's just that there were fireworks going off at the party in my mind and the sparkling lights were spelling out "P*R*E*G*N*A*N*T!"

". . . dangerous for you and the baby, too," Mom was saying when I tuned back in. "You could both die."

I uh-huhed my mother, nodding my head up and down in the appropriate places in the conversation like a good little bobblehead doll. Then I went home and set about conceiving a child with the same singleness of purpose that had served as a survival mechanism my whole life.

Jamey and I didn't tell anyone that I was actively trying to get pregnant. I read all the books and followed all the "conception tips," including propping my hips up on pillows, and even standing on my head in a corner to help things along.

When we found out I was pregnant again, we kept the news to ourselves, though I was so elated the glow on my face could have defrosted a Butterball turkey. We waited until after the first trimester to make sure there would be no miscarriage this time. Then we announced the good news to our families.

About sixteen weeks into my pregnancy, I told Mom. My mother was in the kitchen. I didn't say a word. I just handed Mom a card with a picture of a baby on the front and the words, "Congratulations, Grandma, you're expecting!" written inside.

Mom was dumbstruck. Her initial response was anger—the kind you feel when you find your five-year-old playing in the street. Didn't I realize how dangerous this was! But Mom didn't stay mad for very long.

"Heather, honey . . . did you want this?" she asked.

"More than you'll ever know," I replied.

"But you don't have any idea what this is going to do to your body."

"Mom, think how many times we've gone into some procedure blind, without any idea what it was going to do to my body."

Many of my surgeries over the years had been one-of-a-kind operations, never-before-attempted procedures.

"We didn't know at the Mayo Clinic and we didn't know in Boston," I said. "This baby is a gift from God, a blessing. Please, be happy for me."

Mom put her head in her hands and began to cry.

. . .

The most remarkable thing about my pregnancy was that there was nothing very remarkable about it at all. Oh, I was often in pain. So what else was new? And I had major problems with incontinence. I had to wear thick pads and often leaked urine in the night. The doctors knew I had herniated and we'd have to replace the mesh structure in my abdomen. But we wouldn't know the extent of any other damage the pregnancy may have caused until after the baby was born.

As the months passed, I experienced the normal discomfort of my rapidly increasing size. Other than that, the "medical crisis" of my pregnancy was a nonevent.

But it was a family event of immeasurable proportions. Jamey went with me to every ultrasound appointment. So did Mom and Grandmother. Rebel went sometimes, too, as did Jamey's mother and grandparents. It was an occasion.

When Jamey and I learned our child was a boy, we named him Christopher, after Aunt Nina's son. Aunt Nina was Mom's best friend. Her son, Christopher, had cerebral palsy. He never walked, could barely talk. I had grown up watching Aunt Nina care for the boy, watched her tenderness and devotion. That became my model for what a mother's love ought to be.

My Christopher was a normal, healthy baby. He had all his fingers and toes, plainly visible on the ultrasound images. He was very active, kicking so hard he sometimes woke me from a sound sleep in the middle of the night. But I didn't mind. I would lie in the dark with my baby wiggling around in my belly, my heart so full of gratitude I couldn't go back to sleep. Christopher was a gift from God, and I praised God for him with every breath.

I quickly grasped the implications of this incredible event—Christopher was God's thank-you for my faithfulness! God had performed a miracle and blessed me with a son as a reward, as compensation for all the pain and suffering I had endured in my life.

And he was worth it. Oh, my, yes, he was worth it! The precious child in my womb was worth every tear I had ever shed, every disappointment I had ever endured, every pain I had ever suffered. I would go through every second of it again to gain Christopher as the prize. God's generosity was incalculable: My son was a treasure beyond price.

. . .

Jamey and I lived in what Mom referred to as a "zip-zip" house—it looked like every other house in the subdivision, all built "zip-zip" just the same. Three bedrooms, a bath, 1,000 square feet. Small, but all we needed. Of course, with a baby coming . . . Well, it would do for now. There'd be plenty of time later to think about a yard and other children for Christopher to play with.

We decided to decorate our son's room with clowns. I put up a clown wallpaper border—all primary colors: reds, greens, and blues. We borrowed a crib because we couldn't afford to buy one. I picked out colorful sheets for it and matching bumper pads, and found an adorable clown mobile that danced above the bed.

I loved and nurtured the baby in my belly like I would love and nurture him when I could hold him in my arms. I sometimes went into his room, sat down in the little rocking chair beside his crib, and read children's stories to my tummy.

On a cold February morning about a month before my due date, I began bleeding and having contractions. I was home alone and went next door to ask my neighbor if she thought I should go to the hospital. After all, this could be a false alarm.

I hoped it was. I prayed fervently that it was. I didn't want Christopher to be premature. But he was perfectly healthy, fully developed. If he came now, he would just be a little small, that's all. Lots of babies came out of the oven before the timer went off.

Still . . . I prayed the contractions would stop.

My neighbor called Jamey, and I agreed to meet my husband at the hospital. Soon after I arrived, my entourage turned out in full force: Mom, Rebel, Aunt Laura, my grandparents, Jamey's parents, his grandparents, and assorted friends and ministers. I was admitted and placed in a birthing suite—a large room with a couch, chairs, tables, and lamps in addition to a hospital bed and all the accompanying equipment. The room had a homey feel. The nearby maternity waiting room was full of visitors for me, and they rotated in and out of the suite a few at a time as the day wore on, most coming to take my hand and pray with me.

Just pray the labor stops, I told them all. *Just pray it stops.*

When Grandmother took my hand, she spoke softly: "Whatever happens here, it's God's will," she said. "Don't forget who's sovereign."

I didn't like the sound of that. *God wouldn't dare let anything happen to this baby,* I thought uneasily, then continued to pray that the contractions would stop.

The ultrasound done when I arrived at the hospital showed that Christopher was healthy and strong. He was in the birth canal, head down and engaged, poised for his journey into the world. As soon as I was settled in my room, nurses put a strap around my belly that measured the baby's heart rate, and turned on a monitor that broadcast the comforting sound of its *beep-beep . . . beep-beep . . . beep-beeping* into the room.

As time passed, the contractions got harder and closer together. They didn't ease off as I had prayed they would, and I realized they weren't going to stop. I was going to have this baby early and that was that. It was time. And that was okay. He would be small, but he was fine. A wonderful peace and joy settled over me. I was about to become a mother. I was going to hold Christopher in my arms—today! No more waiting. I would kiss his little face and smell the wonderful baby smell of him and tell him how much I loved him, how I'd been longing for him, how he was a miraculous gift from God.

But my joy was short-lived.

The doctors were anxious about my ability to deliver my baby vaginally. My obstetrician wasn't even completely convinced my pelvis would open. It had fused together after the accident, and nobody was certain what would happen during delivery.

I could sense the growing uneasiness in the room, and naturally I thought it was the doctors' apprehension about my pelvis. But it was soon evident they weren't concerned about me; they were worried about Christopher.

A pediatrician from the Neonatal Intensive Care Unit ordered a monitor placed on the top of Christopher's head, which was now crowning in the birth canal. It would measure the baby's breathing by the oxygen level in his blood. As soon as the monitor began to provide information, the nurses' expressions changed.

"He's decelling," one of them whispered urgently to the other. "Get the doctor back in here!"

Decelling meant that the baby's breathing was decelerating. During every contraction, Christopher's breathing almost stopped. When the contraction ended, his breathing returned to normal. Something was wrong.

I fell from a mountaintop of joy into an abyss of terror, so sickeningly scared I couldn't get enough air to breathe through the contractions.

It wasn't long before what was happening to Christopher was plainly evident on the heart-rate monitor, too, which had been chirping away since the nurse first turned it on.

Suddenly, a particularly strong contraction seized me and the beeping stopped. There was agonizing silence for a few seconds and then it started again. As my contractions grew harder and closer together, the periods of silence from the monitor grew longer. The heartbeat began to weaken, too. After every period of silence, the heart rate came back softer and slower than it had been before.

My body was in a freight-train rush to give birth, and contractions relentlessly grabbed hold of me and squeezed, one after another, like waves in a hurricane crashing on the shore. I was powerless in the grip of childbirth. I couldn't stop the contractions. I couldn't keep the force of them from silencing the echo of life on the monitor. I could do nothing but listen in horror as the sound grew weaker and fainter.

Beep-beep. . . . . beep . . . beep . . . . beep . . . . . . beep . . . . beep . . . . beep . . . . beep . . . . beep . . . . beep . . . .

Finally, a nurse went over and turned off the sound on the monitor.

"What's happening?" I screamed. "What's wrong? Somebody tell me what's wrong!"

I was seized by another contraction and I cried out in pain, unable to speak again until it passed. Doctors and nurses were scurrying around, oblivious to my cries of terror.

"Is my baby dead?" I shrieked. No! No! Nooooo! This couldn't be happening! "Tell me! Is my baby dead?"

Jamey was terrified, too, and totally bewildered. He didn't know how to deal with the horror, and when I looked up, he was gone. Only Mom, Rebel, and Grandmother remained in the room. All of them were sobbing.

"Is my baby dead?" I screamed and screamed. "Is my baby dead?" The furious activity in the room finally wound down. And the inactivity was worse—far scarier than the doctors' and nurses' frantic motion. There was a finality to the stillness that sucked the air out of my lungs.

"Is my baby deeeead?" I wailed, a cry of anguish and fear and despair.

Two nurses exchanged glances. Then my obstetrician stepped forward and spoke as gently as he could.

"I'm so sorry, Heather," he said. "The baby's heart stopped beating. Yes . . . he's dead."

I completely lost it, screaming and sobbing at the same time, crying so hard I could barely breathe, wailing, "No, no, nooooooo! No, no, no, no!" in denial and pain and rage.

Outside the door to my room, Jamey's parents told him that Christopher had died. He didn't move. He couldn't move. He sat with his head down, totally unable to comprehend that his first son was dead.

Inside the room, I was completely hysterical.

"Get out!" I shrieked at my family. "Get out! Everybody get out of here, do you hear me? I don't want you here! Get out!"

In the grip of such powerful grief and rage, I was incapable of rational thought. All I knew was that I wanted everyone in the room to leave. I didn't want my family around me. I didn't want anybody around me!

"Didn't you hear me! I said out. Get out. Get out of here right now! All of you! Get out!"

Mom and Grandmother stepped out into the hallway, but Rebel stopped in the doorway, reluctant to leave me.

One of the nurses—her name was Rose—was a firm, practical, compassionate woman, and hers was the only voice of reason that could get through to me.

"You can't do this alone," Rose told me. "You have to have somebody in here."

I still had a baby to deliver. A dead baby.

I looked up and saw Rebel standing in the doorway, crying.

"Will you stay, Rebel?" I choked out through my own tears. "Will you stay and coach me through this?"

Rebel came to the bed, took hold of my hand, and squeezed reassuringly. If either of us had been aware enough to take note of it, we would have grasped the significance of the moment. Through all our lives, I had looked after Rebel. It didn't matter that Rebel was older; I was tougher, and I was tremendously protective. I had always been the strong one. Now, for the first time in our lives, our roles were reversed. I needed my big sister. And Rebel was there for me.

It took almost an hour for me to give birth to my dead son. Through it all, I raged and sobbed, shrieked out my pain, anger, and grief.

"Why?" I cried out in agony as the pain of a contraction clamped my belly in a vice grip. "Why, God? Why?"

I felt like some demon from hell had reached into my body

and ripped out my heart. Christopher was my gift! He was my gift from God for all the pain and suffering I had gone through in my life. He was my reward. How could he be dead? Why would God let this happen?

"What did I do wrong?" I wailed. "What did I do wrong?"

Rebel held my hand and stroked my head, crooning, "You didn't do anything wrong, Heather. You did everything right! This is not your fault. Do you hear me, this is not your fault! God's got a bigger plan for you and for Christopher."

"You're so stupid!" I screamed at my sister, as another contraction seized me. "And God is stupid. I hate you. I hate you all. I hate God!"

The doctor and nurses were telling me I needed to push, but I didn't want to push. I didn't want to do anything. I had never before felt a pain like the one in my heart, not in all the years and all the surgeries. The agony of my loss hurt so bad I thought the pain would kill me; I hoped it would kill me.

"Heather, you have to push," Rose told me. Rose took hold of one of my legs and held it back. Rebel held the other. And my obstetrician seated himself between them.

"Push, Heather, push!" Rose said.

"Noooooo!" I screamed. "No, no! Nooooo!"

But I did push—one, two, three times—and finally Christopher slid down out of the birth canal and into the doctor's waiting hands.

The doctors and nurses tried to revive the child. They attempted CPR, tried to squeeze the fluid out of his lungs to get him to breathe. But it was a hopeless cause and everybody in the room knew it. The precious child lying limp in an incubator on the other side of the room was dead, and no heroic measures were going to bring him back.

The room was full of medical personnel—my obstetrician, doctors from the Neonatal Intensive Care Unit, nurses, a pediatrician. There were so many people that I couldn't get a good look at the limp child lying in the incubator against the far wall. I was glad I couldn't see Christopher clearly. I didn't want to see him at all. Seeing his lifeless body was to accept the reality of his death, and I couldn't do that yet.

His loss generated a grief so huge I couldn't possibly get my arms around it. But grief wasn't the dominant emotion surging through my body at that moment. The dominant emotion was rage. I was furious! How dare God take my child away! After all I had been through, how dare God let Christopher die!

My physical ordeal wasn't over yet. I still had to pass the placenta. That was like giving birth all over again. More pain, more contractions, more pushing. I didn't want to push anymore. I wanted it to be over. I wanted to go home!

Finally, the placenta plopped out of my body into a big silver dish. When it did, the doctor knew instantly what had killed Christopher.

"Look at this," the doctor said to Rebel, pointing to the two bloody globs of purple tissue lying in a pool of blood in the dish. "The placenta divided in two. The baby suffocated in the amniotic fluid. It happens once in every thousand or so births. It's a random, freak thing; we don't know why it happens. It didn't have anything to do with something Heather did or didn't do. It didn't have anything to do with her injuries. It didn't have anything to do with Heather at all. It just happened."

Rebel tried to relay that information to me but I was totally irrational.

"It is too my fault!" I cried, rising up on my elbows. "It is! If I hadn't gained so much weight, or if I had exercised more . . ."

I listed a handful of other equally absurd reasons why my behavior had somehow affected the child I was carrying. I wouldn't have believed any of those things if I'd been coherent. But in the grip of my shock and pain, I was absolutely inconsolable.

Rebel tried. She wrapped her arms around me and held me, trying to soothe me, telling me over and over again, "It's not your fault. You didn't do anything wrong. It just happened. It's not your fault."

Rose touched my arm and nodded toward the incubator. "Don't you want to see your son?" she asked.

"No!" I cried. "No, I don't want to see him!"

I didn't want to bond in any way to this child I would never nurse, never rock to sleep at night or teach to walk or talk. It hurt too badly already. If I saw him, if I fell in love with him, the pain of losing him would be more than I could bear.

"You need to see him," the doctor said. "You need to make him real for your memories. You need the closure."

"No!" I cried. "No, I don't want to see him. Didn't you hear me, I said no!"

Rebel went out into the waiting room and told the people assembled there—friends, family members, and ministers—what had happened, that my baby had been born dead, and that efforts to resuscitate him had been unsuccessful. They all wept.

Jamey remained in the hallway outside the delivery suite. He couldn't make himself come back in. He tried, got as far as the doorway and could go no farther. He had no frame of reference for such gut-wrenching tragedy, no resources to deal with such sorrow. All he could do was stand there in the doorway, his face ashen, tears streaming down his cheeks.

Mom and Grandmother came back into the room. They were crying, too. Through her tears, Mom told me that I needed to hold my son. I shook my head vehemently and continued to sob.

Mom stood there for a moment, her heart breaking for her grieving daughter. Then she went to the incubator and gently picked up the dead child wrapped in a blanket. Holding the baby tenderly, she sat down in a rocking chair beside the incubator and began to rock Christopher and sing to him.

"Hush little baby, don't you cry, Momma's gonna sing you a lullaby," Mom sang, her voice rough but steady. The song was quiet and intimate, as if Mom and Christopher were the only two beings on the planet. The melody floated out into the room and mingled with the weeping to form a symphony of grief.

"Christopher, I'm your grandmother," she told the child lying in her arms, rocking back and forth, holding the tiny baby close. "I love you so much. And I'm going to miss you . . ."

Rebel, Grandmother, and I were sobbing, but somehow Mom managed to keep her voice steady.

"I wish I could have played with you and seen you smile. I know you're safe in Heaven, but we will miss you here . . ."

She gazed tenderly into the baby's face, memorizing his tiny features. And she rocked him back and forth, back and forth.

Mom told Christopher how much his mommy and daddy loved him, how we all wished things had been different.

"We wish you could have stayed here with us, to grow up with us loving you and taking care of you," she said. "But God had other plans for you, Christopher . . ."

Back and forth she rocked, singing pieces of a lullaby to her grandson for the first time and the last time.

Finally, Mom stopped rocking and got out of the chair. She carried the baby to where I was sitting up in bed.

"Heather, he's so beautiful, you need to . . ."

"Get him away from me!" I sobbed. "I don't want to see him. Just get him out of here!"

But Mom didn't take the baby back to the incubator. Instead, she stepped forward and laid the tiny child down in my lap. Then she turned and walked away.

I stared down at my son, transfixed for a moment totally frozen in time, a moment that could have lasted a minute or an hour. Then I reached down in slow motion, like a sleepwalker or a character in a dream, and pulled the blanket off his tiny body. And suddenly I was seized by an all-consuming need to see what he looked like, what every part of my baby looked like. He was so small, only four or five pounds, but he was perfectly formed, like a miniature baby doll. He had a full head of thick black hair. The right side of his face was perfectly normal, a soft baby pink. But the left half of his face and that side of his body was maroon—colored by the fluid and blood he had ingested before he died.

I counted his fingers and toes, and raised his eyelids to see what color his eyes were.

Some part of my mind registered the question: Why did they put a diaper on a dead baby? I took it off. And I removed the blue, white, and pink T-shirt and matching blue, white, and pink cap.

I was still crying, but softly now, the agony of my grief so profound I couldn't get enough air to cry louder.

"I love you, Christopher," I whispered, caressing the soft hair on his tiny head. ". . . and I'm sorry, I'm sooo, so sorry . . ."

I looked up at Jamey, standing in the doorway.

"Don't you want to see him?" I asked. "Jamey, don't you want to see your son?"

Jamey came into the room then and stood at the edge of my bed. I carefully put Christopher's clothes and hat back on him, and wrapped the pink, blue, and yellow blanket snug around him. Then I picked him up and handed him to Jamey.

Jamey cuddled the child to his chest and sobbed.

"I'm so sorry, Jamey," I kept saying over and over. "I'm so, so sorry."

In the first agony of loss everybody needed somebody to blame. I blamed God, and I felt like Jamey blamed me.

When he had cried himself out, Jamey handed Christopher back to me and went back out into the hallway. Then other members of the family gathered around, held Christopher, and told him good-bye. Rebel. Grandmother. Jamey's grandmother. Aunt Laura.

With tears streaming down her face, Aunt Laura hugged me tight and told me everything would be okay.

I may have been hysterical and irrational, but I was capable of at least one moment of clarity. And in that moment I knew with sickening certainty that nothing in my world would ever be okay again.

THIRTEEN

It was late, getting dark, and everyone in the family was physically and emotionally spent. My doctor gave orders that I be transferred from the birthing suite to a private room—but not on the maternity ward. I told my family to go home, that I didn't want them there, that I didn't want to see anybody. Reluctantly, they left.

A short time later, a nurse came to take me to my room. She pushed my wheelchair down the hall and into the elevator. When the doors opened again, she wheeled me out onto the maternity ward. There was not another room available anywhere else in the hospital.

The nurse settled me in my bed and left. I was alone. I'd been given large doses of tranquilizers and pain medication and

I should have been heavily sedated. But my obstetrician hadn't been around the block with me often enough to understand my body's resistance to medications. Nothing they'd given me even made a dent in my pain or my mood. I was completely alert.

So I lay there in the dark in my room on the maternity ward and hated God. Christopher was supposed to be my gift, God's thank-you for my faithfulness through suffering, my reward. But God had let Christopher die.

"I hate you, God!" I spat the words out of my mouth with loathing, as if they tasted like vomit. "Do you hear me?" I looked around in the darkened room like I might see him there, lurking in the shadows. I wanted to see him! I wanted to scream my rage at him. I wanted to spit in his face.

"I hate you!" I snarled. "I hate you! I hate you! I *hate* you . . ."

Sometime later, there was a knock at my door and a young nurse's aide wheeled a cart into my room. Mothers on the maternity ward were served a special dinner the night after the birth of their babies. The aide didn't know my baby had died.

"Here's steak and lobster for the new mom," the aide chirped cheerily.

My heart tore out of my chest. *The new mom.* I wasn't a mom. Christopher was dead.

"What's the matter with you? Are you stupid?" I shrieked at the aide, who was so startled she almost dropped the lid she was holding. "Are you stupid? Get out of here, do you hear me? Get out!"

The aide backed away toward the doorway as fast as she could, a look of horror and confusion on her face.

"Get out and don't come back!"

I had no intention of eating steak and lobster or anything else. And I didn't eat again for a long time.

The aide left my door open in her hasty retreat, and a few minutes later, I saw nurses wheeling bassinets down the hallway. It was feeding time. One of the babies was crying, wailing that particularly heartbreaking newborn wail. I could see the child—a little boy, I just knew it was a little boy!—through the plastic side of the bassinet, frantically kicking his little legs and waving his little arms. Some mother in another room was waiting to reach out and gather her son into her arms, hold him close, and soothe his tears, shower his little face with kisses, and gaze spellbound at his perfection, absolutely convinced that hers was the most beautiful little boy in the world.

My sense of longing and loss was so intense it was a stabbing physical pain that literally took my breath away. I began to cry again, though I thought I had shed every tear I had. As I did, my rage and hysteria drained away, and I lay there limp, weeping quietly, in total hopelessness and despair.

About midnight, nurses came and moved me to another room. A vacancy had opened up on a medical/surgical ward. But even there, I imagined I heard babies crying.

. . .

Very early the next morning a nurse came into my room to get me to sign some forms. I sat up in bed. My eyes were so swollen from crying I could barely see, and I struggled to focus on the papers in front of me. Finally I saw what they were. One was Christopher's birth certificate; the other was his death certificate. I wanted to cry, but by that time I really was past tears.

Shortly after that, another nurse came in and asked me what I wanted done with Christopher's body. Did I want my son buried or cremated?

I just stared at the woman, too shell-shocked to make a sound. Buried or cremated? How was I supposed to decide a thing like that now, all by myself? But the nurse had to know.

"Buried," I blurted out. "I want him buried." Then I lay back down, turned my face to the wall, and refused to say another word to anybody about anything.

. . .

About midmorning, Jamey came to get me. He had arranged with Mom to take me from the hospital to her house. After work, he would pick me up and take me home to our house. I went where he told me, stunned, a zombie. The doctors had upped my medication significantly once they realized the normal dosage wasn't working, and I was finally so drugged that the slicing edge of the pain was a little dulled, a little distant and other-worldly.

When Jamey and I walked into our house that evening, we were greeted by Butch, our huge rottweiler. The animal was delighted that we were home, and he hopped around us in excitement, wagging the stump of a tail, and licking every exposed skin surface he could find. I sank to the floor inside the doorway, put my arms around the big dog's neck, and began to cry.

When I looked up, I could see into the baby's room, Christopher's room, with its clown border and bright colors. The clown mobile dangled above the crib, waiting to entertain a child who wasn't coming, who would never lie beneath it and watch the clowns dance with big, wide eyes. The house was so small you could see into the nursery from every room. That's one reason we'd picked that room for the baby. We'd wanted Christopher nearby, close, so we'd hear him when he cried, so we could go to him quickly, so we could take such very, very good care of him.

"Close that door!" I told Jamey. He followed my gaze and his own face fell. "Do it! Do it right now. Shut it and lock it. We've got to get rid of all that stuff. I don't want to see any of that stuff ever again."

. . .

The flashbacks began three days after Christopher died.

I was lying on that cot, the stinky cot, with Mr. Jennings sitting on a stool beside me cleaning his gun. I was so afraid of the gun I wanted to cry every time it was near me. I didn't, of course. It always hurt worse and lasted longer if you cried.

Earlier, before he had undressed me and made me lie on the cot, he had put the barrel of the gun in my mouth.

"I'll blow Rebel's brains out just like this," he had said. And he had cocked the gun, watching my eyes grow wide with terror.

Mr. Jennings liked it when I was afraid.

He finished cleaning the gun, stood up, and went to place it on a small table by the cot. He was smiling that smile that never reached his eyes. And he was looking at me, walking toward me, getting closer . . .

I bolted upright in the bed, screaming, jarring Jamey out of a sound sleep.

"What? What's wrong?" he asked, still dopey and disoriented. He put his arms around me, trying to calm me.

But there was no calming me. Mr. Jennings was back! He had crawled like a black, poisonous spider out of a dark hole deep in my mind. And he was there, right there in the room. I could feel his eyes; I could smell his stink!

I kept screaming, my eyes wide and terrified, until I was hoarse, and the screams dwindled down to sobs, and then whimpers. Jamey held me, tried to comfort me. But he had precious little emotional reserve to share with me. He was in shock, grieving, still unable to comprehend the pain that had hit him like a blow to the belly when they told him his son was dead. He did the best he could, tried to be strong and reassuring. But Jamey couldn't give me strength he didn't have.

I didn't go back to sleep. I was afraid to go back to sleep. I lay wide-eyed in the dark, listening to Jamey's even breathing, wishing for the first time in my life that I was dead.

. . .

Mr. Jennings came back the next night.

And the next.

And the next.

I crawled into a shell and shut the world out. I refused to see anybody—my mother, my grandmother, my aunt Laura, my friends, or ministers from my church. They all tried to be there for me, but I shut them all out. I was beaten down by a raging storm of emotions. Grief, anger, and fear were at war inside me, battling for dominance, fighting to see which one of them could make me the most miserable, cause me the most pain. I tried to stand up against them, but they mowed me down, and after a while, I just didn't want to fight anymore.

I had saved enough Vicodin. I asked Jamey to refill the pain medication prescription, and only pretended to take the pills. I had a full bottle. That would be enough—even with my legendary drug tolerance.

I planned when I would do it and how. I yearned to escape into the nothingness on the other side of the bottle; I longed for oblivion. I ached for rest, for long, deep, lasting sleep not framed by tears and terror, sleep that didn't begin in the exhaustion of crying over Christopher, and end in screams, with Mr. Jennings's hands all over me.

One gray, rainy day in early spring, I went into the bathroom and locked the door behind me. Then unlocked it. Why make it hard for them to find me? I filled a glass with water, sat down on the side of the tub, and poured the whole bottle of pills out into the palm of my hand.

"How do you spell relief?" I said out loud. "V. I. C. O. D. I. N."

Relief. Release. Rest. Just a swallow away.

I sat for a long time looking at the pile of white pills in my palm. I was tempted, so very tempted. But I couldn't do it. Oh, this was not some survival instinct taking over at the last minute. It wasn't that I wanted to live. I didn't. But I knew how my suicide would devastate my family and I couldn't do that to them. They'd been through enough. I couldn't ease my own pain by hurting them.

I reached over and lifted the lid on the toilet and slowly poured the pills into the water, watching them cascade off the edge of my hand. That's when I knew I had to get help. Later, I would say that God directed me by divine providence to Karen Lovett. But at the time, I didn't believe that. At the time, I was certain God didn't have the slightest interest in what happened to me. If I had mattered to God, he wouldn't have let Christopher die.

. . .

Karen was a counselor at the Methodist Hospital Counseling Center. I sat in the waiting room that first day, filling out form after form, angry that they wanted so much information and that the questions were so stupid. I didn't put down half of what was going on in my life. I couldn't. There wasn't enough room in the neat little spaces on the forms; there wouldn't have been even if I'd filled up the whole backside of every page.

Karen came out into the waiting room to get me and walked me down the hallway to her office. Even then, even before I opened up my soul and let this little gray-haired woman see who I was, who I really was, Karen's office felt like a safe place. There was a big, overstuffed couch to plop down on, pillows to hold, to hug to your chest when you rocked back and forth sobbing. There were even soft, cuddly stuffed animals.

After she scanned my forms, Karen looked up from the paperwork and smiled. Then she described the playing field and defined the rules of the game.

"What's said in here stays in here," she told me.

I smiled.

"You don't have to smile for me, Heather," Karen continued. "You don't have to put on a happy face for me. You don't have to be okay when you walk through that door. Everything that happens here, everything that's said here is real. Are you okay with that?"

I nodded; I wasn't smiling.

And so the process began.

Week after week, month after month, I cuddled up in a corner of the overstuffed couch in Karen's office and poured my guts out. I relived the horror of Mr. Jennings's abuse in minute detail, unearthing memories I didn't know existed. It was like the mind of that little girl I had been so many years ago had taken mental snapshots of every moment I spent with Mr. Jennings, every incident, every taste and smell and emotion. That child collected books full of those images and hid them in a secret room at the end of a long, dark corridor in my mind. Under Karen's guidance, I found that room, opened the door, and went inside. I picked up every book and looked at every page, inspected every image and read all the contents word for word.

I left Karen's office drained, exhausted, wondering if all the digging and prodding was doing any good, if dredging up all those memories was worth the pain it was causing me.

Karen instructed me to do two things: journal and yell at God.

"You're angry at God—tell him so," Karen said. "God's big enough to deal with your rage. Tell him what you're thinking, be honest about what you're feeling. Don't hold anything back—be real. You can scream anything you want to at God. You can tell him what you think of him. His shoulders are broad. He can take it."

I did what Karen instructed. I screamed at God, cried out my rage and disappointment and hurt. I yelled until I was hoarse, told him I hated him and didn't want to have anything to do with him. I told him to go away and leave me alone and never come back.

But God was there the next day, and I yelled at him some more.

I journaled, too, writing into the wee hours of the morning. That caused problems between Jamey and me. He didn't understand what I was writing, or why I had to write at all. He just wanted me to come to bed. But journaling provided a reason for me to stay up, a reason not to go to bed, an excuse not to be intimate with my husband. I just couldn't do that—not yet. I was too afraid.

I was terrified of getting pregnant again. Oh, the doctors had told me what had happened was a fluke, a chance in a million, that I would never conceive again. And I was taking birth control pills. But it didn't matter. I couldn't go through losing another baby. I couldn't stand it.

But that wasn't the only reason I avoided going to bed. I couldn't be intimate with Jamey because it wasn't Jamey. It was Mr. Jennings. Every time I closed my eyes, I saw Mr. Jennings's face. Every time Jamey put his hands on me, I felt Mr. Jennings's touch. When Jamey reached for me in the night, I cringed and shrank away. Jamey was hurt and confused. And so the two of us grew further and further apart.

My life was spiraling out of control in other areas, too. By the time I sat down on Karen's couch for the first time, I was already in full-blown bulimia.

I had flirted with bulimia at other times in my life. I was skinny as a child, but that all changed at puberty. From that point on, I was never as thin as Rebel or my mother, and sometimes I would lose weight by purging. But I always stopped when I got down to a size 10—or got a new boyfriend.

After Christopher died, my bulimia went totally out of control. I kept a stash of hidden food. When Jamey was at work, I would gorge myself and then stick my finger down my throat to make myself vomit. Binge and purge, binge and purge—I had the drill down. I always carried a ponytail holder in my purse to hold my hair back when I threw up. I carried breath mints, baby powder, and hand lotion, to make sure I didn't smell like vomit. It wasn't long before I was purging everything I ate. When I went out to dinner, I would throw up my meal before I left the restaurant.

Food was my escape. I couldn't control the horrible circumstances of my life, but I could control what I ate, what I put into my body, and what I took back out again.

Months of out-of-control bulimia began to take a physical toll. I developed ulcers in my mouth, and my gums bled constantly. My esophagus was raw from the constant flow of stomach acid, and I became an antacid junkie. I began throwing up blood, and suffered agonizing rounds of diarrhea. I had other physical issues as well. Christopher's birth did a lot of damage to my body. The baby ripped out my vaginal wall flap as he passed through the birth canal, and it required one major surgery and two smaller procedures to put it all back together again.

A few months after I started counseling, Karen gave me a copy of *The Courage to Heal*, a workbook on dealing with the aftermath of emotional and sexual abuse. Using biblically based principles, the book walked me step by step through the healing process.

For eighteen months, I sat in Karen's office once a week, pouring out my heart. Gradually, I got the bulimia under control. The nightmares stalked my sleep for months, but after a while they became less frequent. Eventually, I stopped dreaming about Mr. Jennings altogether. The process was long and painful, but I turned a corner when I was finally able to forgive myself.

Like many other victims of sexual abuse, I had always secretly believed the abuse was in some way my fault. I should have said no. I shouldn't have allowed it to happen. I should have told somebody.

Over time, I learned to accept an accurate view of reality—that Mr. Jennings was a perverted predator and I was a little girl, a child, a small, helpless victim of a sick man's depravity. I was one of dozens, maybe hundreds, of little girls and boys whose childhoods and innocence were stolen from them by a dirty, greasy old man with filthy black fingernails and a smile that never reached his eyes.

I worked all the way through *The Courage to Heal* workbook, and as I did, I healed. I prayed that Mr. Jennings's other victims had somehow found healing, too.

I mourned the death of my son. Over time, my anger at God began to fade, as the wail of a train whistle gets softer and softer as the train moves away in the darkness. God didn't owe me Christopher; he didn't promise me Christopher. What he did promise was that he would always be there, that he would never abandon me. For a time, I turned my back and walked away from God. At least I thought I did. But even when I walked away from God, he never left me. And through all the grief, pain, rage, and despair, I wasn't walking at all. He was carrying me.

FOURTEEN

The first person I told was Grandmother. I wasn't exactly working my way up to my parents one relative at a time, but I did want to start with somebody a little easier than Mom.

"You're going to be a great-grandmother," I said. "I'm pregnant!" I watched the little white-haired woman's face, hoping I'd see joy and approval there. I didn't.

"No! Oh, Heather, honey—no!" Grandmother said, her eyes wide. "You can't do that! It's too dangerous. You don't know what it will do . . ."

Grandmother was watching my face, too, and she saw me flinch at her words, almost as if she'd slapped me. She stopped in midsentence and sat studying me—a dark-haired young woman sitting on the edge of the couch, so vulnerable, with so much yearning in her eyes it broke her heart.

"You need this, don't you?" Grandmother said tenderly. She already knew the answer.

"This will give my pain a purpose," I said.

"Then I'm happy for you," Grandmother told me, and got up and gave me a big hug. It was a lie, of course. She wasn't happy for me. She was scared to death. But she understood that I needed her strength and support right now, not her fear. She'd be happy for me eventually. Until then, she'd just have to fake it. "Have you told your mother yet?"

I shook my head. That was my next stop.

As with Christopher, the harbinger of this pregnancy had been a miscarriage. It had been four years since the stillbirth of my son, and I hadn't been actively trying to conceive. But I had stopped using contraception. If it happened, it happened.

It happened. I hadn't even known I was pregnant. Like the miscarriage before Christopher, it occurred during the first trimester. And it sent me the same message as the miscarriage before Christopher, too—I *can* get pregnant. Conceiving my son hadn't been a fluke, a one-in-a-million shot. I could bear my own child, and I wanted a baby more than anything else in the world. By the time I went back for my six-week checkup after the miscarriage, I was already pregnant again.

I put off telling Mom for as long as possible. I knew my mother wasn't likely to respond positively. When I broke the news, I sat in my parents' living room and told them both at the same time. My father hugged me and told me that it was God's will, that he and Mom would support me and pray for a good result.

Mom didn't say a word. She sat on the couch mute. It was the kind of mute that could signal any number of emotions—disbelief, fear, anger—and I didn't know which one my mother was feeling. Mom didn't know either, not really. She kept hearing my screams—*Is my baby dead? Is my baby dead?*—echoing in the corridors of her mind.

Mom and Jim wanted a grandchild so badly. When Christopher died, they were devastated, too. Mom had been so distraught that Jim went in search of something to raise his wife's spirits. He finally settled on a puppy. He came home one day and handed Mom a cuddly ball of fluff with a tail that never stopped wagging and big, sad eyes. She named the little German shepherd Winnie.

Mom was stroking Winnie's head as she sat on the couch that day, listening to me tell them the best and the worst news she'd heard since the death of her grandson. She cycled through a kaleidoscope of emotions in a matter of seconds, and finally settled on one: hope.

"There isn't anything we can do about it now, so we'll just have to make the best of it," she said. "If it's meant to work out, it will. We'll just pray hard and have a positive attitude. This is wonderful news."

That was a lie, of course. But once the family got used to the idea of a grandchild on the way, nobody had to fake enthusiasm.

Every time Mom saw me, she had a baby gift. A pair of booties. A blanket. A little knit cap. She prayed over every item: "Please, Lord, keep our baby safe. And stand very close to Heather right now, so close she can feel your presence every day. She's going to need your strength. We all are."

After Christopher's death, Jamey and I had moved from our house in Okolona to a farm in Nelson County where I indulged a passion born in a Montana field almost two decades earlier. We bought horses. But the farm near the little town of Chaplin was almost an hour's drive from Louisville. Jamey had farm chores now and the horses to look after, as well as his regular job. Doctor appointments and ultrasounds in Louisville weren't logistically simple anymore, and Jamey didn't come to every appointment as he had with Christopher.

His absence was a symptom of bigger issues as well. Jamey responded to Christopher's death and to the emotional upheaval in my life caused by the loss of our child by working sixty-, seventy-, and eighty-hour weeks. Whenever he had time off, he went hunting. He was avoiding me as well as the grief and pain. I prayed that this baby would draw us back together again, that the child would bring healing to our struggling marriage.

As my pregnancy progressed, I began to make plans, dared to dream again. This time, I decorated the baby's room in pastel colors instead of primary colors. The walls were yellow with a wide wallpaper border of rocking horses. I picked yellow because that color would work for either a boy or a girl and I didn't yet know the sex of the child I carried.

It would have been difficult to find an expectant mother anywhere who better defined the term "high-risk pregnancy" than I did. I had already suffered two miscarriages and a stillbirth, and the injuries I had suffered years ago should have made it impossible for me to carry a child to term. Somehow I'd managed to carry Christopher, but the damage he did to me during birth made this pregnancy even dicier than the first. My doctors monitored me closely, and as soon as there were problems they took quick, decisive action.

About four months into the pregnancy, I began experiencing Braxton Hicks contractions. Prelabor. I was immediately hospitalized at Norton's Hospital in downtown Louisville and placed on medication to stop the contractions. Doctors started me on a course of steroids to beef up the size of the baby. It was a race against time now. Could they get the baby big enough to survive on its own in the amount of time they had before my body expelled the child into the world?

At five months, I had an ultrasound, and Mom was right there with me. All along, Mom had maintained that she didn't want to know the sex of the baby; she wanted to be surprised.

But when the nurse leaned over and whispered it into my ear, Mom couldn't stand the suspense.

"Well, tell me—is it a boy or a girl?"

"It's a girl, Mom," I said, awe and wonder in my voice. "My

baby is a little girl." Jamey and I named our daughter Mackenzie.

I remained hospitalized for twelve weeks—a dozen of the most boring, uneventful weeks of my life. I wasn't sick. I wasn't recovering from some surgical procedure. I was just waiting, like a chicken sitting on an egg. But I had lots of visitors. I'd had surgery at Norton's so often that I knew a small army of medical personnel from every floor in the hospital. They came to talk, to play cards or watch movies. My family came, too. Mom showed up without fail every day. Jim, Rebel, Grampa, Rudy, Aunt Laura, Mamaw and Poppy, Grandmother and Jimmy, my stepbrothers and sisters, my friends Vicki and Teresa, many neighbors from Chaplin, and ministers from my church came to help me pass the time.

Jamey's visits grew less frequent as time passed. With his job and the farm to look after, Jamey usually managed only a brief appearance each day. He'd give me a hug and a kiss, hang around for a few minutes and then go back to work. Some days, Jamey didn't even make it in to see me at all.

I knew that with a couple of phone calls, Jamey could line up neighbors to help with farm chores so he could spend more time with me. Jamey would have been the first to pitch in if a neighbor had asked for his help, but he wasn't the kind of man who could do the asking. So Jamey worked, I waited for our baby to be born, and the two of us drifted further and further apart.

Almost every day, nurses took equipment into my room and performed ultrasounds on me as I lay in bed. I got to watch my baby develop, day by day. That's why it didn't take my doctors long to figure out what was wrong when my urinary system began to back up. The reason was plainly visible on the ultrasound image.

In a normal human body, a long, thin tube called a ureter connects each kidney to the bladder. I had no bladder. It was destroyed in the accident. Years ago, my ureters had been surgically joined together and connected to a tube that drained urine into the pee bag on my leg. One morning after I'd been hospitalized several weeks, I woke up to find the pee bag almost empty. An ultrasound revealed that Mackenzie was clamping my ureters shut. The tiny baby had literally grabbed hold of the ureters and wrapped her little fingers tight around them.

Doctors did everything they could to get the baby to let go. They massaged my belly and tried to turn Mackenzie so she would face the other way. Nothing did any good. No matter what they tried, Mackenzie always went right back to the ureters, holding on as tenaciously as an acrobat to a trapeze bar.

Eventually, my obstetrician had no recourse but to drain urine directly out of my kidneys by inserting nephrostomy tubes into my back. The baby crimping the garden hose caused other problems as well. I developed stones from the urine backed up in my kidneys.

The pain from the kidney stones was excruciating, but I couldn't take pain medication because whatever I took would affect Mackenzie. I had to endure the kidney-draining cold turkey, too. In agony, as doctors stabbed nephrostomy tubes into my back, I forced my mind to focus on the baby.

"We've got to get her here," I thought as the pain seared up my backbone. "We've got to get her into the world—no matter what it takes. We're not going to lose her."

While I was hospitalized waiting for the birth of Mackenzie, my mother's health went south. That's when Mom found out she had multiple sclerosis.

It shouldn't have been a surprise. Mom had had symptoms years before—lost the sight in one eye for six months—but had ignored the symptoms and they went away. Finally, numbness in parts of her body and fatigue drove her to the doctor. The diagnosis simply hung a tag on what was wrong with her; it didn't fix anything. There was no treatment for MS. Some days, the fatigue was so debilitating that Mom would get up, shower and dress, and then have to go back to bed again because the process had so exhausted her.

But I needed her.

So did Jane, Jim's daughter by a previous marriage. Jane was staying with Jim and Mom because she was going through a difficult time in her life. She was pregnant, too, but planned to give her baby up for adoption. Mom was Jane's labor coach. Jane had an appointment to check into the hospital for her obstetrician to induce labor on June 26. My due date was in August.

As June dragged by in a sea of sticky humidity outside my window, my obstetrician grew more and more concerned about my condition. I had toxemia. My blood pressure yo-yoed up and down. My health was deteriorating daily.

My obstetrician, Dr. Vernon Cook, was in the same medical practice as the doctor who had delivered Christopher. He liked me. Over the years, we had become friends. And he knew perhaps better than anyone else that this really was my last opportunity to bear a child. As he monitored the toll the pregnancy was taking on my body, he became certain I could not possibly survive another pregnancy. If I ever got pregnant again, it would kill me.

Mackenzie was my last shot. To give both mother and baby a fighting chance, Dr. Cook had to pull off an incredibly delicate balancing act. Every day—almost every hour—that Mackenzie remained in the womb increased her chances of survival. But every day—almost every hour—that Mackenzie remained in the womb increased my chances of developing all manner of complications. If he waited too long and either one of us started to crash, he could lose us both.

By June 24, Dr. Cook had grown so concerned about me that he refused to leave the hospital. He stayed in or near my room all day. If bad things happened, they would happen quickly. There would be no drive time, no getting-stuck-in-traffic time. There wouldn't be a spare second. He played cards with me for several hours, checked on other patients, and hung out in the nurses' station. Monitors there tracked the heartbeats of every unborn baby in the maternity ward. A half dozen little screens dispensed life-and-death information with wavy green lines and beeps.

It got late. The nurses changed shifts at 11 P.M. Dr. Cook watched the new shift come on. But he didn't go home. The next morning, he was still there. He worked on charts in a cubicle of the nurses' station, made rounds to see other patients on the ward, snagged naps when he could manage it. But he was always there, within rock-throwing distance of my room. Watching.

That evening, Jamey came by to see me for a few minutes, then had to get home to feed the horses. Mom, Jim, and Aunt Laura visited for a while, too. My friend Teresa stayed the longest. She hung out with me watching a late movie and didn't leave until about 2 A.M. Teresa said hello to Dr. Cook as she left. He was sitting in a cubicle watching the monitors, nursing cold, stale coffee in a disposable cup.

Alone in my room, I was trying to wind down and go to sleep. But I couldn't seem to get comfortable. I was so swollen I felt like a beach ball—that was the toxemia forcing my body to retain fluids. I had a monitor strap around my belly and it was hard to find a position where something wasn't jabbing me. I finally snuggled into the right spot and was just dozing off . . .

Suddenly my door slammed open, the lights came on, and Dr. Cook burst into my room. He said only two words, but they froze my heart.

"She's decelling!"

I was so scared, I couldn't breathe.

Decelling. That's what the nurses had said after they put the monitor on the top of Christopher's head to track his oxygen level. Every time I had a contraction, his breathing decelerated. But I wasn't even having contractions now.

"What's wrong?" I cried in terror. "What do you mean she's decelling?"

"The baby's heart rate is slowing down," he said. He reached over and flipped the switch on the monitor next to my bed. Instantly, the green blip appeared, along with the rapid-fire *beep-beep, beep-beep, beep-beep* sound of a baby's heart beating normally, about 120 beats a minute. But to my horror, it suddenly began to slow. Soon the heart rate was less than 100 . . . less than 90 . . . less than 80 . . . going down, down, down . . .

"We've got to get that baby out of there—now!" Dr. Cook told me. "We're doing a C-section. We're not talking about it—no discussion."

I had wanted to have a normal, vaginal delivery, had expected to bring Mackenzie into the world that way. My game plan definitely didn't call for emergency surgery. But it didn't matter what I wanted or had planned.

"We're going to the OR right now, Heather," Dr. Cook said. "If we don't get her out of there—now!—she's going to die."

That's all the convincing I needed.

In the blink of an eye, my tranquil, quiet room was transformed into a scene out of my favorite television show. Frenzied nurses and technicians materialized out of nowhere—just like they did on *ER*. They unplugged all my equipment, grabbed my bed, bounced it off the wall like a cue ball banking off the side of the table, banged it into the door frame, shoved the bed—with me in it—out into the hall, and began pushing it down the corridor at a dead run.

Dr. Cook was at my side, pushing the bed and shouting orders like a Marine Corps drill instructor at a platoon of recruits.

"You," he said, pointing at a nurse, "call upstairs and tell them to get an OR ready. You . . . call the anesthesia service and tell them to get somebody down here . . ."

"Jamey's not here!" I cried.

"We'll call him," Dr. Cook said as he and the bed-racing crew rounded a corner and hit the home stretch toward the elevators. "What's his number?"

I told him the number and he shouted it at a nurse.

"Call this guy, tell him his wife's having a baby!" he said.

"And my mom . . ." I wailed.

"What's her number?"

Dr. Cook shouted the number at a nurse just as the surgery suite doors closed behind him. He took my hand and looked intently into my eyes.

"I'll be right back," he said. "Everything's going to be fine, Heather. I'm not going to let this little girl die!"

The doctor disappeared and nurses helped me onto the operating table and quickly began inserting additional IV lines. I was terrified, crying, begging them all, "Please save my baby! Don't let Mackenzie die!" A nurse gave me a shot of Valium to calm me as other nurses prepared the surgery drapes. Then they sat me up so an epidural block could be administered into my spine. If the block wasn't successful, they'd have to put me out with general anesthesia. I wanted to be awake for the delivery, Dr. Cook wanted me alert, and nobody liked the idea of anesthetizing an already-at-risk baby.

The epidural took.

I spotted my mother and father at a window in one of the doors. They got my attention to let me know they were there, waved and blew kisses, then were ushered off to a waiting room that was beginning to fill with my entourage. Just as Dr. Cook was preparing to make his initial incision, Jamey appeared, dressed in scrubs. He took my hand and Dr. Cook went to work. Within minutes, I felt a gush of warm water as the doctor broke open the amniotic sac.

And then he was holding something up in the air—something blue, something wet, slimy, and covered in blood. The baby! Mackenzie, held up by her feet.

Not making a sound.

Dr. Cook patted the baby gently on her back.

Silence.

He patted her more firmly.

Silence.

Then she coughed, opened her mouth, and let out a wail, a robust, hearty cry that was the sweetest sound I had ever heard. My baby was alive! Mackenzie was alive!

I burst out sobbing, crying hysterically, so out of control I was hyperventilating. I had believed. I had trusted God that everything would be okay this time. But a spider of fear and doubt had still crawled around in the dark recesses of my mind. At the end, I had been so dreadfully afraid, terrified that the nightmare would happen all over again, that Mackenzie would be like her older brother, a limp, lifeless form beyond resuscitation, a tiny baby lying still in an incubator—dead. Now my tears mixed with laughter in a symphony of relief and joy.

A neonatal nurse took Mackenzie from Dr. Cook, cleaned her up, wrapped her snug in a blanket, and placed the baby gently on my chest. She was small, but not as small as Christopher. And she was perfect, with an angelically beautiful face and a full head of black hair. I reached up and gently stroked my daughter's cheek. I planted a kiss on Mackenzie's forehead, and whispered. "I love you, precious. I love you."

Then the nurse scooped up the baby and Dr. Cook was back at my side.

"Heather, we have to put you out now," he said.

I was hemorrhaging, bleeding to death. I had a massive incision that had to be closed, but first a surgeon had to repair the damage Mackenzie had done to my body. The pregnancy had torn out the mesh fabric that replaced the muscle structure of my abdomen. I had herniated in half a dozen places. My urostomy would have to be completely rebuilt. I was in critical condition.

Grabbing Jamey's hand, I uttered a single sentence before I vanished into the cottony world of unconsciousness.

"Don't you leave her!"

"I won't," he promised.

Then everything went black.

. . .

Mackenzie was big for a preemie, weighing in at five pounds, two ounces. She looked perfectly healthy. The nurse gave her to Jamey to hold, then took her out into the waiting room and handed her to Mom.

It was a beautiful moment. The world stopped spinning and Mom cuddled her precious granddaughter, the two of them alone inside a perfect sparkling soap bubble of joy. She showered Mackenzie's tiny face with kisses, delighting in the wonder of a healthy child, a perfect little baby.

Then the perfect little baby in her arms started to change colors.

"She's turning blue!" Mom sputtered. In a matter of moments, Mackenzie's baby-pink skin became as dark as a blueberry.

The nurse snatched the baby out of Mom's arms and cried, "I'm out of here!"

Then she turned and ran with the baby down the hallway. She didn't wait for an incubator or a bassinet, she just ran. Norton Hospital was connected to Kosair Children's Hospital by a pedway high above Fleenor Avenue. With Mackenzie in her arms, the nurse raced across the pedway to the Neonatal Intensive Care

Unit at Kosair—the finest facility for premature babies in the state. Jamey was running right behind her.

Within minutes of her birth, both Mackenzie and I were in critical condition.

And Mom had to leave.

She could still feel the warmth of her granddaughter in her arms when she turned to Jim and said, "I have to go . . . Jane . . . it's time to go get her." It was June 26. Jim's daughter was due at the hospital at 7 A.M. for her doctor to induce labor. Mom was her coach.

My parents stood for a moment in the hallway, looking into each other's eyes, trying to take it all in, sort it all out.

"Pray for . . ." Mom began.

"I'll pray . . ." Jim said at the same time.

They just left the words there, hanging in the air. They didn't finish. They didn't have to. Mom went to get Jane, and Jim went to check on Mackenzie, the "perfect" baby who actually had two holes in her heart and lungs so underdeveloped she couldn't absorb enough oxygen to survive.

Jane's baby, Olivia, was born while I was in surgery. It was a normal, complication-free delivery.

. . .

I woke up in the recovery room after seven hours in the OR to find Mom beside me, the comforting smell of her coffee breath announcing that I had made it. Yet again.

"You had a lot of bleeding," Mom said. "They had to repair your ostomy and replace the wire mesh that was torn out. It was a rough surgery."

I could always count on my mother to tell me the truth still in the husk. And Mom was totally honest that day, too—about *my* condition. But she didn't tell me that my tiny daughter was fighting for her life.

"Mackenzie's alive, sweetheart," Jim told me.

"She's doing good," Mom said.

I closed my eyes and was swallowed up again by oblivion.

"Doing good" was a bit of a stretch. In truth, Mackenzie was just holding on—but with a tenacity that was already beginning to remind her grandmother of me. She was on a ventilator, breathing 100 percent oxygen. The holes in her heart were alarming, but there was an even greater concern. The baby couldn't keep anything down. She vomited everything they fed her. No matter how they tried to get nutrition into her, everything that went down came back up faster than a clown head out of a jack-in-the-box.

I went septic after the delivery. The combination of toxemia, an emergency cesarean section, and all the internal damage from the pregnancy put my body on tilt. My blood pressure went up and down like a fifth-grader's yo-yo, and a massive infection spiked my fever up to 104 degrees.

When I was finally out of recovery and in a private room fully awake, Jim and Mom told me about Mackenzie's condition. I wanted to be with my daughter so desperately I'd have gotten out of the bed and crawled across the pedway to the other hospital just to get a glimpse of her. But it wouldn't have done any good if I had. I was running a fever. No one with a fever was allowed in the Neonatal Intensive Care Unit. No exceptions.

Twenty-four hours went by. My condition stabilized, but still I hadn't been allowed to see my daughter. By 6 P.M. on the evening of the second day after Mackenzie's birth, I had yet to hold the child in my arms. That's when I got a phone call from Susan Harris.

Susan was Mackenzie's primary caretaker in the NICU. But she was more than just a skilled nurse and a strikingly beautiful young woman with flaxen hair and cornflower blue eyes. She was a member of my church, and she made it her business to care for the mother as well as the baby. Susan came to Norton's, introduced herself to me, and told me to call anytime I wanted a report on Mackenzie. I did. I called every hour, all day and all through the night. Susan answered every time, and told me minute details about the tiny baby in her care. That connection to Mackenzie was my lifeline.

When Susan called me two days after Mackenzie was born, her words lit up my life: "You can't come to see Mackenzie, so I'm bringing Mackenzie to see you."

Susan wheeled the incubator, with all its attendant monitors and three separate IV poles, out of the NICU and pushed it across the pedway to Norton's Hospital. She brought with her a set of pediatric heart paddles—charged—and every other piece of resuscitation equipment she would need if Mackenzie crashed. Susan was ready for anything.

No one had held Mackenzie since the nurse clasped her in her arms and raced with her across the pedway to the NICU. When Susan wheeled the incubator into my room, Mackenzie was decked out in the preemie outfit Mom had purchased for her the day she was born. It was white—covered with yellow, hot pink, and purple daisies. So were the matching booties. The tiny baby was bald. Her black hair had been shaved so three IV lines could be inserted into her scalp.

"You have to be the first one to hold her," Susan told me.

It took five minutes to disentangle the tiny baby from all the wires and tubes so Susan could slide her out of the incubator and into my arms.

As soon as I cuddled my daughter close, a peace settled over me and I was no longer afraid. In fact, I was never again afraid that Mackenzie wasn't going to make it—even when the baby's condition continued to deteriorate, even after a month in the hospital when the five-pound, two-ounce baby's weight had dropped to one pound, eleven ounces. I always knew my baby was going to live.

That day, when I first held the tiny little girl in my arms, it was as if God said to me, "She's going to be fine." Oh, I didn't hear an audible voice. But it wasn't like it was with Christopher, when I convinced myself God wouldn't dare allow anything to happen to the baby. This time, I didn't conjure up an obligation on God's part. I didn't see Mackenzie as payment for being good or brave or faithful. Mackenzie wasn't a reward; she hadn't been earned. She was a gift, a precious gift, a free, no-strings-attached gift. I didn't believe God owed me Mackenzie's life. But I believed with all my heart that God was telling me Mackenzie would not die.

Mom had felt the same peace when she knelt beside me as I lay bleeding in the street. Mom knew, she just *knew* her little girl would be okay; I knew mine would be, too.

Mackenzie stayed cradled in my arms for more than an hour. I nursed her, but the baby had no more success keeping that down than she did when she was fed from a bottle. As soon as I sat her up to burp her, everything Mackenzie ate came right back up.

As soon as the baby was placed in her care, Susan recorded—and reported to the doctors and to me—that Mackenzie's heart rate and blood pressure were erratic, sometimes fluctuating dramatically. But as long as Mackenzie nestled in my arms, her heartbeat and blood pressure were stable.

The peace I felt when I held my daughter the first time lasted long after Susan took Mackenzie back to the NICU and I could no longer feel the baby's warmth in my arms. It continued even though doctors warned that the child's prognosis was not good.

She's going to have permanent brain damage.

She's going to be permanently developmentally delayed.

She's not going to make it.

But I knew better. I was certain Mackenzie would be fine. So was Mom. Both of us were realists, of course. We knew it was going to be a long, hard fight, but Mom and I had been in long, hard fights before.

I knew the naysayers predicting gloom and doom had no idea how tough my daughter was.

"She'll show you," I thought. "She's a piece of me. She'll fight. She'll make liars of you all."

Susan brought Mackenzie to me daily as long as I was running a fever and unable to visit the baby in the NICU. As soon as my fever broke, Jamey and I spent as much time with Mackenzie as the hospital would allow. For each visit, we had to put sterile suits over our clothing—gowns, gloves, and masks—like the suit I had worn when I hid in the playroom closet waiting for Tony so many years before.

I was hospitalized for a month, recovering from the cesarean section and the repair surgery. When I was released, Mackenzie was still hospitalized. The baby was not growing. In fact, she was getting smaller, not bigger, and doctors were trying one medication after another to deal with the problem, though they didn't know for sure what the problem was.

Mackenzie's pediatrician, Dr. Wendy Daily, checked on the child every day, without fail. The neonatal doctors gave the baby steroid injections directly into her heart to close the holes, and the medication worked. Gradually Mackenzie's lungs matured. She was off the ventilator in a couple of months. Slowly, she was inching toward improvement except in one vital area: She couldn't keep food down. If the medical team couldn't find a solution for that problem, none of the rest of it would matter. Mackenzie would starve to death.

After the baby's weight fell below two pounds, her doctors gathered to compare notes and come up with a Plan B. Obviously, Plan A wasn't getting the job done. Dr. Daily, Mackenzie's surgeon, Dr. Sheldon Bond, and Dr. Donna Volk, a gastroenterologist, discussed the baby's condition for hours and determined that the baby needed surgery. They theorized that Mackenzie's esophagus must be so premature that it was not closing properly after she ate, that it was too large at the bottom and too small at the top. When Mackenzie was four months old, they performed a surgery to correct the problem.

Now Mackenzie could retain food. She could absorb nutrients. She could gain weight. She could . . .

She could have done a lot of things after the surgery if she hadn't caught an infection called RSV, an airborne respiratory virus. The infection is fatal in 80 percent of the babies who catch it. And Mackenzie was so little, so weak.

It should have been such a scary time for me and my family. And we were concerned. But there was that peace . . . By that time, Mackenzie had become a real person. She had started smiling and cooing. She recognized her mother and father and grandmother. I told one of the baby's doctors, "We've bonded with this little chick and she's not going anywhere."

Slowly, Mackenzie got better. She had to be fed through a feeding tube directly into her stomach. She spent so long without eating that she lost the ability to suck and couldn't be fed with a bottle. She didn't eat food like a normal child until she was three years old.

Once she had kicked the infection, Mackenzie was transferred from the NICU to a private room on a ward. That meant I could stay with her. And I did—24/7. I didn't even leave the baby's room to go to the hospital cafeteria. I lived on McDonald's cheeseburgers and Domino's pizzas!

Mackenzie's first Thanksgiving was spent in the hospital. Her first Christmas was spent in the hospital. Her first New Year's was spent in the hospital. Mackenzie and I spent all day, every day in an 8'×12' room. Our only relief was cruising the hospital hallways with Mackenzie propped up on pillows in a Radio Flyer red wagon with wooden side rails. The hospital offered no privacy. Nurses were in and out at all hours of the night checking the baby's temperature and blood pressure. I didn't get a good night's sleep for almost a year.

After eight and a half months in the hospital, Mackenzie finally hit the magic number. She weighed five pounds. She could go home. So I took my baby to the little farmhouse near Chaplin. But things were not good on the home front. The months had pulled Jamey and me further and further apart. Jamey had spent his days working and taking care of the farm; I had spent every day and every night at the hospital. Our marriage was in trouble.

The strain of caring for a sick baby at home added even more stress to our relationship. Mackenzie had sleep apnea. Sometimes when she went to sleep, she stopped breathing. She wore a monitor that sounded an alarm when her breathing stopped, and I had to leap out of bed three and four times a night when the alarm sounded. Nobody in the family was getting any rest. Nerves frayed; tempers flared. I had to take Mackenzie back and forth to the hospital for one thing after another, week after week, and it was an hour's drive.

Finally, I decided to take Mackenzie and move in with my parents in Louisville. Mom would be there to help with the baby, and I could finally get some rest. Of course, that wasn't the only reason for the move and everybody knew it.

Before Mackenzie's first birthday, Jamey and I filed for divorce.

FIFTEEN

Mackenzie and I lived in the basement of Mom and Jim's house in Louisville for the first two years after Jamey and I divorced. They were tough years. I had been body slammed before, but this time was different.

In the past, the tragedies in my life had been out of my control. I hadn't chosen to be crushed under a car tire. I didn't put a checkmark beside "undergo 187 surgeries" or "die on the table half a dozen times," or "be molested" or "birth a dead baby" as my choices from the Experiences I'd Like to Have Before I Turn Thirty list.

But I had chosen marriage. I had picked Jamey. I had tried as hard as I could to make it work, and the very best I had to offer wasn't good enough. I had bombed at the most important thing

I'd ever decided to do. I had left my dream behind on a small farm in central Kentucky. I had left my horses—right outside my back door, there to ride whenever I wanted. I had left my vision of what my life was supposed to be. I was supposed to get married, have children, take care of my family, and raise horses. It was supposed to work out. Happily ever after.

Only it didn't.

No matter how many times the circumstances in my life slugged me in the jaw, I had always staggered to my feet convinced that "next time" it would be different. Next time, the surgery would succeed and I really would be normal, regular, just like everybody else. Next time, I'd go back to school and not blow through ten maxipads and a change of clothes before lunchtime. Next time would be the last time I ever had to count backward from one hundred.

For much of my life, I had lived for next time.

This time there would be no next time.

I had tried, I had failed, and I wouldn't get a do-over. My marriage was gone. I had swung with all my might and missed the ball. Game over.

Now what?

I didn't know the answer to that question, but I knew who did. I knew who would take care of me and keep me going while I sorted out the pieces of the tattered fabric of my life. As always, I found comfort in God's strength. But this time, I went looking for more than that. For the first time in my life, I searched for direction in his sovereignty. What did God want me to do now? What was his will for my life? I hadn't exactly done a spectacular job of charting my own course. What was God's plan?

And I knew he had a plan. Certainly, nobody would ever have mistaken me for a Bible scholar, but I knew the promise in the book of Jeremiah in the Old Testament, and I clung to it and the light of hope it shone into my darkness.

"For I know the plans I have for you, declares the Lord. Plans to prosper you and not to harm you. Plans to give you hope and a future" (Jeremiah 29:11, NIV).

God had a future out there for me somewhere. And I'd just have to hang tough until he was ready to show me what it was.

For the short term at least, I had plenty to do just figuring out the present. It was as tangled up as last year's Christmas tree lights. The biggest knot was Jamey's visitation rights with Mackenzie.

The issue was geography. Jamey lived on the farm. In my mind, the farm wasn't just a fifty-minute drive from Louisville. It was a fifty-minute *ambulance* ride from Louisville. And an ambulance an hour away was no ambulance at all if Mackenzie needed emergency attention. I was terrified every time Jamey took her with him to Chaplin. It had nothing to do with trusting his care, and everything to do with my hard-earned understanding of health issues. I knew what was a crisis and what wasn't. I had taken a pediatric CPR class. Our baby had a boatload of special needs that would be a challenge for any parent.

For one thing, a feeding tube was Mackenzie's only source of nutrition. She couldn't eat solid food, couldn't even drink liquids. She got no nourishment at all by mouth until she was three years old. She had missed a critical developmental stage as an infant. When a baby is supposed to learn to suck, she didn't, and it's not a skill that can be taught later on. Though the immature esophagus that caused her to vomit everything she ate had been surgically repaired, the tissue inside it was so tender it bled when food passed through it. So doctors had to go around it, inserting a tube into Mackenzie's side so she could be fed directly into her stomach.

In the beginning, she was fed through the tube around the clock. When she began to crawl, she wore a little backpack with a container of formula, so it could drain directly into her stomach 24/7. And for a year, she remained on a heart monitor and a sleep apnea monitor.

That was a lot of medical equipment for anybody to handle, and the farm was too far from help if Mackenzie had a problem. I didn't think it was safe for her to visit her father—unless I went with her. Sort of.

For almost two years, I spent every other weekend in the home of my former neighbors in Chaplin. Staying there, I was right down the road if my daughter needed assistance, day or night. And Jamey sometimes called and asked for my help. There was animosity between the two of us to be sure, but we could always agree on Mackenzie: We both loved her and wanted what was best for her.

Eventually, Mackenzie's health improved and I was able to go back to work. I had been a unit secretary at Frazier Rehab, but had to quit when I was hospitalized before Mackenzie's birth. Now, I was a single mother with a child to support, and I began scouring the classifieds in the local newspaper. I quickly found a position that sounded interesting, went for a job interview, and was hired on the spot.

The next week, I went to work as a headhunter. Not the aborigine-with-a-spear kind; the employment-firm-with-a-job kind. I worked for a company that located attorneys, law clerks, and legal secretaries to fill vacancies in local firms. The job was a good fit for me. I was personable and relational, I knew a lot of people, and my sister, Rebel, was an attorney. I also was well acquainted with the medical community, and the firm wanted to expand into health-related services, too.

What made the position an even better fit was my relationship with the owner of the company, Susan Woods. She and her husband, Gary, were a Christian couple who went out of their way to be kind and supportive. Though it was a small firm, the company provided good health insurance. Unfortunately, providing medical benefits to me was pouring money down a mine shaft, and my employers took it on the chin when I ran up soaring medical bills. Even so, the couple always made certain I remained employed—and insured—even if Susan's assistant, Donna, had to bring me a computer so I could work at home.

Donna and I shared a great passion—horses. Donna owned several and she invited me to ride with her often. It seemed to me that God always gave me horses during the darkest times of my life to grant me peace and to help me heal.

I needed healing emotionally and spiritually. Soon, I needed it physically, too.

I hadn't been working at the job long when I was rushed to the hospital for emergency surgery to repair a bowel obstruction. I remained hospitalized for one hundred days. The incision had to heal from the inside out, and I suffered excruciating pain—weeks and weeks of it that maximum doses of morphine and Dilaudid couldn't relieve. Friends and family members kept round-the-clock vigils in my room. Susan and Gary, Donna and her husband, Craig, Aunt Laura and my cousin Rachel took turns staying with me.

For the first time in my life, Mom couldn't care for me. Her MS had worsened. The fatigue was so debilitating that she wasn't physically able to help.

"Take care of my baby for me," Mom told the others tearfully. "Take care of my baby."

When I was released from the hospital, I went home, to my own home. In 1997, Mackenzie and I had moved out of my parents' basement and taken a 700-square-foot apartment in Okolona, the suburb of Louisville where Jamey and I had lived when we first married. The place was tiny—I joked that I didn't even have enough room to change my mind. But it was perfect for a single mom and a little girl. The man who owned it, J. W. Compton, was a member of my church, and when I couldn't scrape together rent money some months because of my medical bills, he pretended there wasn't any rent to pay. He was one of the ways God looked after me.

There were other ways, too.

In fact, as I learned to depend on God and trust that he would take care of me, I marveled at the "coincidences"—I called them "Godincidences"—that provided just what I needed just when I needed it.

I had no furniture to speak of when I moved into the apartment—just Mackenzie's bed, a burgundy loveseat and rocker I got from Grandmother, and a bed I purchased at a yard sale. My tiny television rested on a TV tray in the living room. The first Christmas we lived in the little apartment, I had no money to buy presents, or anything else for that matter. All I could manage was a scraggly little tree with a handful of decorations and one string of lights that went instantly dark as soon as I plugged them in. When I stood back to survey my work after I decorated the tree, I knew I had seen it before. I had Charlie Brown's Christmas tree.

But that was okay. I had Mackenzie and my own place, and the rest was icing. For the first time in my life, I really understood what "peace on Earth" meant, at least what it meant to me.

When Mackenzie asked me, "Mommy, what's Christmas?" I answered the two-and-a-half-year-old as simply as I could, and then realized I'd said everything that needed to be said.

"Christmas," I told the towheaded little girl with the wide brown eyes, "means that God's here, and he's on our side."

A few days later, I heard a knock at the door, and opened it to find a rosy-cheeked J. W. Compton, his breath frosting, stomping his feet to keep the circulation going. He was grinning so wide I was afraid the corners of his smile might meet behind his ears and the top of his head would fall off.

"Merry Christmas!" was all he had time to say before he had to jump out of the way so the two men behind him carrying a couch wouldn't mow him down.

I stared gap-jawed as Steve and Jerry Sample maneuvered a beautiful black and tan sofa carefully through my front door and sat it down in the little living room.

"But . . . what?" was all I could manage before the men went back out to the U-Haul parked out front and carried in a matching chair and footstool. Then they went back out and brought in even more stuff.

Mackenzie squealed with delight!

"Look, Mommy!" she cried. "Look at the pres-nents!"

Indeed, there were pres-nents to look at—bright packages wrapped in paper with shiny Santa Claus faces, snowmen, and Christmas trees, with big, colorful bows on top. There were boxes almost as big as Mackenzie. And there were smaller boxes, too. Boxes only big enough to hold a food card so I could buy some groceries. Or a gasoline card so I could put gas in my rattledy-bang old car.

There was a winter coat for Mackenzie. Shoes. Clothes.

And there were lamps, pictures, and candles, too.

Tears welled up in my eyes and I scooped my tiny daughter up into my arms and gave her a gigantic hug.

When the men were finally finished unloading the truck, they refused to hang around for protracted thank-yous.

"Tell these fine gentlemen, 'Merry Christmas,' Kenzie," I said, the lump in my throat making it hard to talk.

"Merry Tris'mas!"

I locked eyes with J. W. standing in the doorway. He nodded slightly.

"Happy birthday, Jesus," he said, and then the three men vanished into the night like the wise men who had left presents for the Christ child 2,000 years before.

. . .

Not long after Christmas, I learned that The Legal Edge was about to be sold, and I went looking for another job. I landed one with a nonprofit agency, and became the district director for an organization that raised research funding for fifty neuromuscular diseases.

And suddenly I didn't just have a job; I had a career. The position was like a suit that had been measured, cut out, and sewn to fit me perfectly. I was working with sick kids, conducting support groups for their families, and using my relational gifts to increase donations to the research charities. The agency's budget was $417,000 when I started; a year later it was more than $1 million.

Finally, I was earning a good salary. But I was also working sixty hours a week. My assistant, Willa, even brought work to me when I was hospitalized, which I was time and time again.

The job consisted of nonstop fund-raising. The flagship fund-raising event was an annual twenty-four-hour telethon on the local television stations. I managed it for several years—arranging entertainment, speakers, volunteers to man the phone lines, setting up the stage area and tearing it all down when the telethon was over.

I also raised money by hauling upstanding citizens off to jail, using real officers from the Jefferson County Sheriff's Department. The strategy was simple. Sheriff's deputies showed up at the offices of Louisville attorneys, insurance agents, real estate brokers, car dealers, school principals—even university presidents—and "arrested" them. The "criminals" were handcuffed, put into squad cars, and taken to "jail," which was an area in some public building where my crew and I had constructed a holding cell—complete with bars. The inmates had to remain in the cell for one hour, during which they phoned all their friends and urged them to make donations to bail them out.

It was during one of the lockups that I met a police officer named Bobby. He wasn't the first man I had dated since my divorce, but Bobby wasn't like any man I had ever known. He built up my self-esteem, made me feel pretty and desirable—for the first time in so long I had to haul the feelings out of a dark closet and blow the dust off them. We dated for six months, and then I was hospitalized for an emergency surgery. When I was released from the hospital three weeks later, Bobby had decided we would be better off "just friends."

Bobby was honest. He told me he couldn't handle my medical issues, and he wasn't ready to be a stepdad. I was stunned. Heartsick, I poured out my pain and disillusionment to my aunt Laura.

"How will I ever find somebody to love me?" I cried. "I don't just have to sell myself—with all my medical problems. I have to sell Mackenzie, too. We're a package deal. Maybe there's not a man out there who can handle everything I bring to the party."

And I brought a whole lot more than Fritos and bean dip.

Fact: At any given moment something could malfunction in my mangled internal organs and I could require immediate emergency surgery.

Fact: I would need repeated surgeries for the rest of my life.

Fact: My medical debt was more than three quarters of a million dollars and going nowhere but up.

Fact: I had massive scars and a permanent urostomy.

I had run up the white flag of surrender on the urostomy when I was twenty-six. Of all the surgeries I had undergone in the two decades after the accident, more than half were an effort to avoid a permanent pee bag.

Over the years, I was willing to undergo any procedure any doctor anywhere could devise to rebuild my destroyed urinary system so I wouldn't require a bag. I had spent my childhood incontinent, constantly wetting myself, smelling like urine, going through ten, twelve, fourteen maxipads a day all because I was determined to be normal, to be "regular." And a regular girl didn't have a tube permanently inserted into her side draining pee down a clear plastic tube into a bag.

In 1994, I finally ran out of options.

I had tried everything. Every surgery. Every procedure. Every creative plan devised by the best minds in urological surgery in the country. And none of them worked.

My surgeon, Dr. Tony Casale, sat me down and spelled it out for me.

"Heather, a urostomy is the only way you're ever going to be dry," he said. "It's the only way."

So I had agreed to a urostomy. When I woke up from surgery, I refused to look at my new "permanent appendage." I refused to touch it or clean it. I went into a funk that lasted for months, until a friend from church came to visit me, unzipped his pants, and showed me his colostomy, the result of a perforated bowel.

His name was Kenny Wilburn.

"You'll get used to the tube and bag," he said. "If I can, you can."

He told me that his wife loved him just as much after the colostomy as before.

"Heather, any man worth having loves your insides, not your outsides," he said.

So I had coped. I'd adjusted. But now, as a single woman, all the old self-image and self-esteem issues reared their ugly heads again, and it took several months after my breakup with Bobby for me to get my emotional footing back under me.

But I was finally beginning to come around. There was bounce in my step and a light back in my 1,000-watt smile. Then, one morning after I had worked late at a charity event for the agency, my whole abdominal wall collapsed and I was rushed to the hospital for emergency surgery.

I had pushed too hard. I had ignored my limitations, and now I was paying the price. Organizing and running fund-raisers was hard work. It required lifting and hauling, unloading folding chairs and tables, and loading heavy boxes and decorations. I never should have done those things, and I knew it. I wasn't supposed to lift anything heavier than a gallon of milk. But I loved my job and I refused to listen to what my body was telling me until it yelled so loud I couldn't ignore it anymore.

When I recovered, I had to shake hands with a grim reality. If I wanted to live long enough to raise Mackenzie, I would have to take better care of myself. That surgery was a wakeup call. I would not survive another abdominal collapse. Like it or not, my working days were over. Reluctantly, I applied for disability through the Social Security Administration.

I was approved, and my income plummeted from $40,000 a year to $15,800. The annual cost of my medications and ostomy supplies alone was more than $7,000. My financial ship started taking on water way faster than I could bail it out. That's when God sent out another life raft. His name was Phil Campbell.

Phil owned the Harley-Davidson dealership in Louisville. I had called on him when I worked for the agency, but he had seen too many fund-raisers come and go over the years. He told me that if I was still around in six months, he'd talk to me then—not before. Six months to the day later, I walked into his dealership with six colored balloons.

Phil adopted my whole family. Mackenzie called him Papaw Phil.

In 2002, Phil and some of my other friends—Vicki, Susan, Lee, Caroline, Beverly, Kenny, and Mike—organized a benefit dance for me. Kye Cohain, who owned two huge reception halls across the Ohio River from Louisville in southern Indiana, donated use of one of the facilities. A band donated music. Merchants and friends donated items for a silent auction: trips, jewelry, golf equipment, sports memorabilia. More than 600 people bought tickets, and when the dust had settled after the auction, organizers presented me a check for $20,000.

But the fund-raiser gave me something far more precious than a check. It gave me hope. Seeing hundreds of people, friends, family, and total strangers band together to help sent me a powerful message—I mattered!

The money from the dance provided me a few months' breathing room. It was the last time I would ever feel financially secure.

SIXTEEN

He'd only known me a little over a week, but he'd already figured out there was absolutely no telling what I might say or do. That was part of the charm, the allure. He'd have bet a hundred bucks I couldn't surprise him—and he'd have kissed five twenty-dollar bills good-bye.

Oh, he knew I'd been in some kind of accident as a kid, got hurt really bad. But to look at me, you'd never know it. I looked fine. In his eyes, I looked *mighty* fine! I looked beautiful.

And then, out of the blue, I showed him scars, a tangled mass of white lines and puffy flesh that reminded him—he couldn't help it—of a road map of West Virginia. He didn't say that, of course. He knew I definitely wasn't in the mood for humor.

In fact, he knew exactly how important his response was. He

knew I had bared more than my belly, more than my scars. I had bared my soul. How he handled that precious gift of vulnerability would color every day of the rest of my life. And maybe his life, too.

He didn't know what to say. But whatever it was, it had better be good.

. . .

DeWayne spotted me the moment I walked into the wedding reception. I was wearing a sheer white blouse and silky black pants, and my long, black hair made me stand out. But it was my face—and my figure—that riveted his attention. He thought I was just about the most beautiful woman he had ever seen. He couldn't take his eyes off me, and when he got the chance, he made certain I knew he was interested. He didn't waste time being subtle.

As I stood talking to some friends, DeWayne sauntered by me, stopped, pulled his wraparound sunglasses down on his nose, and checked me out.

I laughed, a little embarrassed, but flattered, too. Though I didn't stare at him quite so boldly, the instant attraction went both ways. I saw enough in a casual glance to know that the big man with the boyish smile possessed the two characteristics I liked most in a man—tall and tall. Even at five feet, eight inches in my bare feet—and I wasn't in my bare feet—I was looking up at him. That was a good thing.

I turned to my cousin Rachel and asked who he was.

"Oh, that's DeWayne Bland," Rachel said. Then she saw the gleam in my eyes. "You be careful," she said. "He's a player."

Translate that: He's a guy who goes through women faster than a Little League team goes through snow cones. That assessment didn't put me off. On the contrary, it intrigued me. I knew I could handle myself with a player. Well, I was pretty sure I could handle myself. Actually, come to think of it, I wasn't sure at all that I could handle myself, but I didn't have a chance to ponder how well armed I might or might not be for the battle of the sexes because suddenly he was standing beside me.

"Hi, my name's DeWayne," he said. "And I know I've never seen you before. I'd remember."

"I'm Heather."

"Would you like to dance?"

I nodded, sat my punch glass down on a nearby table, and allowed the big man to fold me into his arms. I fit perfectly there.

When that dance was over, we danced the next. And the next.

Then we sat and talked. I told DeWayne about my childhood; he told me about his. His parents, Joe and Virginia, were from Marion County, in central Kentucky. His father had been a game warden and taught him to hunt and fish and love the outdoors. He was the family's "wild child," he said, the only boy, with three sisters. We talked about DeWayne's job as a truck driver, about the University of Kentucky basketball team, and country music, about our lives and our vision for the future.

I didn't tell DeWayne about the accident or about all the pain in my life that followed it. I wasn't ashamed of it, or embarrassed by it. But I felt a sudden need to be normal—or at least to look it for the time being. I wanted to be like any other young woman who'd just met a man who lit a fire in her heart. I wanted to be regular, without all the baggage my past had saddled me with. Just for a little while.

When I introduced DeWayne to Mackenzie, she asked him to dance. The little blonde girl and the tall, handsome man made quite a pair on the dance floor. I sat alone at my table watching them, tickled by the expression of studied concentration on Kenzie's face—she wanted to get all the steps just right—and the look of relaxed good humor on DeWayne's.

"He likes kids . . ." I said softly, my words swallowed up by the blaring music. Then I completed my thought in my head, where no one else could hear: ". . . and I like him."

I was in DeWayne's arms as the band played the final song of the evening. When the music stopped, he held me there for a moment, a beat or two in the silence, before he released me. Then he asked if I'd like to go to dinner and a movie with him the following night. I said yes.

. . .

We ate at Dillon's Steakhouse, then saw *Hollywood Homicide.* Well, *Hollywood Homicide* was on the screen. It's debatable how much of it I actually saw. It was hard to concentrate with an alarm going off in my head.

This was not good.

The bond, the connection I was feeling to the man sitting beside me crunching popcorn in the darkness, had sprung up quicker than dandelions after a spring rain. And that was definitely not a good thing.

I was doing fine alone. It had taken years as a single parent, years of maturing spiritually, but finally I had grown into an awareness that I didn't need a man in my life. I would like to have one, sure. But I didn't need one. And the difference between wanting and needing was huge.

Mackenzie and I were living rich, full lives all by ourselves. I felt closer to God than I'd ever felt in my life, and that peace filled up my whole soul. I knew that no matter how far down a dark hole I might sink, God would meet me there. Eight years on my own had taught me that.

So why set myself up to get my heart broken? I absolutely did not need the hassle of falling for some guy who would hit the door as soon as some part of the plumbing in my belly broke down. I knew it would, and I knew he would. So why get into a relationship that would only cause me pain?

Still . . . he was so cute! And we had so much in common. We laughed easily and often. He . . . well, for lack of a better word, DeWayne felt safe. It was like I had known him my whole life.

When he walked me to the door after the movie, he asked me for another date. Then he kissed me good night.

That's when I knew I was in serious, serious trouble. The fireworks that kiss set off in my heart lit up the sky all the way from my front porch to the Tennessee border.

. . .

We dated every night after that, and the tension inside me grew daily. Finally, I could stand it no longer. One evening, when we were watching television in my living room, I excused myself and went upstairs to my bedroom, where I sat down on the bed and called my closest friend, Vicki DeWitt.

"I'm in trouble," I told Vicki miserably. "I am totally in trouble. I'm falling for this guy big-time, but he doesn't know a thing about me—about, you know, all the medical stuff. The surgeries, the bag, the medical debt."

"Then tell him," Vicki said.

"What do you mean, 'tell him'?"

"How many things can 'tell him' mean?"

"Funny. Very funny," I said, though I failed to see any humor in the remark.

"Come on, you know what I'm saying. Go down there and tell him about yourself."

"Just like that? Just, '. . . So, DeWayne, would you like another soft drink, and by the way, I've been split open from stem to stern 187 times, I have a permanent pee bag taped to my side, and a million dollars in medical debt . . . and do you want Pepsi or Mountain Dew?' "

"Funny. Very funny," Vicki said.

"I can't just waltz in and dump all that on him! What if he can't handle it? What if he leaves?"

"What if he does? Come on, Heather. If he can't handle all that's happened to you, he's not the right guy. He can't possibly be part of God's plan for your life if he can't deal with the pain in your past. You're a whole lot better off finding out one way or the other right now, before you're really nuts about him."

"I'm already really nuts about him. That's the problem. But I hear you. The longer I wait, the harder it's going to be. I can't keep putting it off. I have to tell him . . . now . . . right now. Pray for me, Vicki."

I hung up the phone and sat there on my bed, my heart pounding like a snare drum in a marching band. What would he do? What would he say? What would I do if he bailed? So I prayed—brief and to the point. "Father God, I like this man. I like him a lot. I think I might even love him. Well, okay, I guess I do love him. I didn't plan for this to happen, but here it is and I've got to deal with it. Help me do this. And help me suck it up and go on if he walks out the door when I'm finished."

I took a deep breath, opened my bedroom door, and went down the stairs. DeWayne looked up and smiled at me when I entered the room. His smile turned quizzical though, when I walked over to the television and turned it off, crossed to the couch were he was sitting, and just stood there in front of him.

"I have something to show you," I said.

I pulled my jeans down just far enough so he could see the tangled mass of scars on my belly and the bag on my side. I turned slowly around to show him the scars on my hips, back, and legs, then poured out the whole story in one long stream. Well, the high points anyway. The accident. The surgeries.

"I've been operated on more than 180 times, and it's not over. It'll never be over. I'll always have to have surgeries. The bag is permanent, too; it won't ever go away. And I owe more than a million dollars in medical debt."

He listened, but didn't say a word.

"DeWayne, I have a major crush on you," I said. "If you can't deal with all of this, I understand. You won't be the first person in my life who couldn't. But I have to know—now. If you can't handle it, I want you to leave, just don't be here when I come back downstairs."

I turned without a word and went back upstairs—and called Vicki.

"What did he say?" Vicki asked.

"He didn't say anything. He just sat there and let me do all the talking. I don't know what that means."

"Heather, you always do all the talking. It doesn't mean anything at all. How did he react?"

"I don't know," I said. "I really don't know."

"Then go back down there and find out."

I hung up the phone and took another deep breath. I opened my bedroom door and started down the stairs, praying on every step, "Lord, if he's not there, help me deal with it . . . If he's not there, help me deal with . . ."

DeWayne was still sitting on the couch. But he had taken his shoes off and had his feet propped up on the coffee table. He had the remote in his hand and he was channel surfing.

"DeWayne . . ." I said tentatively. I went to the couch and stood in front of him again. "Are you sure . . . ?" I didn't finish the sentence. I didn't need to. We both knew what I was talking about.

"Those scars and that bag, they're what give you your heart, baby," he said. "You're beautiful. And you're even more beautiful on the inside. I've been looking for you my whole life."

I started to cry.

"Don't cry," DeWayne said, alarmed. He always felt awkward and tongue-tied when a woman cried. "At least . . . can you wait until a commercial? I just found a fishing tournament on the Outdoorsman Channel."

I smiled. He knew I would.

"Here, sit down by me," he said, moving over to make room for me on the couch. Then, out of nowhere: "I love you, you know. I'm going to marry you."

The look of stunned surprise on my face must have been comical because DeWayne's grin widened.

"Oh, don't worry. You don't have to say anything right now. One of these days I'm going to ask you to marry me. And when I do, I'll keep asking until you say yes."

. . .

A week later, I was rushed to the hospital for emergency surgery to remove a bowel obstruction. The surgery was serious. DeWayne paced the floor in the waiting room for hours, and was waiting in my room when I was wheeled in from recovery. He didn't leave for a week.

All day and all night for seven days, DeWayne cared for me, taking a week off from work without pay to stay with me. Friends brought him clothes, and he caught a little sleep here and there in a recliner in my room. The chair clearly had been constructed for a person a foot shorter and seventy-five pounds lighter than he was.

In the beginning of my twenty-nine-day hospital stay, I was in serious condition. I could not get out of bed even to go to the bathroom. DeWayne took care of me, helping me onto a bedpan, holding my hair back out of my face when I vomited, spoon-feeding me soup, and urging me to take "just one more bite" to help me get my strength back.

When I was feeling better, DeWayne went back to work, but he still spent every night at the hospital. As soon as his shift was over, he clocked out, went home, showered, gathered up a change of clothing, and headed to my room. He picked up some dinner on the way—usually a pizza or something else he could share with me once I could eat regular food. He stayed in my room until it was time to go back to work the next morning. We watched television and movies together, and played games. But mostly, we just talked, way into the night, sharing our lives and our hearts, our hopes, our dreams, and our pain.

The day I was released from the hospital, DeWayne was there to take me home and get me settled. He carried my belongings into my townhouse, put them away in my bedroom, and made sure I was comfortable. Then he went downstairs to confirm that I had plenty of food in the cabinets and the refrigerator before he left.

Alone in my bedroom, it suddenly occurred to me that the man who had been at my side every night for a month would no longer be there to talk to if I woke up frightened in the midnight dark. He was going home. The intensity of my sense of loss surprised me. It wasn't that I couldn't manage on my own. I'd be fine. But I wanted him there!

When he came up to my bedroom to tell me good-bye, he found me crying.

"What's the matter, baby?" he asked.

"You're leaving," I said, sniffling.

"I have to go home now. I wish I didn't, but I have to." He took me in his arms and kissed the tears off my cheeks. "You know, I wouldn't have to go home if you'd marry me."

DeWayne had asked me to marry him so many times it had become a joke between us. That's why he was totally unprepared for my response.

"Okay," I said.

"Okay what?

"Okay, I'll marry you."

"Do you mean it?"

"Yes, I mean it." And I did. I meant it. For the first time since the night I had shown DeWayne my scars and bag, I finally let go and allowed myself to believe. To believe that I was lovable, and that this great big adorable man genuinely thought I was the most beautiful woman he'd ever seen. I had found my soul mate.

"When?" he asked.

"You tell me."

"How about right now?"

"We can't get married right now—it's Sunday."

"Okay, how about tomorrow then?" DeWayne had known he loved me the first time he took me into his arms and we danced at the wedding, a two-month lifetime ago. He had been asking me to marry him almost daily ever since, and he didn't want to give me a chance to change my mind.

"Well, I don't know. Can you get a license that fast? And what about our families?" I asked. Then I called my mother.

"Mom, DeWayne and I are getting married next week," I said.

Mom wasn't surprised. She had known from the very

beginning that DeWayne was my gift from God. And her response didn't surprise me. We knew each other so well, had been through so much together. I could almost have predicted what my mother would say—and how she would say it.

"Well, that's wonderful, sweetheart, but I can't possibly do it any day next week except Tuesday," Mom said. "I'm booked up every other day."

I smiled.

"Okay, Mom, Tuesday it is."

DeWayne and I were married at Waterfront Park on the banks of the Ohio River two days later. DeWayne's sister Angela stood up for him; Vicki stood up for me. DeWayne wore khaki shorts and a silk shirt; I wore a black T-shirt and a skort. It was a simple ceremony, with family and a few close friends.

Smiling down into my upturned face, DeWayne promised to love and to cherish me, "for better or for worse, for richer or for poorer, in sickness and in health, as long as we both shall live."

He thought he understood how difficult keeping that promise might be. But he had absolutely no idea.

DeWayne made promises to Mackenzie, too. He got down on one knee and gave her a ring, a miniature version of the one he had given me. He looked deeply into her big brown eyes and promised to take care of her and be a good father. He and I would never have children together, and DeWayne wanted the gap-toothed little girl before him to understand that he intended to love her as if she were his own.

If "honeymoon" is defined as taking a trip together right after you get married, then DeWayne and I didn't have one. DeWayne had used up all his vacation time when I was in the hospital. He couldn't even have his wedding day off. We got married at noon and DeWayne went back to work at three o'clock.

But if "honeymoon" is defined as the magical time a couple has together when they have just been joined to each other in a holy union so that "the two shall become one flesh," then our honeymoon was breathtaking.

As we stood beside my bed that night, DeWayne told me in a husky voice that he wanted to take my clothes off. Before I could protest, he kissed me, and as he undressed me, he continued to kiss me, from the top of my head to the bottom of my toes. He kissed every scar on my belly, my back, my sides, and my legs. He kissed my bag. He told me over and over and over again that I was the most beautiful woman he had ever seen. He told me I was perfect.

Tears streamed down my cheeks. DeWayne kissed the tears away, but I couldn't stop crying. Something long frozen inside me was beginning to thaw. For the first time in my life, I knew with absolute certainty that I was not only lovable but loved. The magnitude of that discovery melted the protective shell I had built around my heart. It had shielded me from feeling the pain Mr. Jennings inflicted upon me. It had shielded me from feeling the rejection I expected from any man who saw me, really saw me, saw how disfigured and damaged and ugly I was.

But DeWayne didn't see my image of myself; he saw the woman he loved, his wife, standing naked before him—vulnerable, open, and receptive for the first time in her life. He held the treasure of that vulnerability as tenderly as he held me, and as he made wildly passionate love to me, I felt like a woman, a beautiful, desirable woman, for the first time in my life.

Our first weeks together were a blur of joy. I remembered my parents dancing with no music on, how I would walk into a room when I was a kid and Jim would be holding Mom in his arms, the two of them dancing to the rhythm of nothing but their own heartbeats. That's true love, I always thought. That's being married to your best friend. I never dreamed I would ever find that kind of love in my own life. Now, DeWayne came up behind me while I was doing dishes and took me into his arms and waltzed me across the kitchen floor. He knew what that act symbolized for me, and he wanted me to know he was every bit as much in love with me as Jim had ever been with Mom.

I had never been so happy. Maybe that's why it took me so long to notice that I was running a fever. It was odd. I couldn't seem to shake it and I didn't know what was wrong.

Along with the fever, there was unexplained abdominal

pain. It came and went, but when it was there it was excruciating. The symptoms had appeared a month or so before I met DeWayne. Oh, I'd had abdominal pain before. I lived with it every day of my life. But this pain was different somehow, and I couldn't quite put my finger on how. It was just . . . different. And as the weeks passed, it didn't go away. It didn't get better. It got worse.

SEVENTEEN

I sat in my Jeep watching the cardinal perched on a tree limb outside my window. The bird was looking at me, too, cocking its head to the side in that herky-jerky way birds move. I decided I didn't like any creature that looked at me with only one eye at a time, so I made a sudden movement and the bird fluttered away.

My cell phone rang. It was Tracy.

I listened, then asked a single question.

"How bad is not good?"

Tracy responded. I thanked her, pushed the button with the little red telephone symbol on it, and sat staring into space, not seeing the birds or the squirrels or the people hurrying past me on the sidewalk, people with places to go and lives to live.

"I'm sick," I said softly, speaking the words out loud to give them substance, to make them real. "I'm dying. I'll be dead in three months."

. . .

I didn't know when it happened. I'd had three surgeries within a six-month period in 2002 and 2003, so there was no way to tell for sure. But during one of those surgeries, I had contracted a deadly staph infection that spread through my internal organs like termites swarming through a woodpile.

It was a long time before I found out what was happening to me. The infection went undiagnosed, then misdiagnosed, then treated with all kinds of the wrong drugs.

By the time it was finally clear what was causing the symptoms attributed to everything from kidney stones to my imagination, the doctors told me it was too late to do anything about it. I had finally met my match, they said. I may have amazed and confounded surgeons for three decades, but the voracious virus chewing its way through my belly would do to me what the front tire of a Dodge Charger had failed to do. It would kill me.

It started with a fever I couldn't shake. Chronic fever that sometimes spiked up to 103° and seldom dropped below 100°. I suffered through bouts of nausea that left me unable to keep food down for days at a time. The pain was the worst part. I lived with chronic pain. I understood it; pain was an old, old friend. But the excruciating pain that unexpectedly stabbed like a sword into my abdomen bent me double in agony and sent me yo-yoing in and out of emergency rooms.

I couldn't go for answers to the doctors I loved and trusted, the ones who had cared for me since I was a child. After I left the nonprofit agency and went on disability, I had scratched together the money to pay for my health insurance under COBRA. But the medical insurance coverage expired after eighteen months.

Without private insurance, the only medical care available to me was in a whole new world, a world I hardly knew existed—the world of free clinics.

Every hospital in Louisville had one. They were manned by a merry-go-round of doctors, foreign doctors with accents so thick it was almost impossible to understand what they were saying, and dozens of local doctors donating three hours a month of their time to care for people with no health insurance.

I made one appointment after another at the free clinics, trying to find somebody who could tell me what was wrong with me—and do something about it. I would show up for my appointment on time, and then wait two, three, four hours to see the doctor. Sometimes the doctors had emergencies that delayed them. Sometimes they got caught in surgery. Sometimes there was only one doctor to see all fifty of the people with appointments and all the walk-in patients off the street as well.

Waiting along with me was a cross section of society. Hallucinating alcoholics and junkies with lice in their hair and crack up their noses. Homeless people in ragged clothes sitting beside college students whose ragged clothes were a fashion statement. Young couples, old people, and middle-class people whose private insurance ended when their COBRA ran out. There was also a large contingent of illegal aliens who could neither speak, write, nor understand a word of English.

When I finally got a chance to describe my symptoms to a doctor, I had to back all the way up to "and God created the Heavens and the Earth." I unloaded my whole medical history—from "my mother ran over me when I was four years old" through more than 180 surgical procedures—on every doctor I saw. I had to—because during the two years I went to free clinics, I never saw the same doctor twice.

After I went through my extensive medical history, the doctor would examine me and pronounce a diagnosis. It was never the same as the diagnosis of the doctor the week before, and the doctor the next week would be certain I was suffering from something else entirely.

One doctor determined that I had Crohn's disease. The next said I had irritable bowel syndrome. Most believed my pain was caused by some combination of kidney stones, hernias, scars, and adhesions.

One even told me I wasn't really suffering any pain at all; I was imagining it.

Certainly the kidney stones/hernias/scars/adhesions diagnoses made the most sense. I had suffered some degree of chronic pain from those ever since the accident. A mesh fabric had long ago replaced my abdominal wall. The mesh sprang leaks like the plumbing in an old house, herniating in two or three places at a time. The scar tissue and adhesions in my belly were legendary.

My abdomen had already been opened and closed more often than the front door at the Ritz-Carlton by the time I started first grade. Making an incision was like cutting into concrete. In all, surgeons had sliced into the mother of all scars that ran from my sternum to my pelvis more than seventy times. My damaged urinary system was the perfect breeding ground for kidney stones. Of course my belly hurt!

I had lived every day I could remember with abdominal pain, but I knew this was different. It didn't feel the same. I couldn't seem to convey how it was different to a new doctor every week, but it was different. I knew it. And it was getting worse.

I could do nothing to relieve the increasing agony. I couldn't take the amount of pain medication I needed for relief without being almost comatose, and I had to pick up Mackenzie from school every day. I had a life—a husband, a child, church and school functions. I couldn't fit drugged-out zombie time into my schedule.

The problem was my resistance to anesthesia and pain medication, which was as legendary as my granite belly. Mom once had back surgery, and her doctor gave her 2 mg of morphine for pain relief. She slept for twelve hours. Whenever I had surgery, my doctors started me at 18–20 mg of morphine just to take the edge off, and then they worked upward from there.

Desperate for relief from the strange new pain in my belly, I went to my pain management doctor, Dr. Dean Collis. He was the only one of my original doctors who continued to see me even though I had no private health insurance and little hope of ever paying my bill. He prescribed muscle relaxants, and different combinations of pain medications. Nothing worked.

The pain grew so severe that Dr. Collis put me into the hospital for forty-eight hours and inserted a tube into my spine with a pump that delivered morphine around the clock. It didn't help.

Then the pain, fever, and nausea were joined by a fourth symptom—rectal bleeding. Sometimes it was old, black blood. More often than not, it was bright red.

For months, I endured the unexplained symptoms. Some days were better than others. Occasionally, I went weeks when there were hardly any symptoms at all, and DeWayne and I celebrated a great first Thanksgiving and first Christmas together. But when the symptoms returned after the first of the year, they returned with a vengeance. So I made the rounds of the free clinics again. The doctors there quacked out one diagnosis after another like lost ducks in high weeds, but not a one among them had any idea where the pond was.

I was hospitalized once for routine tests and the doctor decided to call in an infectious disease specialist to take a look at me. He ordered lab work, looked at the report, and pronounced that I had a staph infection. There are forty different strains of staph, and I had one of the milder forms, he said. He gave me antibiotics, told me I'd feel better soon, and sent me home.

And I did feel better. For a while. Then the symptoms returned. I orbited in and out of the hospital, where doctors tried various combinations of antibiotics. None of them worked for very long.

By this time, almost a year after I first began experiencing symptoms, I was growing more concerned by the day. I had been around the medical block often enough to know that steadily worsening symptoms were often a one-way ticket to a toe tag.

It was an Indian doctor in a free clinic who finally named the dragon.

"You have very rare form staph infection," he told me. His accent was so thick I could barely understand what he was saying. "Only one thousand people in whole world are having it. It is not survivable."

I didn't catch everything the little man said, but I understood the last part.

"What do you mean, 'Not survivable'?" I asked.

"You are not getting better from this," he said. "Always people are trying, but no one is beating this."

"Are you saying I'm going to die?"

"Yes, that is what I am saying. I am sorry. Are you having a family?"

"Huh?" My head was spinning. Dying? I had some fatal disease and I was *dying*?

"A husband? Children?"

". . . Uh . . . yes. DeWayne and I are newlyweds, sort of. And Mackenzie, my little girl, is nine years old."

"You should be taking them and going this summer to have much fun together," he said. "Liquidate your belongings and make beautiful memories for your child . . . because you are not being here in September."

. . .

My first reaction was not fear. It was anger. I got up and marched out of the examining room. If I had stayed there another minute, I would have done some serious damage to a little Indian doctor.

What do you mean "dying?" I screamed in my head as I shoved past people in the hallway. *These doctors have told me I have every disease from gastroenteritis to post-nasal drip, and this guy thinks I'm going to believe him that I'm dying? How many times has some doctor said I was going to croak . . . and I'm still here, aren't I? I'm still here!*

Then my anger went in another direction.

I just found DeWayne! I just found my soul mate, the love of my life. I can't die now! *I can't leave Mackenzie without a mommy. And Mom needs me now. Her MS is getting worse. I can't die!*

I got to my Jeep and used my cell phone to call Tracy, a nurse I had known for years; our friendship extended way beyond the clinical.

"Tracy, have you ever heard of a staph infection that's so rare only something like a thousand people in the whole world have it?"

"Spell it."

"I don't know how to spell it," I said. "I don't even know its name. But this clinic doctor says that's what I have, that it's really, really rare . . . and it's . . . fatal."

"I'll see what I can find out and call you back," Tracy said.

Tracy called me back in five minutes.

"He's right. There is a form of staph that only a handful of people in the whole world have," Tracy said, her voice so serious and somber, I felt suddenly cold. "And if that's what you have, it's not good."

"How bad is not good?"

"Very bad."

I hung up the phone and sat still in my Jeep. Images of DeWayne and Mackenzie and my mother filled my vision.

"I'm sick. I'm dying. I'll be dead in three months."

Saying the words out loud made them real. But it didn't make them true.

"No. It's not going to happen," I thought fiercely. "I'm going to grow old with DeWayne. I'm going to dance at Mackenzie's wedding. There's got to be medicine somewhere that will beat this thing. And I'm going to find it!"

. . .

I didn't tell DeWayne right away what the doctor had told me. It was the first secret I had ever kept from him. I just couldn't bring myself to do it. I'd been sick ever since I met him! What would he say when I told him a doctor had just given me less than six months to live? Dealing with a sick—and maybe even dying—wife was not what he'd signed on for.

Would he leave when I told him?

But I couldn't keep it from him. He had a right to know, and I needed his support.

I couldn't look at him when I said it; I just stood there staring at the pattern in the rug on the living room floor. He didn't say a word at first. Then he stood up and folded me into his arms and held me tight, too tight, like he was determined to keep me safe there, out of harm's way.

"What do the doctors know?" he said into my hair. "They've been wrong before. You've beat everything else and you'll beat this, too. We'll beat this—together."

I could hear tears in his voice.

I had never expected that my future would be any different from my past. I had already undergone hundreds of surgeries. Absent God's miraculous intervention, I would likely undergo hundreds more. I constantly herniated. The mesh lining that formed my abdominal wall developed holes and had to be repaired or replaced. I produced kidney stones on a regular basis, and my urostomy would always require surgical maintenance work. I knew I would always have to deal with medical issues. For me, that was the price of admission to life, and I paid it willingly.

But I had always been *injured*; I had never been *sick*. Sick was harder. Way harder.

Tracy and I went online to find out everything we could about the latest developments in the treatment of staph infections. We discovered that Johns Hopkins University was studying an experimental medication that was demonstrating some success.

I had to pay more than $1,000 for testing, labwork, and biopsies to determine if I was a candidate for the study, which had space for 175 people. When I heard from Johns Hopkins again, they informed me that I was number 152 on their waiting list, which meant 151 people would have to die before my name made the top of the list.

I went back online and kept looking. I found an experimental drug that was being tested in Canada that looked promising, but it was outrageously expensive. Then I heard through the grapevine that a local hospital was conducting its own study of that same drug. I pulled some friendship strings in the medical community and snared a space in the study.

It was a regional study. People with staph infections came from as far away as Indianapolis, Cincinnati, and Nashville for treatments at the University of Louisville Hospital free clinic. Over time, we bumped into each other in the waiting room, hallways, treatment rooms, and bathrooms of the facility and developed friendships.

I knew just about all the people in the study eventually, but I became particularly close to two of the other staph sufferers—Caitlin and Winston.

Caitlin was a beautiful young woman in her late twenties, bubbly and cheerful. She was devoted to her husband, who accompanied her to every treatment, and to their tiny baby daughter. She had contracted staph during the emergency cesarean section that brought her little girl into the world.

Caitlin told me that she and her husband had spent everything they had on fertility treatments so she could conceive. Neither of them had good health insurance. When Caitlin got sick after her maternity leave was up, she lost her job. So they ended up at the free clinic, trying to fight Caitlin's infection with the experimental medication dispensed there.

I was in the bathroom draining my bag one day when Caitlin came in, and we struck up a conversation.

"I felt so bad after the baby was born," Caitlin said. "I knew something had to be wrong. I had a fever, and was sick to my stomach all the time."

She said she'd noticed "dark stuff—like old blood" in her stool, then she pulled up her shirt and showed me the wound on her belly that wouldn't heal.

"I guess I picked up some kind of infection," she said. "The doctor said this medicine was what I needed, but it sure doesn't seem to be working very fast."

I was horrified. It was obvious Caitlin had no clue how serious her condition was—didn't realize that the small infected hole in her belly was the tip of an iceberg of staph beneath it.

I bet if I stuck a Q-tip in there, it would go all the way to her backbone, I thought. *Why in the world has nobody told her she has staph?*

Caitlin's condition deteriorated quickly. She died three months after I started the study.

I went to the funeral home to see Caitlin's husband, but he wasn't there. The family said he was not doing well, that he blamed himself for his wife's death and wanted nothing to do with the baby that had killed her.

They said that Caitlin had been out to dinner with her husband and her parents when she collapsed, dead before she hit the floor. The staph had gotten to her heart.

I knew the same thing could happen to me. At any minute, the staph could reach my heart and I would be dead, too. I also knew that I should be seeing some improvement in my condition, that I should be getting better. But I wasn't. I was getting sicker.

I watched helplessly as CT scan after CT scan revealed the relentless march of the infection. It invaded my liver, my pancreas, my intestines, my lungs. I had it in more organs than Winston did, and he didn't seem to be getting any better either.

Winston was a tall, handsome black man in his midforties who had blown out a knee years before playing college basketball. He contracted staph during knee replacement surgery.

Winston had been a shift supervisor at the Louisville Ford Motor Company plant, had a big house, drove a fancy car, and was up to his big brown eyes in credit card debt.

When Winston lost his job because he couldn't work with a bad knee, he kept his health insurance under COBRA until it expired. Then he let his coverage lapse, and when he tried to get private medical insurance again later, it wouldn't cover his preexisting condition. That's how he ended up at a free clinic.

Winston always wore silk shirts, baggy black dress pants, and shiny black-and-white shoes. The cane he used to keep the weight off his bad knee had a gold handle and a gold tip, and he drove a black-on-black Cadillac STS.

One afternoon, I saw Winston pull up in the parking lot. When he came into the clinic waiting room, I asked, "Was that you I saw driving that fancy pimp mobile?"

He looked me up and down and smiled.

"Hey, now, don't you be calling my car a pimp mobile," he said. "I go to church!"

"I go to church, too," I said, "but I know a pimp mobile when I see one."

Winston laughed out loud. He hobbled over and sat down beside me.

"What do you know about cars?" he asked.

"Everything," I told him matter-of-factly, and proceeded to prove it by rattling off a stream of automobile-buff trivia that left Winston breathless.

From that moment on we were friends, sitting together talking about cars—and eventually about life—whenever we happened to show up at the clinic at the same time to get our treatments.

We compared symptoms, and drug side effects, and talked about how the experimental medication was working. Winston had the same symptoms as I did—fever, abdominal pain, bleeding. His knee incision didn't appear to be infected at all. Apparently it had spread out quickly into his body from that site.

We both suffered severe nausea from the medication, and usually vomited for an hour after we left the clinic. And neither one of us thought the medication was working well enough or fast enough.

I tried repeatedly to get the doctors to increase my dosage of the medication; they refused. Maybe they feared what a larger dose might do to me. Maybe they wouldn't increase the dosage because the drug was expensive and it was cheaper to dole it out in small portions. I never knew which. What I did know was that I wasn't getting any better, and neither was Winston. In fact, Winston was going downhill fast.

The doctors had told Winston the same thing they told me—that he wasn't going to make it. After Caitlin died, he started to believe what they said. In six months, I watched him change from a handsome, healthy-looking ex-athlete into a bitter, feeble old man.

Nobody told me he died. I overheard two nurses talking about it when I went in for my treatment, and tracked down the name of the funeral home. As soon as the drug-induced vomiting passed after my treatment, DeWayne and I went to visitation.

The room was full. DeWayne hung around the edge of the crowd. It had been a major concession on his part to agree to go with me. He didn't do funerals.

I made my way to the open casket and stood there looking down at Winston, a single thought chasing its tail around and around in my head: *He didn't have to die!*

Winston's wife came to stand beside me. I had only spoken to the woman a couple of times when she accompanied her husband to his treatment. I didn't recall her name and didn't quite know what to say to her. But I didn't have to say anything. Winston's wife did all the talking.

"I guess we'll all be going to your funeral real soon," she told me. "You had it longer than Winston and worse than he did. I'm surprised you're still up walking around."

I turned and walked away, my face flushed, my eyes moist. I felt like the woman had slapped me.

But she was right! I had had staph longer than Winston. I'd had it longer than Caitlin, too, and Caitlin didn't last three months.

The experimental medication in small doses was working for a few people—people who obviously had less-virulent strains of staph than I did. But Winston's was the seventh funeral I had attended for members of the study group, and I didn't intend for my own to be the eighth. I wasn't getting well taking the low doses of the experimental medication provided by the drug study. If the doctors wouldn't increase my doses, I'd just have to find a way to do it myself.

I went online and tracked down the manufacturer of the drug. It was a pharmaceutical company in Germany. Two of my physician friends made phone calls, called in some favors, and found out how to purchase the medication directly from the company in Germany.

I bought a month's supply. It cost $1,200. Once the doctors had the additional medication, they immediately doubled the amount of it I was taking. Soon, they doubled it again—giving me the absolute maximum dosage.

"They've created a monster," I told my aunt Laura. "When I get through this, when I get to the other side, I'm going to find a way to make enough money to start a foundation for people who can't pay for their medicine, people who're treated like subhumans because they can't afford to pay for private insurance. I want to help the Winstons and the Caitlins of this world. I want to be able to just cut them a check. They didn't have to die!"

Meanwhile, I had more immediate concerns. Where was I going to find enough money every month to pay for my own medicine? And how sick would I get taking four times as much of it?

EIGHTEEN

I might have been more comfortable lying down, but I always opted to take my staph infection treatments sitting in a recliner. I had spent quite enough of my life in hospital beds, thank you very much, and anytime I could avoid one, I did. The nurses made me as comfortable as possible by placing a pillow under my knees, and I hugged another pillow to my chest, like a little kid clinging to a teddy bear.

Sometimes I thought that getting stuck was the worst part. Even in the face of the debilitating side effects of the experimental drug, there was something about being jabbed with a needle over and over and over again that just made me crazy.

Every morning, I woke up dreading the needles. Every morning for so long that normal life had grown vague and shadowy in my mind, I had to force myself out of bed to go downtown to take the medication from Germany that was my only hope of staying alive. Every morning—unless one of "my nurses" was on duty—I could count on being jabbed and poked, and often ignored.

Why did some nurses refuse to believe I knew my own body? Why wouldn't they listen to me when I told them it was useless to try to get a needle in an arm vein, that the only good IV real estate left on my whole body was between my toes? I chafed at the condescending smiles I got from fresh-out-of-nursing-school twenty-somethings who thought you had to have four years of medical training to tell one end of a stethoscope from the other. They'd ignore me and jab the needle in and dig around, then jab it in somewhere else and dig some more, and finally end up putting the line in between my toes just like I said.

The problem, of course, was my bad-and-getting-worse-by-the-day veins. They'd been punctured thousands of times over the years and now almost uniformly refused to accept the presence of an IV needle without collapsing. Sometimes, I had to go from one hospital to the next, driving all over Louisville in the wee hours of the morning, before a nurse could find a functioning vein—or I could find a functioning nurse.

I had been cared for by dozens, maybe hundreds of wonderful, skilled, compassionate nurses in the past three decades. Why was it that in the middle of the night I always seemed to wind up with a turkey?

As soon as the IV needle was finally lodged in a vein, the medication flowing into my body would make my skin tingle.

The hot flashes would begin about half an hour into the treatment. Suddenly, I'd feel like a flare had been set off in my chest, blasting heat into my face, arms, and legs like a flame thrower, bathing me in sweat. Soon, the heat would be replaced by cold. Chills would seize me, and I'd have to grit my teeth to keep them from chattering. As the experimental concoction flowed through my body, I'd alternate, hot to cold, cold to hot, like a case of the flu on steroids.

Usually, the nausea reported for duty about ninety minutes after the medication first began to drip down the clear plastic tube. Even though nurses administered 50 mg of Phenergan as soon as I was settled in the recliner, and six more 25-mg tablets, nothing could avert its relentless attack. First came the gagging, as wave after wave of sickness hammered me. Within minutes, I'd be in full-blown vomit mode.

I quickly learned the location of every trash can between the admitting area and the parking garage of every hospital in Louisville. I vomited my way to my car in the parking garage every morning, throwing up a noxious combination of stomach bile and blood. Old blood, thick and black at first, then bright red.

In its ruthless assault, the staph infection was eating through the walls of my organs. I was bleeding internally, rectally, and into my stomach.

I had sudden nosebleeds half a dozen times a week, was constantly searching the glove box of my Jeep for napkins or in my purse for tissues to stanch the flow before it ran down my lip and dripped off my chin onto my clothing. There was blood in my urine, and in my incessant diarrhea. Everywhere I could bleed, I bled.

I would long since have bled to death without constant transfusions of both blood and platelets—six, seven, ten pints some weeks.

I was spending more and more of my time at the hospital. Staying alive was becoming my full-time job, and I reported for work every morning at 12:30 A.M. When all went well with my staph medicine treatment, I was home by 5 A.M. and had enough time to wind down a little, eat a cracker, and try to get my stomach settled before I woke up Mackenzie, fixed her hair, fed her a cereal bar and a sausage stick, and packed her off to school.

Of course, all never went well.

It was a rare morning when I managed to go back to bed, even for a nap, after I took Mackenzie to school. The four hours of sleep before the alarm jarred me awake was all I got. Life happened—errands, groceries, working as a tutor for special children at Mackenzie's school. Increasingly, my days were becoming a blur of transfusions, tests, biopsies, and doctor appointments. And after a while, finding people willing to pay for my medication consumed virtually every waking moment.

Quietly, without fanfare, DeWayne stepped in and lightened my load wherever he could. Even though he was working fifty to sixty-five hours a week to pay the mortgage, put food on the table, and buy my urostomy supplies and daily medications, he did the laundry, cared for Mackenzie, washed the dishes, and cleaned the kitchen. I never asked; I never had to ask. He was just there.

After we got married, DeWayne called me from work two or three times a day just to check in, just to tell me he loved me. Even after the newlywed glow wore off, he still called; he wanted that connection. As my condition worsened through the fall and winter, the two or three calls became four or five—sometimes more. He didn't say anything profound or fancy. A simple, "I love you, baby." Or "I was thinking about you." Some days, the strength of DeWayne's love was all that kept me going.

What kept DeWayne going were new friends he made when he changed jobs. God placed Tristen and Jimbo in DeWayne's life to help him bear the burden of uncertainty and fear he admitted to only a few people. Their wives, Kim and Sherry, pitched in to help, too. They took me to doctor appointments and picked Mackenzie up at school when I couldn't make it. In the evenings, we often got together to hang out, play cards, or watch ballgames. And we laughed. That laughter breathed springtime into our ever-darkening lives.

[Journal entry] *September 1, 2005*
It's September. And I'm still here! Hey, little Indian doctor, wherever you are—I'm still here!

Almost every day, a test, biopsy, scan, transfusion—or some combination of them all—earned me a seat in a free clinic somewhere in Louisville, where I sat waiting for hours. Predictably, I worked the room. That's how I met Wendell, a six-foot, two-inch homeless man who wore a U.S. Army trench coat no matter how hot or cold it was outside, and slept under the Market Street overpass. The day I met him, he hadn't had a full meal in two weeks, and he was picking lice out of his hair as he sat beside me.

Wendell had sickle-cell anemia, and had to have blood transfusions several times a week. The tall, lanky derelict frightened most people, and the ones he failed to scare off, he ran off. His social skills were lacking in several key areas. And his face twitched. No, it did more than twitch. It vibrated, gyrated, and danced at odds with itself to a melody only he could hear. He called me Baby Girl; I called him Big Boy.

He might once have been an educated man, I often thought. A history teacher or a businessman, maybe. Or perhaps he'd been some kind of scientist or mathematician. He could add numbers in his head as fast as a calculator.

My heart went out to the odd, crazy-looking man who was as glad to see me as a basset hound puppy every time we happened to show up in the same waiting room. After our first meeting, I went home and gathered a sackful of goodies to give to him the next time I saw him. It was nothing elaborate, just useful, everyday items. I brought him flea and tick shampoo, and a Rid kit for lice, blankets, a couple of DeWayne's old jackets, and a pile of tube socks.

There were other regulars in the free clinics as well: defiant prisoners in orange jumpsuits complete with handcuffs and ankle chains, proud old people with chronic illnesses, young mothers with tired eyes who always had at least one sick kid among the half dozen who roamed undisciplined around the waiting room. None of them saw the same doctor twice, none of them expected, or got, the care they would have received if they'd've had private health insurance.

As I sat there beside junkies, crying babies, and Wendell, his face twitching so fiercely it threatened to jump off his head, I grew angrier by the day at the system that made me and these other people second-class citizens. If I'd had private health care, I wouldn't be here, fighting for my life. How many of the others in the room had similar stories?

[Journal entry] *September 8, 2005*
My doctors have dumped me. They've decided I'm not going to beat the staph, and they don't want the liability of me dying on their watch. So they won't sign off on the medicine anymore. I can't take my treatments without a doctor's okay. If I stop taking treatments, I'll be dead in a month.

When the doctors who were treating me refused to continue to approve my use of the German drug, it's not like I could have gone to the free clinic and enlisted the aid of some other doctor there. Only sixteen infectious disease doctors in the country were licensed to dispense experimental medications. And I had to find one of them willing to take my case—fast.

My friend Tracy, who had been my nurse for fifteen years, was so outraged she resigned. She said she couldn't work for doctors she didn't respect, and she couldn't respect physicians who were more concerned about covering their backsides than they were about helping a woman fight for her life.

Though Tracy maintained she didn't believe in God, she said she saw God in me. Whenever bad things were going on in her life, she always asked me to pray for her. She was absolutely convinced that I had a direct line to the red phone on God's desk; she believed I was going to beat the staph infection because of my faith.

In desperation, I got on the Internet and sent out e-mails to hospitals across America—Mount Sinai, Massachusetts General, the Mayo Clinic. Tracy had once worked with an infectious disease doctor in Atlanta, and she called him asking for help. He said his specialty was strep, but the "best staph man in the country" practiced in his office. That doctor agreed to take a look at me, and flew to Louisville to see me.

. . .

I met him at the airport. He was easy to pick out of a crowd—six feet, five inches tall, wearing a Stetson hat and cowboy boots.

When he got into the front seat of my Jeep, I gave him a 100-watt smile.

"Nice to meet you, Big Jeff," I said.

"I'm always up for a challenge," Dr. Jeff told me as we drove toward the hospital in downtown Louisville. "I take all the cases nobody else wants."

"Well, nobody wants my case, that's for sure," I replied. "Nobody wants the responsibility of taking care of me. They pass me off as fast as they can get rid of me so I don't die on their shift. But I don't intend to die on anybody's shift."

I told him about my life and carefully watched his reaction. His demeanor softened.

He's human: There's a chance for me! I thought.

. . .

When we got to the hospital, Tracy joined in the telling of my story. Soon we both were crying.

"Okay, Okay, that's enough, you two," Dr. Jeff cut in, a bit rattled by such intense emotion. "Here's a box of tissues. Wipe your faces and blow your noses—we've got things to do."

The doctor scanned me, scoped me, scraped my throat for tissue samples, and did biopsies of my stomach. He looked at old scans, old tests, and ordered new ones—blood, urine, stool. To determine the damage already done to my vital organs, he performed a pressure test that was the most painful examination I had ever endured. The tests showed staph in my bowel, and in my liver, lungs, stomach, and pancreas—organs not injured in the accident, but now being damaged, maybe beyond repair, by infection.

When I left the hospital at 5:30 A.M. after a full day and night of testing, I had no idea what Dr. Jeff was thinking. I couldn't read him; he was all business. I knew only one thing for certain: If the big man in the cowboy hat refused to take my case, I would die.

There was no point in going to bed when I got home. Kenzie had to be up by 7 A.M. to get ready for school. So I had time for a long talk with God. I put everything in his hands; I knew he would make a way for me. As I was helping Kenzie finish her math homework, the phone rang.

"I guess my conscience is bothering me," Dr. Jeff said. "I can't sleep. So, here it is—I figure we don't have anything to lose by going for it."

The medication at its present dosage was barely holding the staph at bay; I was gaining no ground, and time was on the infection's side. Sooner or later it would get me. So Dr. Jeff intended to double my current dose.

"I need to be sure you understand that I don't know what taking that much medicine is going to do to you," he said. "I don't know of anybody else in the world who is on doses as high as I'm going to give you. But if you're willing to chance it, I'm willing to sign off on it."

He told me it was reasonable to assume that whatever side effects I was currently experiencing—nausea, sores, pain—would be twice as bad on the double dosage. And he said he was leaving orders for me to receive injections of the drug directly into both lungs and my stomach in addition to taking the medication intravenously.

My lab work would be done in Louisville, he said; he would monitor the results by phone, and he'd be back to check on me.

"I don't know what this is going to do to you . . ." he reminded me. But I knew. It would either cure me or kill me.

[Journal entry] *September 25, 2005*

Rachel called me on my cell phone today and asked what I was doing. I told her I was in the bathroom at the bank cursing Dr. Jeff.

I had gone to put DeWayne's check into our account. Drug side effects—squared—had nailed me while I was standing in line. An uncontrollable wave of nausea swept over me—six hours after my treatment was over!—and I barely made it to the bathroom in time to throw up. I vomited bright red blood so violently that it splattered all over me. So violently, in fact, that the heaving dislodged the urostomy bag and urine soaked my shirt.

My cell phone rang while I was trying to figure out how to get out of the bank with my dignity intact and dash home to change clothes. I had to be at the football field at 6:15 for cheerleading practice.

The great delight of Mackenzie's life was cheerleading.

Though I was sick, bleeding, and in pain, I was the cheerleading coach for the Jeffersontown Youth Football League. Mackenzie had plenty of difficulty in her life; this was a source of joy. No matter how bad I felt, Mackenzie's excitement put a smile on my face.

On the way to the football field, we always stopped to put drinks and ice in a cooler. Mackenzie knew the drill. She had to charm whoever was working behind the counter in the grocery store into carrying the loaded cooler out to the car because I couldn't lift anything heavier than a two-liter Coke bottle.

September in Kentucky is sometimes as hot and muggy as August. It was that year. Even October was a scorcher. I had made it home from the bank, changed my clothes, and rushed to cheerleading practice. I sat on the bleachers at the empty field in the blazing sun, waiting for the little girls to straggle in.

When they were all present, there were sixteen of them—including five Hannahs, four Mackenzies, and two Tories—ranging in age from eight to fourteen. At every practice, the girls warmed up with twenty-five jumping jacks and bend-and-stretch exercises. Then they ran the bleachers, all the way to the top and back down five times. I ran a tight ship.

"Let's make sure we understand each other," I told the girls the first day of practice. "Give me mouth or attitude and you have to do five more reps up and down the bleachers. Eye-rolling gets one warning. After that, you have to sit out for five minutes and run the bleachers five times or you're off the team. Are we clear?"

Sixteen little heads bobbed up and down in a communal yes.

A cheerleader in middle school and president of the pep club in high school, I had volunteered to be the coach because nobody else would do it. All the other mothers were way too busy or would just be too tired by the end of the day to handle it. Either I coached the squad or Mackenzie didn't get to cheer. So I did it, standing in the muggy afternoon heat three times a week teaching the girls forty different cheers.

"Okay girls, get in your set positions," I called out, my voice raspy from the ulcers lining my throat. I joked that I had prayed all my life for a deep, sexy voice and God had finally given me one.

Sixteen preadolescent girls scurried to their spots, feet together, hands at their sides, eyes forward, stiff as robots.

"Let's do All Across the Nation," I said.

One of the girls called out, "Ready? Hit it . . . 5 . . . 6 . . . 7 . . . 8."

"All across the nation is a Bulldog sensation," the girls chanted in unison, executing the moves I had taught them to go along with the words.

"We're gonna take you for a ride. We're gonna move you side to side . . . a boom-boom, hey, can't you feel it? A boom-boom, hey, can't you feel it?"

On the "boom-boom," I had instructed the girls to "shake

your booties." They tried. Some of them were more successful than others.

In rapid succession, the girls did three more cheers—Let's Get Fired Up, VICTORY, and Split That V. I sat in the sweltering heat, the makeup that had given color to my pale face long since washed off by sweat. As I watched the girls, I was engaged in a mighty struggle not to burst out laughing. Little kids with no rhythm trying to dance was a riot!

The laughter I didn't let out of my mouth warmed my heart just the same. It was hot and I was sick—but I was glad to be alive! This was one of God's precious gifts of joy, and it was a treasure of incalculable worth.

When they finished the last cheer, I stood to teach them a new one. The girls wouldn't dare loaf. They knew my health issues, and when I performed the movements flawlessly, they were awed.

"Come on, you can do this," I encouraged them. "I can do it and I'm thirty-six years old. You're twelve. You don't have any excuse."

Between cheers, the girls unloaded on me the trauma in their private lives, babbling about daddy's drinking problem, or their parents' crumbling marriage, or their older brother's stash of drugs under his bed. I just listened. I didn't give the girls pat answers. I understood pain and I respected theirs enough not to try to relieve it with hackneyed platitudes.

I left the ball field about nine P.M. utterly spent and pumped up at the same time. I had lost myself in the fun of being with those sixteen little girls. For a little while at least, I hadn't given a thought to staph or medicine or finding the money to pay for it. But I had to be back at the hospital for my treatment in a little over five hours. And I was tired, so very, very tired.

[Journal entry] *October 18, 2005*
Mackenzie had a grand mal seizure at school today.

Mackenzie had epilepsy, but it was controlled by medication. She hadn't had a seizure in more than a year. Suddenly, out of nowhere, the seizures returned worse than they'd ever been. The child was experiencing other frightening neurological symptoms as well—tingling down her arms, numbness in her face.

My world turned upside down. Some mornings I'd have to leave the hospital in the middle of treatments because Mackenzie was at home with DeWayne having one grand mal seizure after another: *bam, bam, bam!* Over and over again, I bolted out of an examining room—after a nurse had worked for half an hour to get a needle into my vein—and dashed to the school to pick up my daughter. Later, when the crisis was over, I had to go back and finish the treatment or transfusion or test I had left behind.

I took Mackenzie and made the rounds of neurologists, trying to find out what was happening to my little girl. For weeks,

I spent almost every waking moment in a hospital or clinic somewhere—for treatments, tests, transfusions, or Mackenzie.

Then the child came down with a viral infection and a stomach ulcer, and was so sick she couldn't keep down any epilepsy medication. For one horrible weekend, she had so many different symptoms I couldn't keep track of them all.

The burden of caring for a sick child took a toll on my strength. Gradually, Mackenzie got better, but I didn't bounce back with her.

I told Vicki one day in November that the doctors keeping tabs on me for Dr. Jeff wanted to admit me to the hospital and keep me there to monitor my reaction to the experimental medication.

"I can't afford to be in the hospital, and even if I could, I wouldn't go," I said. "The hospital is where I caught the staph infection in the first place!"

There was an even more profound reason why I wouldn't allow myself to be hospitalized. I believed that if I ever went into the hospital, I would never come back out.

"I have to be here, out in the world, to keep going," I said. "I have to force myself to get up and go get treatments every day. It's something I have to do on my own. If you're in bed, you just lay there, passive, with people doing things to you and for you. You get depressed. And you die."

I didn't intend to do either.

NINETEEN

Early on, I had to face a reality almost as frightening as the staph itself: If I intended to stay alive to raise my daughter and grow old with my husband, I would have to swallow my pride and ask people to buy the experimental medication for me. I certainly couldn't afford to buy it for myself. There was absolutely no way around it. I didn't have to like asking for help, but I did have to do it. If I didn't, if I couldn't, I would die.

At first, the drug cost $1,200 a month. Then the dosage was doubled, and doubled again. How was I going to find people with that kind of money? Where? The magnitude of the task took my breath away. And scared me to death.

God will provide, I told myself fiercely. I do not believe that

God got me this far to let me die from a staph infection. I do not believe God's anywhere near done with me yet!

And God did provide, in unconventional ways that amazed and delighted me, and confirmed his constant presence and love. Somehow, the medication was there. Every month—somehow!—it was there.

I started by asking family and close friends. I hated to ask my parents—they had spent so much on me already. But I had no choice. I went to my grandparents as well. A close friend who had known me all my life bought medicine every month. And when I was short, a friend of hers made up the difference. I never found out who he was.

As the months dragged by and the stakes got higher, I had to reach out further than my inner circle. I went to the people I'd worked with when I was a headhunter and a fund-raiser. I went to nurses and aides and people I met at the hospital.

Members of my church had jewelry parties and Home Interior parties and used the proceeds to buy medicine. One of those church members was Mackenzie's teacher at Middletown Elementary School. Linda came up with a novel fund-raising project the school could conduct—a butterfly release. For weeks, the children sold paper butterflies to their parents, grandparents, and neighbors. Then one spring day, the whole school turned out to free hundreds of real butterflies the paper ones represented. The event raised $10,000, and the school used it to pay our house payment and utility bills for a year—so we could use more of our income to buy medicine. I spoke at Christian Academy of Louisville, and afterward the teenagers collected $3,400 and used it to buy medicine for me. The Good Samaritans matched their collection, and purchased an additional $3,400 worth of medicine.

But when Dr. Jeff doubled my medication in September, I found myself fighting a war on multiple fronts. I was getting sicker by the day from the drug's side effects, and weaker by the day from the assault of the staph infection. At the same time, I had to find the strength to drum up donors willing to buy medicine for me—every month! The penalty for failure was death.

I tried to recall all the people over the years who had told me, "You're such an inspiration to me, Heather. If you ever need anything, just call. I'll be glad to help." So I called them. And some of them came through. Most didn't.

God never let me down, but people did.

They turned away or stopped taking my calls.

I learned that most people's compassion had a very short shelf life.

Every morning, I woke up with a cold, sick fear in my belly. It was like I could hear a clock *tick, tick, ticking* down the days until the deadline. As I stumbled from one, "Sorry, I can't help you," to another, I became more and more frightened.

For the first time in my life, I was dependent on other people for survival. In the past, I leaned on God for strength and then just sucked it up and did whatever I had to do. Now, I couldn't do it on my own. I discovered that needing other people was the loneliest feeling in the world.

Sure, I knew I ought to trust God. He'd never let me down before. And I tried, I really did. Some days, I was able to claim God's strength and peace. Other days, I was just too scared and too sick.

In September, a friend maxed out a credit card and bought medicine for me.

In October, dozens of people made small medicine purchases.

In November, a church minister knocked on my door. He told me he had taken up a collection in a men's Bible study and raised enough for a month's supply of medicine. He also said he was proud of me, that he was certain God had a purpose for my pain.

In December, three businessmen purchased most of the medicine, and other friends made up the difference.

The medication came in. Somehow, it came in. But it didn't all come in every month. I had to go off the medication time and time again because there were weeks when I could find no one to buy it for me.

[Journal entry] *November 18, 2005*
They had to drain fluid off my lungs three times this weekend. I can't breathe and I'm scared.

[Journal entry] *November 30, 2005*
I had to take six pints of blood last week, and I'm already up to five pints for this week. How long can this go on?

[Journal entry] *December 12, 2005*
This medicine is kicking my butt!

As autumn turned to winter, and winter trudged toward Christmas, I grew sicker and weaker. I was throwing up more and more blood. One lung or the other repeatedly collapsed. I had to take a steroid inhaler six times a day and three daily breathing treatments. I tried valiantly to put a good face on it, but as I passed 300 straight days of treatment without a single break, I felt as worn down as a pencil eraser.

On Christmas Eve and Christmas Day, I was in and out of the hospital three times because I couldn't breathe. Oh, I was never admitted. You can stay in the hospital for eighteen hours without being officially admitted. So I stayed that long, went home for eight hours, and then yo-yoed in and out again. Beginning back in October, I had been required to sign a form every time I left the hospital stating that I was leaving AMA—against medical advice.

At the beginning of the new year, I took stock of my situation. Sober and unemotional, I tracked the downward spiral of my condition. I understood that something would have to happen soon, one way or the other. The downward spiral could have one of two outcomes. Either I would die or I would start getting better.

The second week of January, something wonderful happened.

It was the first wonderful thing in almost a year. Dr. Jeff reported to me the results of my latest CT scan. My liver was free of staph! So was my pancreas, stomach, and bowel! The infection was gone from every organ except my lungs. Dr. Jeff told me he believed that treatments for another couple of months would do it, that I was on my way to accomplishing the impossible. I was going to beat it!

I did a gut check. I didn't feel appreciably better, I was still bleeding internally and throwing up blood, still unable to breathe, still getting my butt kicked every day by the medication.

But finally there was a light at the end of the tunnel—and it wasn't the headless horseman with a lantern. I couldn't wait to tell DeWayne! That night as I lay beside him while he slept, I made a decision: Tomorrow, I'm going riding!

In my condition, horseback riding wasn't an activity I could decide on the spur of the moment to do. I had to get my body ready. When I went in for treatment that morning, I took a 10 mg shot of morphine, an 80 mg pill of OxyContin, and 75 mg of Phenergan. I had to get out in front of the pain because I wouldn't be able to ride if I let it catch up with me.

The day was cold, but I only wore a light jacket. The medication in my body was like a well-stoked blast furnace. I drove my Jeep out of Louisville through a little town called Fisherville to the farm where I kept my horse—a black Tennessee Walker whose shiny coat was the same color as my hair.

When I got out of my Jeep, I called to the horse from the yard, and the mare came running up to the gate. Her name was Grace.

I put a halter on her, led her to the barn, and fed her sweet feed while I groomed her, brushing her black coat to clean the mud off so the big mare wouldn't be uncomfortable when I placed the Western saddle on her back and tightened the cinches. Then I had to force a bit between her teeth, pinching Grace's nose to get her to open up. She hadn't been ridden often enough and her mouth was tender.

My only concession to my injuries was the step stool I had to use to mount. I couldn't grab hold of the mare's mane and haul myself up into the saddle like a normal rider. My belly was mesh from hip to hip, sternum to pelvic bone. It wouldn't stand the strain.

I didn't often ride alone. DeWayne didn't like for me to be out by myself. But today I wanted solitude. When I guided Grace out into the field behind the barn, I longed to cut the horse loose and let her race to the other side. But for me, riding had become a delicious drink—I could chug it all down in one gulp or enjoy it for a long time in little sips. The pounding my body would take atop a running horse would shorten the amount of time I could ride.

So I walked Grace along the fence line, ducking the bare limbs of dead trees. The winter sky was a blue so bright and crisp it almost hurt my eyes. The familiar motion of the horse soothed me. Real peace was a rare and infinitely precious commodity, and it was always waiting for me on the back of a horse.

I looked up and saw Reisha riding up to me on Desert Dancer, a small Rocky Mountain walking horse. Reisha was DeWayne's cousin, a beautiful girl, model gorgeous, who had been riding since her father first set her on a horse's back before she could walk. The farm was hers, and she and I had ridden many a mile on it, talking, laughing, crying, yelling at God, and praying out loud. Reisha understood the healing power of riding, and she knew I wouldn't have been out there by myself if I hadn't needed time alone. But she also knew that solitude was almost always better shared.

We rode along together in silence.

Finally, Reisha spoke.

"How's it going?" she asked.

"Good," I told her, and fell uncharacteristically silent. I would share with my friend the good news later. Right now, I was content to treasure it quietly in my own heart.

Thinking about the test results set my mind whirring.

If I could get rid of the staph before the bleeding became uncontrollable, I could have surgery to repair the damage the infection had caused.

If I could scrape up medicine for just another couple of months . . .

If I could just hang on for a little while longer . . .

If . . .

A brilliant splash of scarlet caught my eye. A cardinal, sitting on a bare limb, puffed out its feathers to stay warm, looking like a miniature fat man in a red suit.

And scripture memorized in some long-ago Sunday school class came to my mind: "Look at the birds of the air; they do not sow or reap . . . yet your Heavenly Father feeds them. Are you not much more valuable than they?" (Matthew 6:26, NIV).

I smiled.

Reisha noticed.

"What?" she asked, looking around. "What are you smiling at?"

"I'm smiling because God is God, and I'm not," I said. "He's running the universe—so I don't have to."

[Journal entry] *February 10, 2006*
If I'm getting better, why don't I feel better?

That day riding Grace through the field under an achingly blue sky was a gift so precious it shone like a sparkling soap bubble in my memory, giving me strength to hang on as winter plodded on toward spring—and the path I thought would get easier didn't. It got harder.

About a month after Dr. Jeff gave me the good news, he delivered the bad news. He told me he wanted to double the dosage of my staph medicine. Again. Repeated scans returned the same results. There was no longer any staph in any of the major organs of my body—except my lungs. But it was hanging on tenaciously there. There was no gradual improvement as the weeks went by. There was no improvement at all. Dr. Jeff finally concluded that to beat it, to knock the staph out of my lungs, he would have to hit it with a larger dose of the experimental drug.

I was certain he had totally lost his mind.

"You said I'm the only person you know who's ever taken doses this high of this stuff, and now you're telling me you want to double it? You're joking, right? Twice as much as I'm taking now . . . that much will kill me!"

Dr. Jeff cocked his head to one side and grinned.

"Heather, I'm just about convinced that nothing in this world can kill you," he said. Then he grew serious. "We're not beating it this way. Nothing's changing. I keep pumping this stuff into you and nothing's changing."

"How on earth . . . ?" I said aloud, more to myself than Dr. Jeff. It was all I could do to find enough people to buy a month's supply of medicine now. How on earth could I find enough people to purchase twice as much? The cost was such an absurd figure that all the synapses in my brain stopped firing and resolutely refused to process it. God had done one miracle after another to get me this far. But how . . . ?

"If we're not winning this battle, we're losing it," Dr. Jeff said, speaking quietly, patiently, as if he were talking to a small child. "There's no such thing here as a draw."

I walked out of the hospital that day with a sense of unreality. This couldn't be happening. It just simply could not be happening. Not now. Not after all I'd been through. I knew with absolute, complete, and total certainty that there was no way for me to come up with enough money to buy all that medicine. It was impossible. But I also knew with absolute, complete, and total certainty that if God wanted it to happen, he would make a way. And I just couldn't believe that God was finished with me yet.

And so the crocuses poked their yellow noses out of the dark earth, buds showed up on the cherry trees and the dogwoods, the bluegrass shed its drab winter coat and painted the meadows turquoise . . . and God provided my medicine. Somehow, God made it happen. But I was never able to remain on the medicine consistently. Because there were times when I could find no one to purchase it for me, I would be on the drug for six weeks, then off it for two, back on for three weeks, and off a week. I was unable to stay on the medication without a break long enough for it to heal me.

When I was capable of rational thought, I was overwhelmed by the magnitude of what God was doing. But I wasn't often capable of rational thought. I was sicker than I ever dreamed a person could be and not die. My days became a blur of pain and nausea and exhaustion. I fell into a well of suffering, a deeper, darker well than I had ever known in my life.

By May, I had to have a break. Just twenty-four hours. Just a day, one day of light to carry back into the black hole with me. So I arranged to go on a ten-mile trail ride called the Relay for Life—a fund-raiser for cancer research—in Bardstown, Kentucky. Grace needed to be ridden as much as I needed a break. Even at my sickest, I made it out to the farm to see the black mare a couple of times a week. But I was way too sick to ride her. And I noticed she was gaining weight, from inactivity,

I supposed. We both needed some sunshine, fresh air, and exercise.

The day provided plenty of all three for our enjoyment, only Grace didn't do much enjoying. We hadn't ridden more than a mile before I figured out that something was majorly wrong with my horse. She was like a different animal. Cranky. Uncontrollable. Skittish. She kicked like a mule at every male horse that came near her. The ride was a struggle every step of the way, and I left her in the barn that night convinced that I absolutely had to find more time for her. I made myself a promise that somehow I would find a way to ride her more often.

But riding Grace quickly ranked down on my to-do list below what suddenly became my number-one concern—trying not to bleed to death. The bleeding I'd been battling with transfusions for months was getting markedly worse. The doctors weren't sure whether the staph or the experimental medication had eaten holes in my internal organs, but I was bleeding all over. I was taking several pints of blood and platelets every few days. Something had to be done to stanch the flow.

So Dr. Jeff decided to stop up the largest hole, which lay at the base of my stomach where it joined my small intestine.

"What I'm going to do is like patching a pair of blue jeans," he said. "I'm going to take a two-inch by two-inch piece of old scar tissue and stitch it over the hole to close it off."

He paused then, and looked at me hard.

"You know we can't use general anesthesia, don't you?" he said.

Yeah, I knew. I understood far better than he did what that meant. I couldn't be put to sleep for the procedure. They would dope me up the best they could, give me maximum doses of all the pain medication they could find, but I would be awake and aware. I would feel everything. And with my body's tolerance for drugs, I was certain I was in for a rough ride. There was no way around it. I'd just have to gut it out, that's all.

It was going to hurt. Oh, my, yes. It was going to hurt! I knew that and I thought I was prepared for it. But I was wrong.

With my backside in the air, Dr. Jeff inserted a dilator into my rectum to keep it open and then . . .

The pain was absolutely excruciating. Unbelievable. Unbearable. Cold, hard instruments. Poking. Prodding. A scalpel cutting. A needle stitching. Blood everywhere. The agony was indescribable.

And so I left. I had to take myself someplace far away or I couldn't stand it. So in my mind I climbed on my big black mare and rode her through the woods in the spring sunshine. Or I lay in bed on a Saturday morning talking and cuddling with DeWayne. Or I curled up on the floor beside Mackenzie watching a movie and eating popcorn.

Scissors snipped tissue, a needle stitched the patch in place, blood poured down my legs and dripped onto the floor . . .

One part of me shrieked and sobbed in agony. But the other part of me, the part that mattered, was far, far away.

The first patch held for a few days and then came loose. So the whole procedure had to be performed all over again. The second patch held.

[Journal entry] *June 6, 2006*
I'm done!

A few weeks after the patch finally stanched much of my internal bleeding, I made a major decision. A life-changing decision. I decided I was finished. No more staph medication. No more treatments. I had reached my limit. Four hundred and fifty days of treatment was enough. One way or the other this had to end. It had to stop. It had to be over.

When I told Dr. Jeff, he pitched what Grandmother used to call "a conniption fit."

"You can't do this, Heather!" he actually shouted at me. "There's still staph in the bottom of your right lung. Didn't you see it on that last scan?"

"Yes, I saw the shadow in the bottom of that lung," I said. "But every time I take a scan, there are shadows in different places. Are you certain they're all staph? You keep telling me that if we just double my drug dosage, I'll be free of staph in a couple of months. So you double the dosage, a couple of months pass, and it's still there. So you double the dosage again. And again. And again. And it's still there. So tell me this: Are you sure that shadow isn't just dead staph collected in the bottom of that lung? Or something else entirely? Are you absolutely certain?"

"No, I'm not absolutely certain," he admitted. "But it is my best professional opinion that it is live staph, and if you go off this medication now, it will start growing again and you'll be right back where you started, with staph in every organ of your body." He paused for effect. "And this time, Heather, you won't make it."

That was definitely the wrong thing to say.

"I've had doctors all my life telling me I wouldn't make it," I fired back. "Telling me I can't do this or I'll never be able to do that. Telling me no. But you know what, when they said no, God said yes! You're not in charge, he is. I'm telling you, I'm going off this medicine. You work out the tapering off schedule so I can be done with it by the middle of July."

"But, Heather . . ."

"I said I'm going to be off this medicine by the middle of July! I'm not negotiating. That's the way it's going to be."

I had discussed my options for weeks with DeWayne, friends, and family members, and they were solidly behind me. They knew how sick I was of being sick. They knew I had to have a break. Mom said she was certain I understood the functioning of my body better than any doctor ever would.

I had long talks with God about it, too.

"Lord, you know me better than anybody else, you know how many hairs I have on my head, and you know I'm at the end," I prayed the night before I confronted Dr. Jeff. "I just can't keep this up. I'm tough, but not this tough. It's got to stop. Here, now, it's got to stop. I need strength and courage to do this, and you're the only one who can give it to me. I trust you, Lord. More than any doctor, I trust *you.* You've never let me down."

On July 2, I got a call from Reisha.

"Heather, I know what's wrong with your horse," she said. "Grace is pregnant."

"She couldn't be!" I said, totally flabbergasted. "How could Grace be pregnant? She hasn't been anywhere near a stallion."

"Heather, I'm telling you, she's pregnant," Reisha continued urgently. "And not just a few months along. She's ready to foal. She's got milk . . . it's running down her leg."

"I'll be right there."

The equine veterinarian confirmed Reisha's suspicion. Grace was pregnant all right, and ready to deliver any minute!

I moved the mare to the farm next door to Reisha's, where Roger and Caroline, friends from church, graciously provided a double stall in their barn large enough for the big horse to deliver her baby in comfort. And then I waited.

And waited.

The horse who was "ready to deliver any minute" held on to her foal for five days, and during those five days I was never more than a hundred yards from her stall. I moved in with Roger and Caroline, slept in an apartment in their basement, and checked on Grace every hour. My nurses brought my medication and administered it to me there.

On July 7, I went to see about Grace at 2:30 A.M., then rode the four-wheeler back up to the house to get a little sleep. I was just nodding off when I was jarred awake by excruciating stomach cramps. I dashed to the bathroom, but I wasn't sick. How odd, I thought. I looked at my watch, saw that it was 3:15 A.M., and figured that since I was wide awake, I might as well to go back to check on Grace again. I hopped on the four-wheeler—didn't take a flashlight or my cell phone—and headed down the hill to the barn.

When the four-wheeler's headlights lit up the stall, I saw Grace down on her side, with the hooves and top of the foal's head sticking out of the birth canal.

I raced back to the house and in the front door, yelling, "The baby's coming!" I hollered at Caroline to get my phone, grabbed a flashlight, ran on foot back down the hill, jumped the fence, and dashed into Grace's stall.

By then, the foal was halfway out. But he wasn't moving his front legs. He was still, too still, and it didn't take me but a few seconds to figure out why. He was being held prisoner by the birth sac.

A pregnant mare must be taken off a feed called fescue for the duration of the pregnancy because the feed makes the lining of the birth sac so thick the baby can't break through it. Grace had had no prenatal care of any kind. She was eating fescue just last week! Her birth sac was so tough the baby would never be able to kick out of it. And if the foal couldn't kick out, he would die.

I looked around the stall, frantically searching for something sharp to cut through the sac. There was a tool for that purpose in the birthing kit the veterinarian had given me the day he walked me through step-by-step instructions on how to deliver a foal. But I couldn't locate the kit, and time was running out. The baby was way too still.

So I grabbed the sac containing the half-born foal and dug my fingernails into the membrane. It was, perhaps, an inch thick, as tough as a tire inner tube. But mine was the strength of desperation, and somehow I managed to poke a hole through. Liquid and blood came gushing out as I tore with all my might to open the slimy sac and release the foal. All the while my heart was pounding in my chest and I was shouting frantically at God.

"Oh, please, don't let this little horse die, please, oh, please, take care of him, help him! Let him live, please, God, let him live!"

I picked up a towel and began rubbing all of the foal's body I could reach—trying to stimulate him. The baby had begun making gurgling noises but was not breathing. The veterinarian's instructions came back to me when I needed them: If the foal doesn't breathe, put your hand over his muzzle, cover up one nostril, and blow hard into the other one.

My hands trembling, I did what the vet had told me to do, and several things happened at once. The foal coughed up fluid and took a big gasp of air. Grace had a burst of energy and gave a mighty push, and the foal plopped out onto the soft hay. It was a male, a colt.

I remembered the vet's words: "Don't help the foal. He has to kick out of the sac by himself."

So I backed off and left him alone. He began to kick, little movements at first that quickly strengthened. Within a minute, he was kicking the membrane away from his legs, and Grace was reaching around licking him, tearing at the sac with her teeth to help him get untangled from the last stringy pieces.

And then he was trying to stand up on his little stick legs! Teetering this way, tottering that way. He got all the way up with three legs under him, then fell face first in the hay on his little gray nose. Immediately, he tried again, got his front legs under him . . . then his back legs . . . trembling . . . shaking . . . standing! Standing and lurching forward to take a step. And another.

I just sat there in awe, watching it happen. I didn't even realize I was crying until I tasted the salt of my own tears. And I didn't realize I was praying until I heard the sound of my own voice.

"Oh, Lord, would you look at this!" I sobbed joyfully. "Would you just look at this! Only you could have come up with a gift like this. I never would have asked . . . never would have dreamed . . . but you always give me more than I dare to ask or imagine."

As I sat crying, laughing, and praying at the same time, I understood a fundamental truth. Despite decades of suffering, pain was not the driving force of my life. It never had been. I had been propelled through life by the engine of joy.

Over the years, I made thousands and thousands of individual decisions not to be controlled by pain. If I had been unwilling to suck it up and go on, if I had allowed self-pity and bitterness to snag fishhooks into my soul, I would have missed everything. Everything that mattered. I certainly wouldn't be gazing at a precious, still-wet foal—with a wonderful husband and a beautiful daughter at home waiting for me to tell them all about it.

I thought back over the events of the last year, the hardest year of my life, and I was filled with an overwhelming gratitude. The bleaker my life got, the brighter God's incredible gifts of joy sparkled in the darkness.

The little foal grew more sure-footed by the minute, and I began to consider what I would name him. Nothing cutesy. His name had to proclaim that he was a great gift from the Lord. Eventually, I decided to call him Maximus, which means "the greatest."

The sun began to paint the eastern sky pink as I sat in the damp hay watching Max teeter around the stall on his little toothpick legs. I took a deep breath, let it out slowly, and relaxed. I wasn't afraid anymore. I knew he would be fine.

This little foal would be just fine.

And so would I.